Routledge Revivals

Scepticism and Construction

Originally published in 1931, this book follows the sceptical principles of Bradley to their logical conclusions, pushing them even further than Bradley was willing to go. The argument selected as a starting point is the one used in Note A of the appendix to Appearance and Reality. The author argues for a return to the position of Kant, and opposes the central conception of Absolute Idealism, arguing for a metaphysical scepticism.

Scepticism and Construction
Bradley's Sceptical Principle as the Basis of
Constructive Philosophy

Charles A. Campbell

First published in 1931 by George Allen & Unwin Ltd

This edition first published in 2024 by Routledge
4 Park Square, Milton Park, Abingdon, Oxon, OX14 4RN

and by Routledge
605 Third Avenue, New York, NY 10158.

Routledge is an imprint of the Taylor & Francis Group, an informa business

© 1931 Charles A. Campbell

The right of Charles Campbell to be identified as the author of this work has been asserted by him in accordance with sections 77 and 78 of the Copyright, Designs and Patents Act 1988.

All rights reserved. No part of this book may be reprinted or reproduced or utilised in any form or by any electronic, mechanical, or other means, now known or hereafter invented, including photocopying and recording, or in any information storage or retrieval system, without permission in writing from the publishers.

ISBN 13: 978-1-032-94187-5 (hbk)
ISBN 13: 978-1-003-56937-4 (ebk)
ISBN 13: 978-1-032-94200-1 (pbk)
Book DOI 10.4324/9781003569374

SCEPTICISM
AND CONSTRUCTION

BRADLEY'S SCEPTICAL PRINCIPLE
AS THE BASIS
OF CONSTRUCTIVE PHILOSOPHY

BY

CHARLES A. CAMPBELL

LECTURER IN MORAL PHILOSOPHY IN THE
UNIVERSITY OF GLASGOW

Glasgow University Publications

LONDON
GEORGE ALLEN & UNWIN LTD
MUSEUM STREET

PRINTED IN GREAT BRITAIN

PREFACE

As this study purposes to be constructive no less than sceptical, and as the claim to unite construction with scepticism savours somewhat of paradox, I think it will be well to offer what preliminary explanation is possible by outlining the general character of the view of experience which the text aims at establishing.

To consider, first, the sceptical aspect of my thesis. My starting-point is Bradley's epistemology. I state and defend the central tenet of that epistemology, and endeavour to show, at the same time, that the implications of the Bradleian Absolute in the way of metaphysical scepticism are a great deal more far-reaching than Bradley is himself ready to admit. But although the argument from the nature and demands of knowledge is my starting-point, what I am especially concerned to maintain is that the essential result of the epistemological argument (*i.e.* that the ultimate nature of reality is 'beyond knowledge') is supported in the most striking way by considerations drawn from aspects of experience other than the cognitive. In pursuance of this task, I take up in turn three basic forms of our experience — the experience of 'self-activity,' 'moral' experience, and 'religious' experience—and I try to show that in the case of each the experiencing subject is compelled by the very nature of the experience to make affirmations which imply the conviction that reality is 'beyond knowledge.' If these affirmations are really ineradicable from these forms of experience, and if (as I expressly argue in regard to moral experience and the experience of self-activity) these forms of experience are really basic in our nature, then we seem entitled to say that the assertion of the 'supra-rational' character of reality is an assertion which 'our nature' obliges us to make.

Metaphysical scepticism is thus, in my view, the converging point of a variety of independent lines of thought. We are guided to it by the evidence at once of cognitive experience, of the experience of self-activity, of moral experience, and of religious experience. The path of epistemology is but one of many paths all leading to the same terminus.

So much for the 'sceptical' aspect. But what room does this leave for 'construction'? None, it is obvious enough, for a constructive philosophy which aims at knowing the ultimate nature of things. But for a constructive philosophy with less exalted, though still, as I believe, vitally important aims, there is room. The third chapter, that on 'Noumenal and Phenomenal Truth,' may be taken as an attempt to bridge the gulf between scepticism and construction. When once we realise (it is there urged) the full implications of the fact that 'Noumenal' Truth, Truth in its ideal or ultimate form, can have absolutely no positive or concrete significance for the finite intellect, the concept of 'Phenomenal' Truth, Truth in that degraded, but by intellect not positively transcendible, form of itself in which it does have concrete significance for the finite intellect, takes on a real importance. For this 'Phenomenal' Truth has its own standards, and we, as finite intellects, cannot afford to view with indifference the measure in which our thinking attains to, or falls short of, these standards. It is with the endeavour after 'Phenomenal' Truth only that constructive philosophy can, as it seems to me, concern itself; and its highest achievement lies in the articulation of what I have called 'final phenomenal truths.' A proposition has 'final phenomenal truth' if it be such that it is manifestly insusceptible of revision or modification under the conditions of finite experience: if it be 'intellectually incorrigible' (to use Bradley's phrase), though not (for this it could not be without becoming a 'noumenal' truth) 'intellectually satisfying.' It is possible, I believe, to arrive at a number of these propositions which, while not fulfilling the full demands of 'knowledge,' are yet such as cannot be significantly questioned under the conditions of finite experience. To this category belong, it is contended, the 'ineradicable affirmations' already alluded to (the explicit formulation of which, however, it would be premature to attempt here). And while these 'final phenomenal truths' must always remain, in one sense, 'illusions,' they are certainly not to be classed with 'mere' illusions. There is obviously a vast difference in status between illusions corrigible by fuller and better thinking, and illusions which belong (as these do) to the abiding framework of human experience. The term 'illusion,' as applied to the latter class, can retain little of its customary dyslogistic significance. It will seem to retain progressively less, I should hold, in proportion as we achieve the reorientation of attitude to 'man's place in the cosmos' which the suprarationalist premises make necessary.

This bald outline must suffice by way of indicating the central purport of my thesis. I am only too acutely conscious that that thesis involves (as will already be in part apparent) subscription to a goodly number of tenets now commonly deemed unrespectable. The temper of modern philosophy is not congenial to the reintroduction of an Absolute—and the prefixing of the qualification 'supra-rational' will probably seem to aggravate rather than to extenuate the crime. It would be futile to attempt to anticipate here the justification in the body of the work of these and other heresies, but I should like to say just this with regard to the central 'heresy' that the ultimate nature of reality is 'beyond knowledge.' There is a tendency to stigmatise doctrines of this kind as 'escapist'—as though they stood for a somewhat craven retreat from the admittedly tremendous difficulties of the metaphysical problem. This attitude seems, on the face of it, radically unfair. The mathematician is not suspected of intellectual cowardice if he declines to wrestle with the 'difficulties' involved in squaring the circle. It is recognised that he has satisfied himself, after due consideration, that the 'difficulties' are just not surmountable, that the problem is in principle insoluble. Ought it not to be accepted, as at least a provisional hypothesis, that the metaphysician who pronounces ultimate reality to be 'unknowable' is in precisely the same case?

Turning now to more general matters, the problem of presentation has, I must confess, troubled me a good deal. As the very essence of my thesis lies in the peculiar relation of reciprocal support which, it is claimed, holds between different branches of philosophical inquiry, it has been necessary to try to comprehend here a much greater variety of fundamental issues than can conveniently be treated within the covers of a single volume. One result is that I have been able to give but scant space to the examination of competing theories. In the main, I have thought it best to concentrate upon the positive development of my own position, and to pause over competing theories only where these have gained so large a measure of authority that their neglect might be deemed inexcusable. In the case of 'theory of knowledge,' however, the prevailing anarchy makes a condensed treatment more than usually unsatisfactory, and it has only been possible to avoid giving to epistemology what I should regard as a quite undue predominance in the total argument by a largely dogmatic acquiescence in certain traditional presuppositions. On that account no more can strictly be claimed for this phase of the argument than that, granted the general validity of the Idealist mode of approach to the problem of knowledge, a 'sceptical' solution is logically inevitable. To many this result will doubtless seem to be in itself a refutation of the Idealist approach. But if I am right in my contention that the evidence of other basic aspects of our experience conducts us to the same sceptical conclusion, then the terminus of the epistemological argument must appear in the light of a verification, rather than a refutation, of its premises.

It will be in place here to say a word about my general relationship to the Idealist (by which is meant, here as throughout, Absolute or Objective Idealist) philosophy. In a manner, the whole book is a sustained attack upon Idealist doctrine. I have defined my several positions, almost always, by contrast with the corresponding position in Idealism. On the other hand the very adoption of this method of presentation is in itself an earnest of my substantial adherence to the Idealist tradition in philosophy. I do not apologise for this adherence. The reaction in contemporary thought against Idealism seems to me to have passed beyond all reasonable bounds. To wipe the slate clean and start all over again—this ideal of 'modernism' may be picturesque, but it is of doubtful wisdom as a method of philosophy. The majority of Idealism's critics are surely in real danger of throwing away the baby with the bath-water—if the well-worn metaphor may be allowed. No doubt the critic will reply that there isn't any baby, and never has been, that it is all bath-water. Perhaps (though I am convinced of the contrary) this is so. But it seems fair to insist that something more than the very cursory glance which is commonly bestowed upon the scene is a *sine qua non* of the pronouncement of any opinion which deserves to be listened to.

If the reader of these pages finds in them more than he thinks proper about the Idealist philosophy, he will also, it is to be feared, find much less than he thinks proper about those startling developments in science which occupy the central place in so many recent philosophical works. He will find, indeed, almost literally nothing at all about them. Here again I am quite impenitent. I do not believe that on any single major issue raised in this book has the scientist any relevant comment to make. Philosophy's present preoccupation with, and humility before the claims of, physical science—part cause and part effect of the recoil from the too confident syntheses of Idealism—is, in my judgment, a disaster to philosophy; and perhaps, in encouraging the diversion of so much scientific energy into channels where progress is impossible by the methods of science, a minor disaster to science also. It is easy enough to understand why the scientist should have been temporarily intoxicated and the philosopher temporarily intimidated; but it is surely more than time now that philosophy reasserted its autonomy. The philosopher is not a kind of 'odd job man' in the field of knowledge. He has his own province, the province of the 'ultimate'—even though it should prove that it is but a 'human' ultimate of which he can gain positive knowledge. Into this demesne the scientist has, on the basis of a purely scientific culture, no right whatsoever to stray, whether in the interests of a materialistic or a spiritualistic view of life. It is an old story that the abstractness of science, and its dependence upon presuppositions which it is not its business to examine, preclude science from any legitimate claim to ultimacy for its results. Why it should be supposed that recent advances in the *findings* of science—however exciting—should in any way mitigate the disqualifications intrinsic in the *method* of science, is a question which the 'scientific' philosopher seems to me never to face. Not, of course, that the philosopher will omit to utilise with gratitude the accredited results of scientific investigation in any comprehensive cosmic picture which he may eventually feel empowered to offer. But these 'results' as they come from the scientist are one thing: they may wear a very different guise indeed when apportioned to their place in the economy of a system which ignores *no* aspect of experience—not even that 'thinking' through which science itself comes to be.

I should like to append an apologetic word about my adoption of the title 'supra-rationalism' to stand for the metaphysical unity of this study. The pretentiousness of employing a private 'ism' appals me so much that only the intolerable character of the circumlocutions in which I found myself involved in the effort to avoid any such coinage has reconciled me to its practice. The term 'supra-relationalism' would have better satisfied my sense of indebtedness to Bradley. But this term, which would add a syllable to a word already plentifully endowed in that respect, has the disadvantage of suggesting a line of advance in Bradley's thought which, in view of the notorious ambiguity of the term 'relation,' I have been somewhat anxious to avoid.

I pass finally to the pleasant task of thanking those who have helped me with the composition of this book. My obligations are great indeed. The Master of Balliol and Dr H. J. W. Hetherington (both one-time occupants of the Chair of Moral Philosophy in this University) were kind enough to read, and to offer very valuable comments upon, an early draft of the book; and a like service has been performed by Professor A. A. Bowman, Professor of Moral Philosophy, and Professor H. J. Paton, Professor of Logic and Rhetoric, of this University. In its later stages the book has owed most to Mr W. F. R. Hardie, M.A., Fellow of Corpus Christi College, Oxford, whose sureness of insight into what I wanted to say—and, at times, into what I ought to be saying but didn't much want to say—has saved me from many pitfalls. Mr Hardie has also been good enough to share with Mr George Brown, M.A., Lecturer in Logic, and Mr A. L. Macfie, M.A., LL.B., Lecturer in Economics (both of this University), the tedious task of proof-reading. Finally, I am glad to have an opportunity of acknowledging my indebtedness to Messrs Allen and Unwin's Philosophical Reader, whose advice has led to the removal of many defects. To all of these gentlemen I offer my most grateful thanks.

It remains only to add that, in view of the character of the work, I have judged the interests of the reader to be better served by the provision of an analytical table of contents than by an index.

CONTENTS

	PAGE
PREFACE	v–xii

CHAPTER I

THE EPISTEMOLOGICAL APPROACH TO THE SUPRA-RATIONAL ABSOLUTE

Section 1. *Introductory* 1–5

Contemporary neglect of Bradley's sceptical arguments—three causes of this adduced—task of present chapter defined.

Section 2. *Contradiction and the Non-contradictory* . . 5–14

Philosophy's need of preliminary investigation into what will finally satisfy the intellect—'the real' must at least be 'non-contradictory'—the nature of the 'contradictory' considered—how 'unite differences' without contradiction?—the only solution—hence the formula of judgment Xa is Xb—'common-sense' objection to the alleged demand for mediation of differences—answer to this objection—the ultimate defect of Dualism in metaphysics.

Section 3. *The Non-contradictory (and therefore the Real) in Principle Unattainable by Thought* . . . 14–20

Non-contradictory complex must be a unity exhibiting perfect mutual implication of differences within it—the intellect's way of advancing to the goal makes attainment impossible—the 'partial externality' of all 'grounding'—an illustration developed—for intellect, the unity remains always partially external to the differences—contrast between what the intellect wants and what the intellect can achieve—discrepancy *in principle* between the real and any thought-product—consequent rejection of doctrine of 'Degrees of Truth.'

Section 4. Untenability of Doctrine of Degrees of Truth. Criticism of it from (a) *the Pluralist,* (b) *the Supra-rationalist, Standpoint* 21–37

Short statement of doctrine of 'Degrees'—the general nature of the Pluralist's criticism—the cardinal defect in that criticism—Mr Russell's attack on 'internal relations' considered and rejected—Mr Moore's attack likewise—common failure of Realist critic to appreciate ground of Idealist's acceptance of all relations as internal—the Supra-rationalist criticism of doctrine of 'Degrees'—'noumenal' and 'phenomenal' self-consistency—how does Bradley justify his subscription to the doctrine of 'Degrees'?—criticism of Bradley's self-defence—Bradley's verbal oscillation between Idealism and Supra-rationalism—latter the more central element in his thought.

Section 5. Bearing of the Metaphysical Problem of Error upon the Doctrine of the Supra-rational Absolute . 37–43

The metaphysical status of the false judgment in Idealist metaphysics—but *can* error, properly interpreted, accept this position?—analysis of error, and exposure of the difficulties presented by it for Idealist metaphysic—error, in the end, the affirmation of a self-contradiction—but if so, can reality, which must embrace error, be animated throughout by mind, or the 'spirit of non-contradiction'?—if error, as defined, a fact, then reality not 'rational'—but do not *all* judgments, on our principles, affirm a self-contradiction?—vital distinction between two kinds of self-contradictory affirmation outlined in preliminary fashion.

CHAPTER II

The Supra-rational Absolute and its Critics

Section 1. Note on the Structure of the Total Argument . 44–45

Epistemological result to be verified by examination of freedom, morality, and religion.

Section 2. The Absolute as 'Experience,' 'Self-consistent,' 'One,' and 'All-inclusive' 45–56

Why does Bradley hold that Reality must be at least 'experience'?—one apparent ground considered and criticised—a deeper ground suggested, on basis of Bradley's account of the nature and functions of immediate experience in the knowledge situation—difficulty of accepting Bradley's 'felt many in one'—unity of reality comes to us neither in mere feeling nor mere thought, but in an ideally interpreted feeling—Reality cannot be significantly described as 'experience'—sense in which Reality may be significantly described as 'self-consistent,' 'one,' and 'all-inclusive' must be carefully qualified.

CONTENTS

Section 3. Criticisms of the Supra-rational Absolute—(a) Indirect Criticisms 56–72

Supposed certainty, in post-Kantian Idealism, that 'the real is the rational'—Idealist gloss upon the Kantian distinction of noumenal and phenomenal—substitution of 'identity in difference' for 'abstract-self-identity' does not really overcome the radical discrepancy between the 'world of the understanding' and the 'world of reality'—'otherness' indispensable to thought, impossible to Reality—Bosanquet's attempt to prove 'otherness' to be inessential to self-consciousness in its full nature—the failure of this attempt —'unity' and 'otherness' complementary and alternating aspects of life of self-consciousness—linguistic embarrassments of Idealists in attempting a description of the Absolute's nature—the 'logical' argument that the opposition of 'self' and 'other' is necessarily transcended in self-consciousness, stated and criticised—apprehended distinction of self from object differs *toto cælo* from apprehended distinction of object from object—consciousness that there is an ultimate unity behind differences of self and not-self is not necessarily consciousness of the nature of that unity.

Section 4. Criticisms of the Supra-rational Absolute—(b) Direct Criticisms 72–81

Does our Absolute 'explain nothing'?—this, if meant as a criticism, involves a *petitio principii*—criticism that supra-rational Absolute is 'meaningless' is equally insubstantial—criticism that the Bradleian argument for scepticism rests upon the 'adoption of the logic of abstract identity'—misunderstanding implied in this criticism—criticism that the condemnation of the 'phenomenal' presupposes knowledge of the principle of the 'noumenal'—first answer to this, that the condemnation presupposes knowledge only of what the noumenal *is not*—but is negative knowledge not logically posterior to positive knowledge?—two forms in which this doctrine may be maintained—examination of our own 'negative judgment' in connection with each of these forms, and explanation of its immunity from the orthodox criticism—final criticism, the apparent reduction of 'cosmos' to 'chaos' involved in supra-rationalist theory—answer, that on none but this, or some similar, theory can we *escape* the reduction to 'chaos,' unless the evidence of practical experience be illegitimately abstracted from.

CHAPTER III

NOUMENAL AND PHENOMENAL TRUTH

Section 1. Absolute Idealism's Rejection of the Correspondence Notion of Truth 82–84

Why Coherence is for Idealism the 'nature,' as well as the 'criterion,' of Truth—Correspondence View (Idealist tells us) natural only at inadequate stage of thought's development, and must be rejected.

xvi   SCEPTICISM AND CONSTRUCTION

PAGE

Section 2. *Supra-rationalist Modification of this Rejection.*
  Noumenal (or Ideal) and Phenomenal Truth . 84–90

  On Supra-rationalist metaphysic, the 'union of thought with reality' is a consummation *not continuous with* the intellect's search after truth in positive thinking—hence is *not* what Truth means 'in the end' or 'from a higher point of view'—the point of view for which Truth means this has no 'positive' significance for finite mind—for finite mind, subject-object dualism remains, and so long as it remains, truth must mean some kind of 'correspondence' of ideas with reality—a 'Noumenal' Truth may be posited, in which 'correspondence' is meaningless; but Truth in so far as it has positive significance for human thinking (Phenomenal Truth) cannot dispense with 'correspondence'—brief excursus upon the reasons for postulating some kind of 'ideal intermediary' in cognition.

Section 3. *The Criterion of Phenomenal Truth*—(a) *Correspondence* 91–96

  Analysis of example in which we seem to ourselves to be using 'correspondence with fact' as our test—if concerned with the judgment of another person, we cannot, strictly, use it as a term in the comparison—and the 'fact' with which it is to correspond is itself a judgment—application of correspondence 'test' presupposes the possession of a different test—the 'stronghold' of the Correspondence theory—its defect the same as before—transition to a new view of the test which often underlies the Correspondence view—this view criticised—a final attempt to make Correspondence view plausible—its defects.

Section 4. *The Criterion of Phenomenal Truth*—(b) *Rational Coherence* 97–103

  Our substantial agreement with Idealist theory—difference on our theory as to *what it is* that 'Coherence' tests—application of Coherence doctrine of 'test,' to Correspondence doctrine of 'meaning,' of Phenomenal Truth—impossibility of achieving a content which fully satisfies the test—no 'degrees' even of Phenomenal Truth—but are *all* possible judgments modifiable by advancing knowledge?—preliminary indication of certain exceptions, where what is asserted is 'intellectually incorrigible.'

Section 5. *The Criterion of Phenomenal Truth*—(c) *Immediate Apprehension* 103–106

  Development of the conception of 'intellectually incorrigible' judgments—the characteristics which make them so—'self-awareness' as a humanly ultimate guarantee of the validity of certain assertions.

CONTENTS

Section 6. Phenomenal Truth, as the Intellectually Incorrigible, contrasted with Noumenal Truth, as the Intellectually Satisfactory 106–108

The 'final truths' whose possibility we have maintained belong to the 'Phenomenological' level—they give intellectual incorrigibility, not intellectual satisfaction—what the latter demands not satisfied in the judgments guaranteed by 'self-awareness'—final phenomenal truths not restricted to unimportant matter.

Section 7. Status of 'Geometrical Truths' in Idealism and Supra-rationalism Respectively 108–112

Presuppositions upon which this argument is to be developed—reasons why 'final phenomenal truth' is possible in geometry—the error in the Idealist doctrine of geometrical truth—but, again, the final truth claimed by us here is only final 'phenomenal' truth.

CHAPTER IV

MORAL FREEDOM (I)

Section 1. Introductory 113–115

Apparently inexpugnable character of the belief in freedom—rough statement of the type of freedom to be defended here.

Section 2. Criticism of the Idealist Doctrine of Freedom . 115–127

The doctrine briefly stated—loses point when the Bradleian Absolute is substituted for the Idealist Absolute—no doctrine which considers freedom from point of view of 'Absolute' possible to us—this limitation of ultimacy not a serious defect—Idealist doctrine does not touch the freedom which is a postulate of morality—Idealist metaphysic incompatible with latter freedom—Bosanquet on freedom—some arguments considered in favour of compatibility of Idealist metaphysic with morality—ethical irrelevance of the 'freedom of enlightenment.'

Section 3. Conditions of Problem Surveyed and Method of Argument Determined 128–142

Determinist cannot ignore the 'immediate affirmation of consciousness'—but may argue that this more than offset by the manifold evidences of universal causal continuity—claim to freedom involves claim to be able to interrupt this causal continuity, but is there any evidence that conduct ever does in fact interrupt it?—there is evidence, the only kind in the nature of the case procurable, in the immediate experience of the subject in the 'effortful act of will'—the experience of 'effortful willing' furnishes the most significant positive

b

xviii SCEPTICISM AND CONSTRUCTION

PAGE

assurance of our freedom—analysis of this experience, and of the claims in the way of freedom which inherently attach to it—inquiry begun into the credentials of these claims—why should we *not* believe in them if they are judgments which our nature *obliges* us to make?—no answer at all that freedom is thus made to rest upon a 'mere feeling'—immediate experience or feeling alone *could* furnish positive evidence of freedom, if freedom exists—Libertarian must therefore rely ultimately upon 'feeling,' but this no defect—two reasons why Determinist must actively aim at 'explaining away' this feeling—Libertarian should further show that freedom defended collides neither with observed facts nor with postulates of thought.

Section 4. Criticism of Attempt to 'Explain away' the Sense of Effortful Activity 142–158

Importance of distinguishing between consciousness of self as 'active' and consciousness of self as 'scene of activity'—former involves awareness of acting 'against the line of least resistance'—McDougall's attempt to explain this experience consistently with premises of the 'instinct psychology'—criticism of McDougall's view—Bradley's account of 'perception of activity'—as with McDougall, constituents as stated will not explain the specific experience they are meant to explain—possibility considered, and rejected, that the addition of certain 'bodily feelings' will make account adequate.

Section 5. Recapitulation of General Argument . . 158–159

CHAPTER V

MORAL FREEDOM (II)

Section 1. Defence against 'Caprice' Criticism . . 160–162

Criticism that lack of 'intelligible continuity' between character and act implies that act is not agent's *own* act—answer, that criticism rests upon the postulation of a false dilemma.

Section 2. Defence against Charge of Ignoring the Observable Continuity of Conduct and Character . . 162–165

Freedom here defended not a freedom in which 'anything may happen'—prediction within limits made possible by two factors which our theory can consistently recognise.

Section 3. Defence against Charge of Miracle-mongering . 165–167

Assumption underlying this charge a false assumption—sense in which free will is, and sense in which it is not, 'mysterious.'

CONTENTS xix

Section 4. The Privacy of Will-power. Answers to Objections 167–172

Is expenditure of will-energy something for which the private self is solely responsible?—objection to this view on ground of supposed native differences in will-power—further objection on ground of apparent modifiability of will-power by external conditions—answers to these objections.

Section 5. Summary of Doctrine regarding Will-energy, with some Further Observations 172–175

Five points recapitulated—sixth point, conditions and *raison d'être* of will-energy—seventh point, is there a 'maximal' expenditure of will-energy?

Section 6. Reaction of Present Doctrine upon Problem of Finite 'Individuality' 175–179

What 'individuality' involves—are finite persons real individuals?—Idealist answer to this question—Idealist claim that its answer preserves for finite persons the possibility of all that they most value in 'individuality'—criticism of this claim—the individuality of finite persons in terms of the doctrine of this chapter.

Section 7. Note on Bradley's Criticism of the 'Reality' of the Finite Self 179–183

Nerve of Bradley's criticism—our agreement with it qualified by our doctrine of freedom considered in relation to general supra-rationalist attitude to experience.

CHAPTER VI

The Reality of Moral Obligation

Section 1. Absolute Idealism and the Status of Morality . 184–191

Metaphysical significance of doctrine of present chapter—incompatibility of Idealist's intelligible universe with reality of moral obligation further considered—Bosanquet's vacillating account of the 'bad self'—the account consistent with his metaphysics implies the truth of the Socratic doctrine of willing.

Section 2. The Socratic Theory of the Will . . . 191–196

Origin of the theory which denies possibility of the 'incontinent' act—conditions which it must fulfil to be accepted—attempt to 'explain away' the appearance of 'knowing the better and choosing the worse'—cases which the explanation seems incapable of covering—*caveat* against 'self-deception' as an explanatory principle.

xx SCEPTICISM AND CONSTRUCTION

PAGE

Section 3. Statement of the Problem, and of the Method to be Adopted 196–200

Supposed uniqueness of the experience of the 'ought'—critic of the reality of moral obligation must analyse this experience into non-moral constituents—this fairly commonly believed to be impossible, yet moral experience seldom allowed its rightful place in metaphysical construction—probable reason, that apprehension of 'oughtness' not seen to be 'embedded' in human experience with the security attaching to a supposedly incompatible logical postulate—line of treatment suggested by these considerations.

Section 4. Exposition and Defence of the Idealist Doctrine of Desire 201–211

What is meant by holding that object of desire is a conceived personal good'—the 'self-reference' in desire fundamental—defects in Butler's view of desire—the characteristic unity of a rational being's desires attributable to the 'self-referent' factor—alleged 'egoism' of doctrine we are maintaining—question of 'egoism and altruism' not in fact raised by doctrine—fundamental fallacy in criticism of doctrine is equation of 'aiming at personal good' with 'aiming at future state of satisfaction of private self'—Rashdall's proposed dilemma not applicable to doctrine as here stated.

Section 5. The Contrast of the 'End of the Self-as-Such' with the 'End of Desire' 211–217

How this contrast emerges—'end of impulse,' 'end of desire,' and 'end of self-as-such' illustrated in a concrete situation—the contrast rooted in the structure of human nature—note on its emergence, and special nature, in primitive life.

Section 6. The Moral Authority of the End of the Self-as-Such—(a) *Removal of Obstacles to its Appreciation* 217–227

Impossibility of formal 'proof'—disposal of hostile prepossessions our main task—prejudice due to the religious texture of common moral notions—prejudice due to liability of suggested moral ideal to express itself in materialistic forms—but main prejudice the supposed 'egoism' of the ideal—view defended that ideal *may* express itself in egoistic forms and still be 'moral'—'economic' and 'moral' good—'moral obligation' even to private pleasure a possibility—the limited truth in Butler's 'manifest obligation' of 'Reasonable Self-love'—charge of 'egoism' further refuted—the 'social impulse' in man—'private pleasure' only one of many wanted objects—question whether ordinary moral education does not imply egoism of moral principle in just our sense—note on Intuitionalist's doctrine of 'goods.'

Section 7. *Digression upon the Crucial Difficulties of Intuitionalist Ethics* 227–244

Self-contradiction in the conception of a manifold of moral rules each of which is 'absolute'—Mr Ross's avoidance of this difficulty by conceiving the intuited rules or principles as only *prima facie* obligations—question naturally arises, how determine our 'actual' duty when *prima facie* obligations conflict?—monistic moralist has a single ultimate authority to which to appeal in cases of conflict of commonly accepted rules, but what corresponds to this in Mr Ross's theory?—Mr Ross's first answer seems to suggest that there is no such principle for him, and that none is needed—but later maintains that we have to try to observe the 'greatest balance of *prima facie* rightness over *prima facie* wrongness'—but on Mr Ross's premises it is impossible *in principle* to make this calculation—we cannot by 'taking thought' advance even to 'more probable opinion'—second major objection to Intuitionalism its failure to reconcile the findings of comparative ethics with its definitive set of 'self-evident' obligations—orthodox answer of Intuitionalist (*e.g.* of Mr Ross), that a truth may be self-evident and yet demand a certain 'mental maturity' for its apprehension—but in fact the *kind* of 'mental immaturity' which is ascribable to savages, etc., is not the kind which is relevant to this issue—and not all who dissent from the Intuitionalist's list are 'mentally immature' in *any* reasonable sense—further, what positive account can the Intuitionalist give of the 'contrary' principles which other moral consciousnesses recognise as obligatory?—failure of Intuitionalist to make his list of self-evident principles evident even to fellow-Intuitionalists.

Section 8. *The Moral Authority of the 'End of the Self-as-such'*: (b) *Its Intuitive Appeal* . . . 244–246

'Test Situation' appealed to—obligation towards end of self-as-such intuitively apprehended—obligation is the obligation to respect one's *self*—or, again, the obligation to 'be rational'—ultimate 'explanation' of obligation not possible—'go and *feel*!'

Section 9. *Concluding Remarks on the Implications of the Position Reached* 246–247

The 'ethical argument for freedom' no longer 'hypothetical' only—reality of moral value means rejection of 'intelligible' reality.

CHAPTER VII

The Principle of Moral Valuation

Section 1. *Moral Valuation and 'the Moral End'* . . 248–253

Is problem of principle of moral valuation same as problem of nature of 'the moral end'?—difficulties in so understanding it if term 'moral end' conceived in usual way—

only if 'the moral end' means just that which each agent takes to be morally best can we evaluate conduct morally in terms of it—suggested way of escape through distinction of 'subjective' from 'objective' rightness—ineffectiveness of this device—what *can* an 'objectively' as distinct from a 'subjectively' right mean?

Section 2. *Approach to, and Exposition of, the Positive Theory to be Defended* 254–261

Subject-matter of moral valuation—the two morally relevant aspects of volitional acts—two points recalled in connection with 'will-energy' aspect—classification of possible principles of moral valuation on basis of above 'morally relevant' aspects of volition—exhaustiveness of classification—objections to adopting principles (or theories) (*a*) and (*b*)—conditions necessary to evaluate *personal* worth satisfied only in theory of type (*c*)—propositional statement of main points in doctrine to be maintained.

Section 3. *Discussion of the Difficulties in the Practical Application of our Principle* 261–267

Can we, on our principle, pass moral judgment upon others?—concrete content as a 'clue' to will-energy—conditions of knowledge which must be fulfilled if content is to be a clue—these conditions as a rule fulfilled to an appreciable extent—does our principle encourage 'moral anarchy'?

Section 4. *Reply to Criticism Based upon the Moral Consciousness's Apparent Acceptance of the Relevance of Content.* (*Part I*) 267–274

Enlightenment of content of ideal often taken as adding to the moral value of devotion to ideal, and sometimes taken as the 'predominant partner'—is this an attitude which belongs to the moral consciousness as such?—on the contrary, such judgments occur only when moral consciousness is, in assignable ways, distorted or obscured—argument, with illustrations, in support of this contention—by what criterion do we, in our most serious moments, estimate our own moral worth?

Section 5. *Digression on the Supposed Distinction of Merit from Goodness* 274–276

Statement of the distinction—its untenability as a distinction *within* morality—it really implies the postulation of another intrinsic value besides moral value—origin and validity of this postulation to be considered later.

CONTENTS

Section 6. Reply to Criticism Based upon the Moral Consciousness's Apparent Acceptance of the Relevance of Content. (Part II) 276–279

The false abstraction through which moral value comes to be ascribed to 'content' or 'concrete ends' in their own right—level of moral reflection required to avoid this natural misinterpretation of moral consciousness's deliverances—'pragmatical' value of the false standard.

Section 7. The Fiction of 'Non-Moral' Objective Values . 279–285

How the postulation of Cultural Values, objective but non-moral, arises—the offspring of the error already examined of ascribing moral value to content as such—reply to criticism that to make all value reside in the will to the ideal involves a ὕστερον πρότερον—all *objective, intrinsic* value resides in the will, the object of desire being, as such, merely value-for-self—concept of an objectively valuable emerges only in relation to the categorical imperative—are Truth and Beauty not intrinsic values?—objections to so conceiving them—'trinitarian' conception of the Values incompatible with unity of personality—real value of Truth and Beauty.

Section 8. Metaphysical Significance of Present Doctrine . 285–286

CHAPTER VIII

Supra-rationalism and Religion

Section 1. Introductory 287–288

What is claimed for the argument of this chapter?—its limitations as contrasted with the arguments on freedom and morality.

Section 2. Alleged Contradictoriness of Religious Experience. 'Finite God' Solution 288–292

Two fundamental elements of religious consciousness—their apparent mutual incompatibility exhibited—are they compatible if God is taken as less than the Whole?—'moral dynamic of religion' then possible, but not the 'peace of religion'—'Finite God' cannot be more than a temporary halting-place in religion.

Section 3. The 'Supra-rational God'—the Meaning of the Conception, and its Value as a Solution . . 292–300

God as 'unknowable'; is this a contradiction in terms?—how doctrine may be 'meaningful' without compromising God's fundamental unknowableness—God as 'Infinite in Power, Wisdom, and Goodness' *is* 'unknowable'—sketch of religious man's defence (against allegation of contradiction) on basis of 'unknowable' (or better, 'supra-rational') God—the flaw in this defence—its rehabilitation—historical precedent for holding to supra-rational character of Divine Perfection—impossibility of adopting any other line of defence.

Section 4. Harmony of this Solution with General Principles of Bradley's Philosophy. Bradley's own Solution   300–305

No rationalist philosophy can vindicate religious experience—Bradley's Absolute as the philosophic counterpart of the God of religion—Bradley's statement of the inherent contradiction in religion—his reasons for holding this contradictoriness to be a matter of indifference to religion—criticism of Bradley's view.

Section 5. Relation of Faith and Moral Fervour. Justification of this Relation on the Metaphysical Theory of the Present Work 305–311

The faith which gives 'peace' is somehow an actual *stimulus* to moral endeavour—explanation of this relation from point of view of religion—the explanation involves an assumed affinity, for religion, between God and 'good'—religion need not, but philosophy must, justify this assumption (which looks as though it were in conflict with metaphysics here maintained)—the principle of the justification on Supra-rationalist metaphysics—but no philosophy can 'prove God' save formally—recapitulation of argument so far.

Section 6. Implications of Above Doctrine with Respect to Theology 311–315

Our 'creed' stated—theological 'articles,' in ordinary sense, not possible—possibility that the great historical religions 'differ only in opinion '—' accidental ' character of credal dogma—the only sound principle for the ' grading ' of creeds.

Section 7. Defence against Criticism of ' Undue Abstractness '   316–322

Choice is really between an 'abstract' religion and no religion at all—but does our religion lack anything essential to full 'satisfyingness'?—demand for a personal God considered and rejected—demand for a personal mediator between man and God considered and rejected—note on the demand for assurance of immortality.

SCEPTICISM AND CONSTRUCTION

CHAPTER I

THE EPISTEMOLOGICAL APPROACH TO THE SUPRA-RATIONAL ABSOLUTE

Section 1. *Introductory*

NOT very many, I suppose, of those who are entitled to pass an opinion would dissent from the judgment that the most distinguished figure in the last half-century of British philosophy was the author of *Appearance and Reality*. It is natural to ask, therefore, why Bradley's central doctrine—a doctrine propounded unceasingly, and with the evident consciousness (much as he disdained claims to originality) that herein lay such individual contribution as he could make to the progress of philosophic thought—should at the present day be little better than ignored. For upwards of thirty years Bradley laboured to secure, if not an acceptance, at least an intelligent recognition of the existence, of his epistemological arguments for metaphysical scepticism. But that this aspiration has in any substantial measure been realised no student of Bradley's writings would, I venture to think, be prepared to admit. It is true enough, of course, that contemporary philosophy in this country abounds in allusions to the 'Bradleian scepticism.' But it is, I think, equally beyond dispute that a very small proportion of these references (whose general vein is one of denunciation and summary dismissal) imply more than a casual acquaintance with the grounds upon which Bradley's disconcerting conclusions rest; and that Bradley himself was acutely aware of the virtual irrelevance of most of the comments on his position is, I think, a fair inference from the tenor of his later writings, which are directed not so much to answering professed criticisms of his scepticism as to removing current misapprehensions as to its nature and basis.

This disinclination to treat seriously the distinctive doctrine of a philosopher whose eminence is at least verbally acknowledged on all hands, constitutes something of an anomaly. But it may be explained in part, and in part even excused. I wish here to indicate briefly three influences which have been operative. To grasp them clearly is in some measure to purge one's mind of the hostile bias which they tend to engender.

The first is the general Western prejudice against the very possibility of scepticism as the final issue of metaphysics. It seems to be felt that however subtle and brilliant may be the dialectic which suggests such a result, it must be regarded, after all, as no more than an intellectual *tour de force*. Just as we know that Achilles does catch up with the tortoise, even although we may feel a difficulty in exposing the precise fallacy in the argument which denies it, so we know that Bradley *must* be wrong in erecting a philosophy which destroys philosophy, even although we do not see just how we are to refute him. Western philosophy, it may be suspected, has never quite got over Hegel's ridicule of Schelling's Absolute. A unity beyond the difference of subject and object, a unity in which all the features of our world are transformed out of recognition, is "a night in which all cows are black!" It has become the fashion to look upon this epigram as though, through some magical property, it conveys decisive proof that the view of Ultimate Reality to which it refers is merely absurd: so that frequently philosophical critics appear to consider their destructive purpose satisfactorily accomplished, and further argument to be all but superfluous, if only they have succeeded in reducing the metaphysics of their opponents to something approximating to this ill-starred Schellingian Absolutism. Now in a subsequent chapter I shall try to face squarely the

APPROACH TO SUPRA-RATIONAL ABSOLUTE

genuine arguments which may be brought against the doctrine of a 'supra-rational' Absolute. At present I wish merely to enter a protest against the uncritical tendency to give to Hegel's epigram the force of a conclusive argument. There is nothing self-evidently ridiculous in a view which holds that 'the All' must remain opaque to the categories of the intellect. Those of us who believe it to be the true view are in excellent company. Not only Bradley and Schelling, not only Plotinus, not only—as I should be prepared to argue—Plato in his profoundest utterances, but the whole vast army of mystics of all religions, the persons who, by common consent, embody the religious genius of a people at its highest level, have borne a like testimony. Or again, now that a broader culture is making it evident to all save the incorrigibly parochial that the Oriental absorption in 'the One' is not a symptom of barbaric ignorance or neurotic superstition, but has the support of critical philosophical thinking no less worthy of attention than many admired systems of the Occident, we might appeal to the Vedic literature for impressive evidence of the *prima facie* reasonableness of such a view as that of Bradley. But in truth there is a veritable 'cloud of witnesses.' There have been, I suspect, moments in the meditations of well-nigh every great philosopher in history when the reason-transcending character of Reality has suddenly presented itself, not so much as a more or less defensible doctrine, but rather as sheer platitude. Enough has perhaps been said, however, without attempting further extension of our list, to suggest that those—and they are not few—who would condemn the Supra-rational Absolute without a hearing are on the side of complacent dogmatism rather than of critical philosophy.

A second major influence has been Bradley's own doctrine of Degrees of Truth and Reality. About this I shall have to say a good deal in the sequel. It is enough here to point out that Bradley's adherence to this doctrine has enormously weakened the effect of his statement of the argument for the

Supra-rational Absolute. For whereas every serious student of philosophy is aware that he cannot legitimately ignore Bradley's thought, Bradley has, by his championship of this essentially non-sceptical doctrine, made it possible for friends and foes alike to treat his work as though the really fundamental and significant thing in it were *not* his presentation of the case for scepticism. This attitude to Bradley, which would regard him as characteristically a Hegelian, although subject to occasional wayward aberrations into scepticism, cannot, I am confident, be justified by a survey of Bradley's writings *in extenso*. But the doctrine of 'Degrees' affords strong proximate justification, and Bradley must accordingly accept a fair share of personal responsibility for the misapprehension.

The third influence is this. Bradley has, in the course of his writings, led up to his theory of the relation of thought and Reality in a considerable variety of ways. Now some of these approaches are notably less satisfactory than others. At times the conclusion is made to depend upon, or is at least closely interwoven with, specific doctrines which even those who support Bradley's main contention would without much hesitation reject. Unhappily the most familiar statements of Bradley's position suffer especially from this disability. To mention one conspicuous instance, a good deal of the argument in *Appearance and Reality* is coloured by adherence to the very doubtful doctrine of 'ideality' as the 'loosening of content from psychical existence.' Again, Bradley's doctrine of Immediate Experience bristles with difficulties: yet from the great importance which Bradley himself appears to attach to it, the reader may easily be misled into supposing that the rejection of this doctrine logically involves the rejection of Bradley's whole theory. It is not to be denied, I think, that there are a number of factors in Bradley's presentation which militate against the maximum persuasiveness of which his sceptical proposition is inherently capable.

This last consideration determines the form which the

epistemological part of this essay may most profitably take. My chief interest is not in Bradley's *ipsissima verba*, and I shall make no attempt to sketch his several methods of dealing with his problem. I am concerned with the validity of his sceptical conclusions rather than with the manner of their presentation. For I wish to use these conclusions, in later chapters, as the basis for a constructive treatment of some of the central issues of philosophy. I shall proceed, therefore, by endeavouring to present the sceptical argument in what appears to me to be its least vulnerable form, freed, as far as possible, from all 'appendages' which might provoke independent controversy. I shall, in so doing, utilise principally the important 'Note A' in the Appendix to *Appearance and Reality*. But I shall supplement freely from other sources where this seems desirable.

Section 2. Contradiction and the Non-contradictory

Philosophy, Bradley has said, is an attempt to gain a view of the general nature of Reality which will satisfy the intellect. This definition, which looks innocent enough, nevertheless suggests strongly the necessity of a certain preliminary inquiry as an indispensable basis of all philosophical construction. We ought to ask at the beginning, 'What in general *would* satisfy the intellect?' or 'What are the formal characteristics of that which the intellect is prepared to accept as real?' Just how fruitful such an investigation may prove for subsequent construction will depend, naturally, upon the sort of answer which our question induces. But it is hard to see how any philosophy which pretends to be critical and ultimate—and surely these adjectives are implied in the very meaning of the word philosophy—can legitimately dispense with this preliminary. Our 'scientific' philosophies, of course, do commonly dispense with it. But it may well be asked whether it is not just the nemesis of such a method—or rather lack of method—that their several constructions are in agreement with one another upon scarcely one positive philosophic proposition of importance. Recent philosophy, for all its richness, has exhibited a truly chaotic instability. And the fundamental reason, in my judgment, is the failure to keep firmly before the mind that what is good enough for science is emphatically not good enough for philosophy. It is not science's task to ask of its principles that they should be rational through and through, capable of satisfying in full the demands which the intellect makes upon whatever lays claim to be finally 'real.' But in respect of philosophic principles we can aim at nothing less. We may have to be content with something less. But if so, it will be of the first importance to know that, and if possible to see why, they are less.

It is assumed, of course, that the investigation in question is one upon which we can engage with some hope of achieving results. But this is an assumption which seems hardly doubtful. Thinking is a process directed towards the establishment of truth, of a 'content' which will adequately express the real. And it is a process which is, quite evidently, not haphazard, but marked by a well-defined continuity.[1] To suppose it blind and 'aimless' would be, in effect, to render all argumentation futile, and would imply a refinement of scepticism which it is no purpose of these pages to advocate. It ought therefore to be possible, one may suppose, by careful scrutiny of the process of thinking, to lay bare the criterion which directs its activity and controls its advances from less to greater satisfaction.

[1] It is not so evident, of course, to those who insist upon concentrating attention upon low-grade specimens of thinking, e.g. perception. And it may be remarked in passing that the modern preoccupation with the so-called 'problem of perception' seems out of all proportion to its real importance for philosophy. The manner in which this problem is broached —involving various assumptions of physical and physiological ' truths '— is such that its discussion is necessarily incompetent to make any contribution to the ultimate problem of knowledge. For the veridical character of physical and physiological knowledge is just *taken for granted* as the very basis of the discussion.

APPROACH TO SUPRA-RATIONAL ABSOLUTE

Now there is one mark, albeit a negative one, of the 'intellectually satisfying' concerning which there is no serious difference of opinion. From it we may make our start. The intellect will accept as genuinely expressing reality no content which contradicts itself. Controversy there may be as to what precisely constitutes a 'self-contradiction.' But no one with whom philosophy is called upon seriously to deal will refuse to allow that where there is that which he understands by 'contradiction,' there is defect of truth. Let us begin then by inquiring into the essential mark of the contradictory. Our discussion, as we shall find, will lead on naturally to the apprehension of an indispensable condition of the non-contradictory, and will accordingly yield us not merely negative but also some positive (though purely formal) information as to the general character of that which the intellect can accept as true and real.

What then is Contradiction? Its specific character will best disclose itself by reference to the logical nature of the unit of thought, 'judgment' or 'predication.'[1]

All judgment, all thinking, involves the assertion, in some sense, of 'unity' in 'diversity.' So much is obvious. We cannot possibly dispense either with the differences or with the unity. Unless the differences are pronounced to be in some sense 'one,' we have not got a judgment but, at best, a mere 'association of ideas.' And unless it is 'differences' that we pronounce to be one, there is again no judgment, for there is no movement of thought at all. It is an old story that the formula of thinking cannot be 'A is A.' The predicate may, indeed, be *verbally* identical with the subject, but unless it is *conceptually* distinct we have got, not thinking, but a mere form of words.

Thinking then must unite differences. But if the formula of judgment is certainly not 'A is A,' is it more correctly

---

[1] In what immediately follows I shall be doing little more than restating the gist of ' Note A,' already referred to.

expressed as 'A is B'? If we take this formula strictly as it stands, it seems evident that we are in no better case than before. For B, being different from A, is not-A. What the formula appears to say, therefore, is that 'A is not-A.' But this is to assert and to annul in the same act, which no one supposes to be other than crassly self-contradictory. If, then, the uniting of differents characteristic of thought is to find expression, it cannot be in the simple formula 'A is B.' For this, strictly interpreted, expresses rather what thought characteristically abhors than what thought characteristically affirms.

But, it may be said, no one really supposes that thinking, in uniting differences A and B, pronounces them to be *identical*. This is to misread the significance of the 'is' of the copula. 'A is B' (this rose is red) really means 'A has B' (this rose has red). And with this (as it may be said) we escape the easy reduction to self-contradiction. But do we? On the contrary this new formula but disguises, and in no way removes, the contradiction evident in the rejected formula. Let us suppose that what thought means to assert is that 'A has B.' Surely to assert that 'A has B' is just to assert that 'A is such-as-to-have-B'? We are asserting now the identity of A with 'such-as-to-have-B.' But since 'such-as-to-have-B' cannot be taken to be merely the same as A (for if it were, we should be back to the tautological 'A is A'), it must be something different, must be, let us say, C. Thus what we are doing in our new formula is to replace 'A is B' by 'A is C'—which seems no great advance. We are still saying that 'A is not-A.' Our new formula is still the formula of contradiction.

At a first glance, then, the uniting of differents appears to give us contradiction at once. Yet it is obvious that it *must* be capable of being understood in a way in which it does not give us contradiction. For to unite differences is the very life of thought. It must, then, be only some particular way of uniting differences which is contradictory, and there must also be some way to which thought can give its assent. There must be some way in which A and B may be united without 'asserting and annulling in the same act.' What is this way? How does thought endeavour to effect the union of differents? The answer to this question should throw into sharper outline the precise nature of that union of differents which is self-contradictory, at the same time as it indicates the conditions which must be observed by any union of differents which the intellect can accept as expressing the real.

How then (for this is what we are asking) are differences to be conceived so as to be compatible with their unity? There is, I think, but one answer possible—that found in the idea of 'system.' So long as the diversities in question are thought of as self-contained units, thought recoils, and must recoil, from the declaration of their identity. But it is otherwise if the differences are conceived not as self-contained units but as diverse expressions of a system which is a whole of mutually implicatory elements. If the differences are so conceived, what we are doing when we connect A and B in predication is not to assert that A as such is B as such, but that a system X which expresses itself as A does also and thereby necessarily express itself as B. And there is no contradiction in this if X is indeed a system of mutually implicatory elements. For it is the very mark of such a system that it expresses itself as A only in so far as it is also B (C, D, etc.), in B only in so far as it is also A (C, D, etc.), and so on. In such a whole, diversity, although a fact, *is not a fact opposed to identity*. For there is nothing in the diversities which is external to the system, nothing in them, therefore, which is not derivable from the identity. Once admit into the diversities any element of being *not* internal to the system, and you find that, in sundering the differences from the identity, you have also destroyed the idea of a mutually implicatory system. If, however, we hold fast to the idea of such a system, we find that therein identity and diversity are but obverse sides of the same fact. The variety of the elements has no particle of being apart from their oneness. A and B are, though different, at the same time one, for their whole nature derives from the identity of which they are expressions.

It is under the controlling idea of such a system, accordingly, that the uniting of differences characteristic of thought must proceed throughout. We need make only the simplest 'ideal experiment' to discover that to unite differences *per se*, or simply, is abhorrent to thought. On the other hand, their union as connected expressions of a systematic identity seems not only abstractly intelligible, but also to represent plainly the goal of the intellect in actual practice. For it is clear enough that the constant aim of intellect is to *mediate* connections. It is not content with the conjunction of B with A. It endeavours to offer a ground for the conjunction. And this is just to say that thought endeavours to treat the differences of experience not as entities *per se*, but as members of a system which prescribes their mutual relations. Refusal to do this is tantamount to giving up the business of thinking.

Bringing together the points of our discussion so far, we can now suggest an answer to our question, 'How may differences be united for thought without self-contradiction?' The answer is, only in so far as the differences are conceived as mutually implicatory elements of a system. The whole effort of thought is directed to the establishment of such a system—or, not to prejudge an important issue, of such systems. And it is only in proportion to the perfection of the established system that the differences are with logical assurance pronounced to be one.

The true formula of the judgment then is not 'A is A,' nor 'A is B,' nor 'A has B,' nor anything of a cognate character which treats the terms as simple entities. The formula is $A(x)$ is B, or, perhaps more suggestively, Xa is Xb—X being conceived as a mutually implicatory system such that in expressing itself as A it necessarily expresses itself as B. 'A *as such* is B' gives us, on the contrary, the very essence of contradiction. In asserting differences to be one *per se*, it merely annuls what it posits. They can be 'one' only as differentiations of a system which prescribes their mutual implication. This, if I am right, is what Bradley means when he urges that to bring differences together in 'bare conjunction' is the very type of contradiction.[1] Brought together thus they collide, and must collide. To avoid collision, they must be brought together at a point in which 'internal diversity' is posited; brought together, that is, *within* a system X. Conjoined simply, at a point which has no internal diversity, the differences are denied the sole condition which can save their identification from being a flat self-contradiction.

Let us now notice the kind of objection which will be felt against what I have said from the side of 'common sense.' A brief discussion of it will, I think, assist in elucidating further the particular point I am anxious to make.

'What you are saying,' it may be protested, 'implies that a self-contradictory character attaches to by far the greater part of the affirmations made in ordinary life. Ordinary cognitive experience consists of numberless assertions which connect greenness with grass, a cylindrical shape with this pipe, surliness with such and such a person, and so on, and it is the exception rather than the rule that in cases of the sort we think of the connection as "mediated." As a rule it never occurs to us when we attribute a character to an object that there is any difficulty in the immediate connecting of the differents, or any necessity for this internal diversity in the subject which you claim to be logically demanded. Yet we certainly are not aware of uttering anything that is abhorrent to the nature of the intellect. And if ordinary experience suggests so strongly that the intellect does *not* shrink from a "bare conjunction," does this not throw some doubt upon the result of your logical analysis?'

[1] *Appearance and Reality* (2nd ed.), p. 566.

The answer to this is, I think, not very difficult if it is borne in mind that on the whole man thinks to live, not lives to think. A purely intellectual interest is rare, and is certainly not present in the normal commerce of man with his world. Hence it is seldom indeed that the intellect 'functions pure.' The rational interest is controlled by the practical, and it is enough for us if the connections we affirm are such as to 'work' satisfactorily for the ordinary purposes of our contacts with our natural and social environment. Such satisfactory 'working' is notoriously compatible with gross intellectual falsity.[1] It is, with the ordinary man at ordinary times, only when 'situation' gives the lie to 'expectation,' when, accordingly, established beliefs do not 'work,' that misgivings are aroused and, possibly, an intellectual interest stimulated. We may say, in short, that in respect of the connections asserted in everyday experience, mere pragmatical considerations play a very large part indeed, and that therefore no just inferences can be drawn from the nature of these assertions as to what the intellect does or does not demand.[2] And we must go on to insist upon this. If, as we must in philosophy, we abandon the standard of practical utility and examine these everyday assertions from the point of view of rational tenability—preferably through the medium of some simple symbolism which will ensure that our judgment be not warped by the illusions and prejudices instilled by habitual experience— there can be but one verdict on the matter. So long as mediation, not necessarily explicit but at least implicit, is lacking,

---

[1] *E.g.* the belief that the sun moves round the earth works perfectly satisfactorily for all the ordinary purposes of life.

[2] At the same time I should agree that common-sense's case for the everyday assertion of unmediated connections, as put on the previous page, involves an overstatement. There are traces of an implicit demand for a rationale in, for example, the universal insistence upon 'relevance' of predicate to subject (*vide* Bosanquet, *Implication and Linear Inference*, p. 87 *et seq.*). But my present point is that the plain man's pre-occupation with practice ensures that the demand for a rationale is not 'pushed' as it must be where an intellectual interest dominates.

APPROACH TO SUPRA-RATIONAL ABSOLUTE

these affirmations are reducible to the form 'A as such is not-A,' and their self-contradiction is starkly manifest.

Furthermore if, desiring to observe intellectual process in its integrity, we turn from that sphere in which intellect is a relatively unpredominant feature—the sphere of everyday life—to the experiences which are professedly theoretical in character, such as philosophy and scientific inquiry, it seems clear enough that here the intellect does decline to accept a bare or unmediated conjunction. Whether such a conjunction does or does not happen to accord with a strongly entrenched belief is, for science, immaterial. It is of the nature of philosophy and the sciences to look upon the unmediated conjunction, however widely subscribed to, as an implicit problem. These disciplines differ from 'common sense' perhaps most radically just in their habitual disrespect for the merely *de facto* connection. They insist upon the thorough-going mediation of whatever lays claim to be believed—science, it is true, only within the ambit of its presuppositions, but philosophy absolutely.

And that is why, in the last resort, it is commonly regarded as the failure of any metaphysical system that it should be forced to accept a dualism. For a metaphysical dualism is a dualism of two *ultimate* principles, *i.e.* it consists in the presentation to the intellect of differences which not only do not, but in virtue of their professed ultimacy cannot, find any ground of union in a system beyond themselves. This is the root cause of the mind's dissatisfaction with all dualism. We are offered, perhaps, God on the one hand, matter on the other, neither being reducible to the other nor resoluble into any higher unity. And we are asked to accept the interaction of these two 'ultimates' as the final truth about things. But so long as these concepts are really 'two' for thought, we are aware of failure. We realise that our 'system' bids us to predicate of a subject 'God' something that we do not see to issue from His nature, something that is genuinely different from God, while at the same time we are forbidden to look to any superior principle beyond the differences which might explain and justify the connection. From such *de facto* connections the intellect recoils. It is the very type of the irrational, and the history of philosophy shows that sooner or later the irrationality of it is appreciated. It is, of course, open to the critic to urge that unless, even in the end, there remain real differences for thought, we could not judge or predicate at all. This I believe to be true, and to be of the utmost importance. But what it points to, I shall later argue, is not some irrational necessity of resting in a dualism as ultimate truth, but rather the need of recognising an insuperable barrier which lies in the path of the intellect's search for ultimate truth.

Section 3. The Non-contradictory (and therefore the Real) in Principle Unattainable by Thought

We are now in a position to say something, though of a purely formal character, about the general nature of the true and real. If the intellect rejects as self-contradictory any 'simple' union of differents, and if the only way in which it can avoid self-contradiction in bringing differents together is to connect the differents as mutually implicatory elements of an encompassing unity, then, it appears, no content can be accepted by the intellect as expressing 'reality' unless it be got into the form of a unity which exhibits a perfect mutual implication. Only thus can the intellect's inherent demand be satisfied. Our next task, however, is to see that although such a unity is the inherent demand of the intellect, and thus needful for the assurance of apprehending ultimate reality, it is a unity that is not attainable by intellect. And this failure, it will appear, is a failure not merely in degree. It is a failure in principle. For—and this is the central paradox of human experience—the route which the intellect takes, and must take, in its efforts to realise its ideal, is one which never

APPROACH TO SUPRA-RATIONAL ABSOLUTE

can, by reason of its intrinsic character, lead to the desired goal of mutually implicatory system, or 'unity in difference' —which never can, therefore, yield us apprehension of the real.

The whole issue may be said to turn upon the nature of a 'ground.' We have seen that thought demands a ground for its connections of differences, and that only by positing such a ground does it escape the contradiction of uniting bare A with not-A. But we shall also have to see that what a 'ground' concretely means in actual thinking is always something which remains partially external to the differences it connects. To secure a 'ground,' accordingly, is still to be left with a further question which demands an answer—'How is the ground itself connected with the elements it connects?' Hence is provoked the inquiry after a deeper ground. But since this deeper ground must also be partially a 'third thing' relatively to the elements it connects, a like problem recurs. And this process, it would seem, must continue *ad infinitum*. The further back we push the 'ground' or the 'why,' the more unified and coherent doubtless becomes the system of differences we affirm. But the true manifold-in-unity wherein mutual implication is perfect, the self-explanatory identity in difference which thinking craves and will alone accept as expressing the ultimate real, must forever elude its grasp.

The point may be perhaps best elucidated by means of a concrete illustration, which we shall draw from a familiar sphere. Suppose we are reflecting upon the rational justification of the simple statement that if the carburretor-jet of a motor-car is partially choked there is a tendency in the engine to misfire. We want to understand the 'why' of this situation, to find a 'ground' or intelligible nexus for the connection affirmed. Our first suggestion will be, no doubt, that the ground lies in the ignition system of the engine as dynamically conceived, the special core of the connection being the thinning of the petrol supply to the cylinder. And with this insight the intellect does achieve a partial satisfaction. But, it is plain, only *partial* satisfaction. However adequate the explanation may be for practical needs, from the speculative point of view it at once gives rise to a further problem. For it is certainly not self-evident how the 'ground' here laid bare stands to the 'differences' it connects. It is necessary to ask, Why should a thinning of the petrol supply *result from* a partially choked jet, and why should a thinning of the petrol supply *result in* the occasional failure of combustion? To suppose that these questions answer themselves is sheer speculative blindness.

Since there is nothing in this particular illustration which is not paralleled in every other endeavour of thought to rationalise its world,[1] let us express the situation which has here arisen in the generalised form of symbolic representation. When we say that a choked jet is the occasion of misfiring, we are uniting differences which we may call A and B. But we are aware of the necessity of establishing a 'ground' for the union of A and B. Our initial ground we take to be 'the ignition system of the engine as dynamically conceived.' Here we have the X, or systematic identity, which was alluded to in our early abstract statement of intellectual process. Again, every connection has a special core within the system X. Here, it is the thinning of the petrol supply to the cylinder. We may call this core C. And we may say that what the explanation is doing is to justify the union of A with B on the ground that A is bound up with C which is bound up with B within the system X. But we saw, once more, that the connection of the thinning of the petrol supply neither with a choked jet nor with misfiring is self-evident. That is (continuing our generalised statement) how C is connected with A, and again with B, requires further elucidation, sets for us a fresh problem. Or, expressed in terms of the whole system as apprehended, the systematic identity C is observed not to issue in the union

[1] Certain qualifications of this statement will have to be made later.

of A and B by the *internal necessity of its own nature*. We have a unity which is still partially external to its differences, and which therefore points beyond itself to a higher unity for final intellectual satisfaction.

But let us follow the course of rationalisation a little further in our selected instance. It will elicit no new point of principle, but may assist in making clearer the fundamental defect (metaphysically speaking) which I wish to expose in the process under examination.

We find ourselves asking next, then, 'What is the warrant for the connection of our A with our C?' Superficially, it may seem enough to reply that petrol is unable to flow through a partial solid, such as the dirt in the jet, with the facility of its flow through air. But there is, in fact, nothing like a self-evident connection here. We are still impelled to ask, Why? And if we find our answer now in so-called 'fundamental laws' as to the resistance of masses, etc., what we have arrived at is once more not self-evident truth but a generalisation drawn from a wide, but yet indefinitely inadequate, experience of an abstract aspect of the world. The inadequacy and the abstractness alike force upon our attention the still mysterious nature of the 'matter' which, in our unregenerate moments, we may think we 'understand.'

And similarly when we inquire into the warrant of the connection of our B with our C. How does a thin petrol supply connect with failure of combustion? We may find our ground here in a necessity that there should be maintained a certain more or less definite proportion between the molecules of petroleum and air in order to secure combustion. But why this proportion *should* be necessary for combustion, and so on, and so on, are questions to which, as we push back our analysis, we may find increasingly elaborate answers, but no answer which does not by its very nature set for us a fresh problem. Push back as we may, still we find ourselves faced with a union of differents in which the differents do not spring from the unity, and are therefore partially external to it. And such a complex is not one in which the intellect can find rest.

What we have found in this illustration holds, I maintain (with certain partial reservations to be explained later), for all of thought's endeavours to understand its world. The effort to gain a non-contradictory, and therefore so far a true, view of Reality dissipates itself in an infinite process. And in principle the reason is clear enough. Thought knows nothing of *intrinsic* connections of differents. If differences are to be connected, thought demands a 'ground' of connection. But since the ground must always be other than the differences it connects (if it were resoluble into them it would not 'connect' at all), the intellect is immediately offered a fresh element of difference which must in its turn be connected up through a deeper ground. And to this process there is no end.

Let us put it in another way. What the intellect wants in order to attain to the self-consistency which can alone manifest the real, is a complex of differences so united that the principle of their union is internal to the complex. What the intellect achieves (and the defect is incurable) is a complex of differences which refers beyond itself indefinitely for the justification of the union. The real is unity in difference, a unity which issues forth in the differences by virtue of its own nature; or—from the other side—differences which have no being save within the unity of which they are expressions. Only a complex of this kind will be self-explanatory, provoking no 'why' to which it does not itself supply the answer. But such a complex, if we have been right, it is vain to suppose attainable at any level of the process of thinking.

But, moreover, from the point we have now reached it becomes clear that we must qualify severely the language which we have so far allowed ourselves to use in alluding to the nature of the real. We have spoken of the real, above, as 'a unity issuing forth in its differences by virtue of its own nature,' and again, as a system of differences wherein perfect mutual implication reigns. And we have meant to convey thereby that the real (if it is to satisfy thought's demands) must be a unity which is not external to the differences which it combines. But the negative intention does not justify the positive description, as we now see. The latter may be used only by a licence not in the end permissible. For to speak of a whole wherein perfect mutual 'implication' reigns, is to speak of differences connected by a 'ground' which is wholly internal to the differences it connects. And of a 'ground' of this sort, we have just seen, the intellect knows nothing. The positive description, accordingly, is only a name (suggested by our apprehension of the defects which must be remedied in the 'real') for our ignorance of the kind of unity which is not external to its differences. And it is in the end a misleading name, inasmuch as the use of it must tend to suggest a meaning, in terms of our ordinary conceptions of ground and implication, which can only be a distortion of reality. We must recognise that 'ground,' 'implication,' even 'necessity,' are concepts which cannot with any positive significance be applied to the union of differences in the ultimately real.

Let us gather together our thoughts and observe whither we have been led. I have argued that the path which the intellect takes and must take to avoid self-contradiction—the continuous pursuit of deeper and more adequate grounding for its connections, which is one with the pursuit of 'system' ever more comprehensive and internally harmonious—is not a path which can lead to Reality. Inherent in the very nature of the process is a reference beyond itself which raises fresh problems on the basis of temporary solutions. So far as I can see, one conclusion is inescapable. Reality in its true character must be pronounced to be disparate from each and every thought-product. And the term 'disparate' must be taken in its fullest significance. I do not mean that there is here merely a difference of degree, such as might leave it possible for us to say that certain thought-products reveal more adequately than others, although none with perfect adequacy, the character of ultimate Reality. I mean that there is a fundamental difference in kind, such as renders thought-products and Reality strictly incommensurable. This is metaphysical scepticism—though I hope to show that it is a form of scepticism not open to the objections commonly brought against this type of philosophy. Nevertheless, whether it be in the end defensible or not, it does seem to be the result to which the argument has driven us. For, according to the argument, we must have for Reality differences united in a certain way, and we actually have in thought-products differences united in a quite other way. The 'patterns' of thought-products and Reality—to use a term now much in vogue—are fundamentally diverse. And since the 'pattern' of Reality is one to which thinking gets not one whit nearer, no matter how elaborately systematic its functioning, we seem bound to say that thought by the pursuit of its own characteristic method does not make the slightest advance towards the articulation of the true nature of Reality. To make the concept of 'degrees' applicable, it is plainly necessary that there should be an intelligible continuity of principle between the lower stages and the perfect consummation. But that continuity is just what is lacking in the relation of thought-products and Reality. I find myself compelled therefore to affirm (*a*) that Reality owns a character which transcends thought—a character for which, since a label is convenient, we may use the term 'suprarational'; and (*b*) that there is no possibility of measuring the degree in which any particular content of thought manifests the character of Reality. But since (*b*) clearly carries with it the rejection of the Idealist doctrine of 'Degrees of Truth and Reality,' a doctrine which no one has done more to recommend than the philosopher upon whom my argument so far has been based, it is very necessary to pause here and explain my attitude to this doctrine with some precision.

Section 4. *Untenability of Doctrine of Degrees of Truth. Criticism of it from* (a) *the Pluralist, and* (b) *the Suprarationalist, Standpoint*

A rough statement of the doctrine of 'Degrees of Truth,' sufficient for our present purpose, may be given in comparatively small compass. For if the principle at its base be assented to, the doctrine is (apart from special refinements) simple and seemingly inevitable.

The principle at its base is simply that of the coherent unity of all Reality. Starting from the postulate that the real must be self-consistent, it is urged that self-consistency is not to be found in any finite content, that the finite points inevitably beyond itself for self-completion, and that therefore nothing short of the One Infinite Whole can claim to be fully real. Reality is one, a single all-inclusive harmonious system (to which Bradley, of course, would add 'of experience'). Reality being thus envisaged, it follows with apparent logical rigour that if we are to know the truth about any feature or aspect of Reality, it is in the end necessary to know the Whole. Torn from its context in the coherent Whole, no finite feature will present itself in its ultimate meaning. So far, then, as every judgment, while claiming to portray a genuine character of Reality, omits to take account of the universe in the totality of its self-expression, the content affirmed must be tinctured with falsity. Consideration of those aspects of Reality from which abstraction has been made must, if Reality is a unitary whole, modify to a greater or less extent the content in question. Every finite judgment, then, must fail to portray in its true being the aspect of Reality which it aims to reveal.

But, on the other hand, this inevitable falsity of the finite judgment is not the whole story. There is a positive side, which requires equal emphasis. Judgments are only 'partially' false. They possess also 'partial' truth. We have a criterion which enables us to determine the degree in which our judgments do express Reality as it ultimately is. For the character of Reality we know to be 'self-consistency.' And 'self-consistency' is a character which it is evident that we can, and constantly do, employ in appraising actual judgments. Accordingly it will be proper to say that judgments are true, *i.e.* adequately express the character of Reality, in the degree to which they attain self-consistency, *i.e.* (as it becomes when worked out in Idealist Logic) in the degree to which the connection asserted is informed by a system which is at once comprehensive and internally harmonious. The partial *falsity* of every judgment, then, may be said to reside in the fact that abstraction is always made from at least some features of the Real, this abstraction involving a defect in self-consistency and consequent failure to express the Real as it is. 'Only the whole truth can be wholly true.' The partial *truth* of every judgment lies in the fact that every judgment is, in however crude and inchoate a fashion, the exhibition of a unity in difference, and attains in some measure to the systematic coherence which is the character of Reality.

Now this doctrine of Degrees of Truth is, in my opinion, a valid implication, so far as its general lines are concerned, of any metaphysic which regards the Whole as an intelligible system. It does not even matter in this connection how it may be considered fit to conceive the central principle of this Whole. It is enough, for the point of the Idealist argument to hold good, that it be a Whole which is rationally continuous throughout its manifestations. If criticism of the doctrine is to be effective, it must, I think, be launched against the legitimacy of construing the Whole after this manner. And this criticism may emanate from two sharply contrasted standpoints. It may have its roots in Pluralism, or, on the other hand, in some form of Scepticism, such as the Supra-rational theory here advocated. Since it will serve to place in a clearer light that side of Idealist thought which I am myself prepared to endorse, I propose to say a few words first of all concerning the Pluralist's attack, passing on thereafter to urge, on my own behalf, the Suprarationalist criticism.

(a) *Criticism from the Pluralist's Standpoint*

The nerve of the Pluralist's argument against the Idealist Absolute lies in his denial of the internality of relations. That relations are 'internal,' *i.e.* grounded in the nature of the terms they relate, is, he protests, a mere false hypothesis which the Idealist adopts as if it were axiomatic certainty. Naturally (the Pluralist is prepared to concede) *if* all relations are grounded in the nature of the terms related, then, since every term stands in some sort of relation to every other term, every term depends, for the knowledge of its true nature, upon a knowledge of all other terms. And this leads straight to the Monistic Theory of Truth. But against this it is argued that relations are not, or certainly not all, internal. It may be too drastic to regard Reality, with the earlier Mr Russell, as an aggregate of independent entities standing in purely external relations to one another. But this picture, it is held, is at least as near the truth as that of Monistic Idealism. And the Pluralist proceeds to make good his case, as he believes, by citing a number of concrete instances in which, he contends, it is mere wilful paradox to claim that the intrinsic nature of the term is in any way affected by the relation in which it 'happens' to stand.

I cannot, of course, attempt here a comprehensive consideration of the arguments and illustrations whereby the Pluralist seeks to support the theory that at least some relations are external. The main thing that I wish to do is to set forth the criticism which is implied in our earlier examination of the process of thought, since that criticism is, in my view, fatal to the very principle of the Pluralist's position.

For let us recall what we then found about the attitude of thought to the professed union of differents. Thought, we found, abhors a 'bare conjunction.' It cannot accept a connection without postulating, and endeavouring to explicate, a ground for the connection. For otherwise it is identifying bare A with not-A, and this is self-contradictory. But what, after all, is the assertion of a merely external relation but just this self-contradictory assertion of a bare conjunction? A is affirmed to stand in a relation, say a relation of 'paternity,' to X, and the Pluralist maintains that the nature of A is indifferent to the relation. But if we thus connect A with 'father of X,' insisting that the connection is one of mere fact, devoid of any rationale, this is just to connect differences without the provision of even an implied ground of their union—i.e. simply in and as a bare conjunction. Nor can the Pluralist reply that he does admit a rationale, but that this rationale leaves the nature of A unaffected. If we do indeed have to assume a ground for the connection of A with 'father of X,' then this ground is a system within which A and 'father of X' are implicated elements, or it is no 'ground' at all; and it is absurd to suppose that the nature of A will be the same when apprehended within the system as when apprehended in isolation. There is no choice but either to deny the necessity for grounding of connections outright, or else to agree that the nature of the term cannot be thought of as unaffected by its possession of a relation. The former alternative will support the doctrine of external relations. But the cost will be no less than the suicidal admission that thinking can rest satisfied with a self-contradiction.

The short and easy manner in which many Realists think fit to dismiss a doctrine which is granted by Realists themselves to be the very corner-stone of the Monistic Theory of Truth [1] might reasonably provoke suspicion that perhaps we have in these critics, not a clearer understanding of the issue, but a mere misunderstanding of their opponents. This I believe to

---

[1] B. Russell's *Philosophical Essays*, p. 161. 'Hence the axiom [of internal relations] is equivalent to the monistic theory of truth.'

be the case. But that one's counter-criticism may not lay itself open to a similar imputation, one ought, perhaps, even at the risk of some disproportion, to dwell a little longer upon this *cause célèbre*. Mr Moore and Mr Russell may no doubt be regarded as among the most formidable opponents of the doctrine of Internality, and I shall say something on the views of each. In neither case, as it seems to me, is the real reason for the Idealist's advocacy of the theory grasped and combated. It should be possible, I think, even without entering upon a fully detailed analysis of their respective views, to make clear the fundamental misunderstanding upon which these views rest.

It is noteworthy that Mr Russell's discussion opens with a formal statement of the ground (or, as he believes, *one* of the grounds) for believing in the internality of relations which is verbally unexceptionable. It is only when he proceeds to draw out the implications of the statement that it becomes evident that the interpretation which he places upon his words is far removed from that which the Idealist for his part would place upon them. This is what Mr Russell says: 'If we ask ourselves what are the grounds in favour of the axiom of internal relations . . . they seem to be two, though these are perhaps really indistinguishable. There is first the law of sufficient reason, according to which nothing can be just a brute fact, but must have some reason for being thus and not otherwise. . . .'[1] With the second 'ground' which follows in Mr Russell's statement we need not concern ourselves. For it is what Mr Russell here calls the 'law of sufficient reason' which does, in fact, furnish the real and sole basis of the Idealist 'axiom.'

What defect then does Mr Russell find in this proposed ground? The answer is quite unambiguous. The 'law of sufficient reason' upon which the ground is itself grounded is untrue. For what is the 'reason' for a proposition? 'The *reason* for a proposition is always expected to be one or more

[1] *Philosophical Essays*, p. 164.

simpler propositions. Thus the law of sufficient reason should mean that every proposition can be deduced from simpler propositions. This seems obviously false, but in any case it cannot be relevant in considering Idealism, which holds propositions to be less and less true the simpler they are, so that it would be absurd to insist on starting from simple propositions.'[1]

Now if the 'law of sufficient reason' does in fact mean what Mr Russell in this last citation says that it means, I am ready to grant that it does not hold good. But it is perfectly certain that this is not what the law means for any Idealist who introduces the conception to explain his adherence to the internality of relations. What the Idealist means when he holds that 'nothing can be just a brute fact, but must have some reason for being thus and not otherwise,' is, quite simply, that the intellect cannot accept an 'ungrounded' union of differents, a 'bare conjunction.' But the 'ground' which the intellect posits is not, of course, supposed to be 'one or more simpler propositions.' Indeed Mr Russell shows, in the passage quoted above, that he himself is quite well aware of this, and why he should imagine that his argument still touches Idealism is far from clear. The 'ground' which must be posited on Idealist principles is, as we have sufficiently seen earlier in this chapter, a system within which the differents connected are conceived as mutually implicatory elements. If Mr Russell's criticism is to be relevant to the Idealist defence of ' internality,' what he ought to assail is the line of argument which contends for the intellectual necessity of positing such a ground if differences are to be united in a way acceptable to thought. For if it be true that the union of differences does require a ground of this nature, it is impossible to hold that the possession of a relation, or any other character, by a term 'makes no difference' to the nature of the term.

Let us pass on to consider Mr Moore's treatment of the

[1] *Philosophical Essays*, p. 165.

matter in his well-known essay, 'External and Internal Relations.'[1] We shall see, I think, that Mr Moore is quite as far removed as Mr Russell from an appreciation of the real foundations of the Idealist doctrine.

With Mr Moore's statement of what is meant by 'internality' the Idealist will have no quarrel. After a somewhat lengthy process of eliminating abstractly possible meanings, Mr Moore reaches the position that 'one thing which is always implied by the dogma that, "All relations are internal," is that, in the case of every relational property[2] it can always be truly asserted of any term A which has that property that any term which had not had it would necessarily have been different from A.'[3] This is, I think, a perfectly fair statement. And we can agree with Mr Moore further when he asserts that the 'difference' alleged in the 'dogma' is not merely 'numerical difference' but also 'qualitative difference.'

What then is Mr Moore's own position with regard to the 'dogma' so stated? He is prepared to agree that *some* relational properties are certainly internal to their terms in the sense that the absence of these relational properties necessarily involves *numerical* difference in the terms. He is prepared to agree that it is probable, although not certain, that *some* relational properties are internal to their terms in the fuller sense that the absence of these relational properties necessarily involves qualitative difference in the terms. But he insists that there remain over many quite obvious cases in which relational properties are not internal to their terms, either in the one sense or in the other. And this, of course, is more than sufficient for the denial of the doctrine of internal relations.

The Idealist reader of Mr Moore's essay arrives at the

---

[1] *Philosophical Studies*, chap. ix.
[2] Mr Moore's distinction of relational property from relation is, I think, a contribution to clarity, but does not specially affect our present argument.
[3] *Philosophical Studies*, p. 284.

present stage in a mood of eager expectancy. There is every reason to believe that Mr Moore is about to grapple seriously with a matter which has always been for Idealism of bed-rock importance. But nothing could in fact be more disappointing than Mr Moore's actual treatment. What he has to show, in order to overthrow the opposing doctrine, is that *some* relational properties at any rate are not internal. He proposes to do so by demonstrating that some relational properties are not internal even in the 'minor' sense (*i.e.* entailing numerical difference in the terms), and therefore *a fortiori* not internal in the 'major' sense. But the actual argument is at bottom little more than an appeal to the supposed 'plain facts' of common sense. Indeed the impression with which one is left is that, in Mr Moore's opinion, the main work of refuting the doctrine of internal relations is completed when that doctrine has once been clearly stated (as by himself). When clearly stated it refutes itself.

Take the case of a coloured patch, says Mr Moore, half red and half yellow. Now the whole patch has the relational property of possessing the red patch as a spatial part. This relational property is, Mr Moore agrees, clearly internal in that 'any whole, which had not contained that red patch, could not have been identical with the whole in question.' [1] But to find a relational property that is not internal we have only to turn to the relational property owned by the red patch, that of being a spatial part of this whole. 'It seems quite clear,' says Mr Moore, 'that . . . the red patch might perfectly well have existed without being part of that particular whole.' [2] Yet the 'dogma' of internal relations implies 'that any term which does in fact have a particular relational property could not have existed without having that property.' [3] 'In saying this,' Mr Moore goes on, 'it obviously flies in the face of common sense. It seems quite obvious that in the case of many relational properties which things have, the fact that they

[1] *Philosophical Studies*, p. 288. [2] *Ibid.* [3] *Ibid.*

have them is *a mere matter of fact*: that the things in question *might* have existed without them.'[1]

Is all this in fact 'quite clear' and 'quite obvious'? In truth, the one thing that is quite clear and obvious to the Idealist reader is that Mr Moore is working with presuppositions as to the nature of knowledge which his opponents would never dream of admitting. The argument, as stated, simply does not touch Idealism. For what, on Mr Moore's presuppositions, seems 'quite clear,' seems, on Idealist presuppositions, to involve a plain self-contradiction. A very few words should suffice to show that this is so.

Let us consider the proposition 'the red patch has the relational property of being a spatial part in a certain whole.' For convenience we may convert it to the form 'this red patch is present owner of the relational property, etc.,' and then symbolise the subject of the proposition as A and the predicate as B. Now Mr Moore holds that we can accept the proposition 'A is B,' while also accepting the proposition 'A *might not have been* B.' But this implies, of course, that for Mr Moore the intellect can accept a connection of differents without postulating, much less attempting to explicate, a rational ground for the connection. For it is supposed by Mr Moore that these differences *might* not have been so united: and such a supposition is incompatible with the postulate of a rational ground for the connection (which implies that the connection, if it is at all, is a necessary connection). In other words, Mr Moore's argument implies the assumption that the intellect does not demand a rationale for its connections, but is prepared to accept a 'bare conjunction' of differents. And this, for the Idealist thinker, *e.g.* for Bradley, represents the very essence of the self-contradictory—the direct identification of A and not-A. For the Idealist the intellect can assent to the union of A and B only in so far as they are conceived to be mutually implicatory elements within a system X. For him, therefore,

[1] *Philosophical Studies*, pp. 288-9.

it is just nonsense to assert that A *is* B, and at the same time that A *might not have been* B.

There is no need then for Mr Moore to go on (as he does in the essay from which I have been quoting) to construct an elaborate explanation of the Idealist's obtuseness in failing to recognise the 'obvious fact' that 'in the case of many relational properties which things have . . . the things in question might have existed without having them.'[1] The explanation is much simpler and much more fundamental than Mr Moore supposes. It is just that the supposed 'obvious fact' is in vital contradiction with the cardinal principle in the Idealist's theory of knowledge. Unless this principle is duly examined and found wanting, attacks upon the doctrine of internal relations are so much beating of the air.

As for the appeal to 'common sense,' the Idealist has never denied that for *working* purposes certain relational properties may conveniently be treated as external to their terms. And that is all that common sense is concerned with. Reference to common sense yields some indication as to the pragmatical value or disvalue of an idea. But as to ultimate theoretical validity—which is the concern of philosophy—it is no test at all. Those who appeal to it for support on favourable occasions are just as likely to dismiss it with obloquy when its pronouncements happen to be unfavourable.

The Pluralist's attack upon the Idealist doctrine of 'Degrees' seems to me, then, to miss its target through a radical failure to appreciate what are the basic presuppositions upon which the Idealist superstructure is reared. Let us turn now to the Supra-rationalist's criticism—which ought at least to be free from this particular defect.[2]

---

[1] *Philosophical Studies*, p. 289.

[2] It is, I think, unfortunate that even some Idealist writers have expressed themselves in a way which suggests that they regard the Realist attack upon internal relations as *bene fundatum*. Thus Mr W. E. Hocking, in his brilliant little book, *Types of Philosophy*, p. 368: 'Realism is justified in rebelling against the notion that all relations are "internal." There are external relations, such as make no *significant* differences to their terms.'

(b) *Criticism from the Supra-rationalist Standpoint*

The criticism which has to be passed upon the doctrine of 'Degrees' from the side of Supra-rationalism is, however, so obvious in character that one's chief difficulty lies in understanding how Bradley can have persuaded himself that the doctrine is, for him, tenable. For it is of the essence of Bradley's position to hold that differences are united in Reality in a manner intrinsically different from the mode of union which is characteristic of, and inseparable from, the finite intellect; and that of this ultimate mode of union the intellect can know nothing. How then can it be possible to grade thought-products according to the degree in which they manifest the nature of this unknown and unknowable Reality? The reply might be, and is, given, that at least we know that the nature of Reality is to be 'self-consistent,' and that we can, and do, grade our judgments in a hierarchy of 'self-consistency.' But this, on Bradleian presuppositions, is merely to play with words. For—and here we have the crux of the whole situation—'self-consistency' *means* something different in the two usages. The true self-consistency, that which applies to ultimate reality, Bradley has discovered to lie 'beyond any relational arrangement' (to use his own expression), and to be incapable of envisagement by the intellect. Obviously, then, the ideal of self-consistency which the intellect does admittedly employ in practice in grading judgments cannot be the 'pure'

But if 'making no *significant* difference' means (as it seems to mean in Mr Hocking's subsequent illustration of a ship not ceasing to be the same ship when it reaches a new port) merely that we can abstract from the difference without introducing into our calculations noticeable confusion or error *in the ordinary contacts of experience*—why, this is something which no responsible defender of internal relations has ever challenged. Bradley has himself frequently stated that we do right to regard some relations as merely external for all practical purposes. The issue is not this, but whether such relations can or cannot be regarded as *ultimately* external. No Realist can accept the negative answer, no Monistic Idealist can accept the affirmative. The issue is quite vital; and the attempt to mitigate the rigour of the opposition is not, I think, serviceable to the promotion of a right decision.

ideal. In so far as it is concretely envisaged, and thus able to be used as a positive criterion, 'self-consistency' can only be a defective or degraded expression of the pure ideal. This is the direct implication of Bradley's fundamental contention that the intellect attempts to advance towards the self-consistent after a manner which, although characteristic of it, is not in fact capable of leading to the truly self-consistent. What such a doctrine implies is surely that the ideal as concretely operative in intellect appears in a bastard form. How otherwise could it be guiding the intellect along a path which does not lead to true self-consistency?

In short, we have got to recognise that there are two quite distinct forms of the ideal of self-consistency unmistakably posited in the Bradleian epistemology, whether or not they be always kept clearly in mind by Bradley himself. There is the 'pure' self-consistency which a regress upon the conditions of cognitive experience compels us to posit as characterising ultimate reality, but of whose concrete character we know nothing. This we may call the 'noumenal' ideal. And there is the 'empirical' self-consistency which is the criterion and positive guide in our actual intellectual operations. This we may call the 'phenomenal' ideal. The contradiction in Bradley's doctrine of 'Degrees' is that he uses the *second* form to apportion degrees of the *first*.

Since I reject the doctrine of 'Degrees' primarily because I accept the basic principles of Bradley's epistemology, it will be necessary for me to deal with the relation of these two forms of the ideal at some length in the sequel. Here all that I am anxious to make clear is that in some sense these two distinct forms must be admitted as components of the Bradleian scheme, and that this admission is fatal to the doctrine of 'Degrees.' It may, however, be advisable to anticipate subsequent explanations to the extent of pointing out that, although the 'phenomenal' ideal is here spoken of as being, as it were, a 'transcript' of the 'pure' ideal, it is not to be supposed that

APPROACH TO SUPRA-RATIONAL ABSOLUTE

any conscious process is involved in the 'transcription.' The mind does not *first* of all possess the pure ideal and *then* proceed to construe it in terms of a relational arrangement. The ideal before the mind is from the first envisaged in its phenomenal aspect. We get at the conception of the 'pure' ideal only by a critical regress which discloses to us that the mind cannot attain to the harmony which it itself demands for Reality by following that form of the ideal which is its positive criterion. It seems a valid interpretation of this unsatisfiable demand to say that there is an ultimate ideal possessing the mind (the 'pure' ideal) which is radically distinct from the operative ideal which controls its concrete procedure (the 'phenomenal' ideal).

It is true, however, that Bradley has, in response to criticism, offered to explain the paradox of his doctrine of 'Degrees of Truth.' To notice his rejoinder will, I think, but add confirmation to our view that the doctrine is, on his premises, untenable. On p. 597 of *Appearance and Reality* Bradley tells us, in answer to criticism similar to the above, that, so far as he understands the objection, it 'offers no serious difficulty.' No doubt (he urges) from *one* point of view all judgments are equally false. But there is another no less valid point of view from which it is proper to apportion to them 'degrees of truth.' In theology, he points out, we are not conscious of any incompatibility in maintaining that 'before God,' measured by His Perfection, all men are equally sinners, while also maintaining with like assurance that some men are certainly 'better' than others. Both points of view have their own validity. So too, Bradley suggests, with this apparently incompatible combination of philosophical doctrines —'Degrees of Truth' and the 'Supra-rational Absolute.' The worst fault that can be alleged against his position, Bradley thinks, is that of 'two proper and indispensable points of view,' he may have unduly emphasised one.

In reply to this defence we may certainly admit at once that there are 'two points of view' from which we may regard the status of judgments. I have just been engaged in indicating what they are—that of the 'noumenal' ideal, and that of the 'phenomenal' ideal, of self-consistency. But then what we want in a metaphysical treatise is the metaphysical point of view, and surely *this* is not 'double'? On the contrary, the point of view of metaphysics, if Bradley's doctrine of the Absolute be accepted, is singularly free from ambiguity; and it is to the effect that there is not the vestige of a justification for the attempt to grade thought-products according to the degree in which they approximate to ultimate reality. The other point of view, with its criterion of rational system, may be that which we naturally employ in grading judgments; but if we are to speak in terms of metaphysics we must say that any 'degrees' thus ascertained are not degrees of *truth*. Or, if we do call them degrees of 'truth,' we must confess that we are meaning by the term 'truth' something much less ambitious than is currently signified, something much less ambitious than 'the revelation of the character of ultimate reality.'

To repeat—the 'two points of view' correspond to the two forms of the ideal of self-consistency already discussed. If we could take the self-consistency of *Reality*, the 'noumenal' ideal, as intelligibly continuous with the 'phenomenal' ideal, then the doctrine of 'Degrees' might have some *locus standi*. But if not, if there is no intelligible continuity between the two—and that is certainly the issue of the Bradleian doctrine of knowledge—then 'Degrees of Truth' is meaningless.

I feel bound to conclude, therefore, that Bradley's defence is no defence at all; and that the doctrine of 'Degrees' with which his name is so closely associated is a contradiction of his fundamental principles. The unhappy consequences of his adoption of the doctrine in the way of diminishing the influence which his scepticism ought to have had upon the course of recent philosophy I have already alluded to at the beginning of the chapter. It has served to obscure under a veil of substantial similarity the real enormity of the gulf between the Bradleian metaphysic and that of Absolute Idealism. As a result very little serious attention has been given, even by Idealists, to the foundations of Bradley's Supra-rationalism— although they are in point of fact fatal to the Idealist construction of the universe. Had Bradley consistently followed out the implications of his Supra-rationalism, he would, I think, have been forced into presenting a philosophy whose opposition to Idealism is quite as deep-seated as the opposition offered by New Realism. It is a good deal more than arguable that the real 'Refutation of Idealism' is to be found, not in Mr Moore's *Essays*, but in Bradley's *Appearance and Reality*.

But if Bradley is claimed by Idealists as essentially one of themselves—as a brother whose occasional backslidings are indeed to be deplored but whose heart is in the right place— the fault must be imputed to Bradley himself in no small measure. Quite apart from the incriminating doctrine of 'Degrees of Truth,' Bradley has undoubtedly fallen into a mode of expression in certain passages which lends a great deal of colour to the notion that he is thinking along the lines of Idealist metaphysics. A particularly fruitful source of ambiguity, which it will be worth our while to consider for a few moments, is his use of the expression 'in detail' when alluding to our ignorance of the nature of the transmutation which every, even the highest, object of thought must undergo to become fully adequate to reality. Almost invariably he speaks as if we are ignorant only of 'how in detail' the feature in question must be modified in order to take its place in the Absolute. And the natural inference that the reader makes from this language is that we *do* know 'how in principle' the transformation is to be made. But if we know 'how in principle' finite objects are 'supplemented and re-arranged' so as to become fully self-consistent, then we must be supposed to know 'in principle' the character of Reality or the Absolute itself. The Absolute cannot be the closed book to thought which Bradley's term 'supra-relational' seemed to imply. If, then, this not unnatural construction is put upon Bradley's words, Bradley seems really to be speaking in these passages quite as a good Idealist should. For not even the most Idealistic Idealist would presume to insist, any more than Bradley himself, that we can know 'how in detail' finite apprehensions are to be transmuted in order to become adequate to ultimate reality.

Nevertheless, a closer study of the context of the thought in these passages should, I think, make it quite clear that Bradley is not intending to contrast the 'how in detail' with a 'how in principle,' in the usual meaning of these expressions. The real contrast which he has in mind is the contrast between 'knowing *how*' and 'knowing *that*.'[1] Bradley passes in review the various forms of finite experience, exhibits their inadequacy to the nature of the ultimately real, but urges that, on the view of ultimate reality which he sets forth, there is nothing in these experiences which offers positive opposition to their inclusion within the Absolute, although as to the 'how' of their inclusion we must rest in ignorance. We are entitled to say therefore, he urges, what on general grounds seems certain, *that* these experiences are somehow transmuted so as to take their place within the harmonising Reality. But *how* they are transmuted we do not know. It is, I agree, only by a loose use of words that a mere 'knowing that' can be verbally identified, as by Bradley, with ignorance only of the 'detail' of the transformations. Bradley must, I think, be deemed guilty of a laxity of language on this point. But that he is in his actual thought even violently opposed to the possibility of knowledge of the 'how,' even the 'how in principle,' must, I think, be granted upon any impartial study of the foundational elements in his philosophy.

---

[1] This contrast comes out fairly clearly on p. 242 (*Appearance and Reality*): 'We insisted . . . knowledge.' But even here failure to know 'how' is closely identified with a failure of mere 'detail.'

But perhaps the most conclusive evidence that Bradley does not really mean that we know the 'how in principle' is furnished by his treatment of the metaphysical significance of Error. Error in its full sense, Bradley points out, involves a *positive* discord which forbids it from taking its place as a constituent member of a harmonious system comparable to a relational world of knowledge. Only a harmony that is supra-relational can accept it as a contributory element. But, says Bradley, we do not know 'how' Error is thus accepted, for we cannot, '*even apart from detail*, realise how the relational form is in general absorbed.'[1] Those who are tempted to claim Bradley for Idealism may fairly be invited to explain how this dictum is compatible with the doctrine that we can know Reality 'in principle.'

Section 5. *Bearing of the Metaphysical Problem of Error upon the Doctrine of the Supra-rational Absolute*

The matter just touched upon at the conclusion of the last section—the metaphysical difficulties occasioned by the status of Error—is one the decision of which must have a good deal of weight in determining the rightness or wrongness of the thesis that is to be maintained throughout this work. Is Bradley right in holding that there is an element in Error which makes it incapable of inclusion within an Absolute which is an 'intelligible' Whole? that Error cannot be apprehended as contributing to any kind of harmony that is analogous to 'rational system' as we know it? If he is right, then here is confirmation of the position independently arrived at, that Reality is 'supra-rational.' Error must (like all else) belong to the Whole. But it discloses within itself, so it is claimed, a positive opposition to a Whole which is rationally continuous. Let us address ourselves then to a discussion of this important problem.

It is necessary to see clearly first of all what it is that

[1] *Appearance and Reality*, p. 196 (my italics).

the alternative metaphysics of Absolute Idealism must here maintain. For Idealism, every judgment is, in its logical character, partially true and partially false. It is true in so far as it attains to, false in so far as it falls short of, that systematic wholeness that is characteristic of Reality. But if we now view the judgment in its metaphysical rather than in its logical character, view it as a concrete actuality which belongs to the order of Reality, every judgment must, it is evident, be regarded by Idealism as an individual manifestation of the one animating principle of Reality, the Absolute Mind or Spirit which is the soul and the source of all that is. There can be no judgment, therefore, however misguided it may seem to us to be, which is not (for an ultimate vision) an expression of the Supreme Mind, and which does not ultimately contribute to its life as a necessary 'moment' or 'emphasis' of its self-expression. The 'irrationality' which we are apt to ascribe to such judgments we shall have to understand as consisting in an inadequacy of Reason, not in an antagonism to Reason. For a perfected view would reveal to us that the spirit of Logic, or—to use a favourite expression of Dr Bosanquet's—'the spirit of non-contradiction' is the all-pervading principle of the universe.

Now the question is as to whether we can really fit Error into this logical bed of Procrustes. Mr Joachim has in *The Nature of Truth* laid bare the difficulties of any such resolution with a detail and a candour that are the more impressive in view of the author's well-known philosophical sympathies. I am not able to go quite all the way with Mr Joachim in his treatment, but gratefully avail myself of some of the chief points which he brings out.

It is distinctive of Error in its proper nature, Mr Joachim urges, that the judging subject must not *know* he is in error. He must be making his assertion in the confidence of inviolable truth. A and B may make what is verbally the same judgment, 'the sun travels round the earth,' but these judgments must not be hastily labelled as alike 'erroneous' apart from consideration of the psychical conditions under which they are made. A, let us suppose, is fully aware of the limitations of his astronomical knowledge, and makes his assertion with the consciousness that it is no more than provisional, that it awaits supplementation and revision from a fuller experience of the relevant data. B, on the other hand, is completely free from misgivings, and judges without entertaining the faintest doubt that what he asserts is an ultimate truth. Only in the latter case, Mr Joachim points out, can we say that we have got Error proper. A is under no delusion. He 'knows that he may be mistaken: and *with this knowledge* the "mistake" (if so it prove) is not an "error"'.[1] B, on the other hand, 'plunging into the wrong road with the untroubled certainty that it is right,' definitely misleads and deludes himself. A's state is one of ignorance. But in B we have 'that ignorance which poses, to itself and others, as indubitable truth.' This last is the mark of Error proper.

Now whatever we may say of the metaphysical status of A's judgment, there do seem to be insuperable difficulties in the way of understanding B's judgment, or Error proper, as a contribution to the harmonious self-expression of Absolute Reason. A's judgment, it is conceivable, does not positively *collide* with truth. The meaning it affirms is not antagonistic to a 'higher point of view.' But how can we maintain this in the case of B? Here we have a certain content which cannot as such be accepted by Truth, not held in suspense as a provisional hypothesis, but uncompromisingly asserted as unshakably true. B's judgment, we seem therefore bound to say, is not just an inadequate manifestation of the Reason whose self-expression is Truth, but is a definitely hostile element which opposes itself to Reason. And with this we are left with the alternatives of either denying the existence of Error as diagnosed—which seems to be to fly in the face of facts—or of giving up our dogma that Reality is a systematic Whole

[1] *The Nature of Truth*, p. 141.

every one of whose phases is a manifestation of the Reason which is its animating principle.

This anti-rational aspect of Error proper appears with peculiar force when considered in the light of what was said in Section 2 on the nature of logical contradiction. We saw that the essence of contradiction was the connecting of differences without provision of a 'ground' for their union. But it further follows, since in practice every ground attainable fails to be an adequate ground, and but adds a fresh point of difference, that any assertion of a connection of differences through a ground, *which takes that ground as final*, is still a connecting of differences (although of *different* differences) without provision of a ground of union. Thus any connection of differences, however systematically mediated, is, if offered as final truth, a self-contradiction.

But if this is so, then Error proper, which we saw to have as its distinctive mark the claim to absolute finality, is a judgment of the very type of the contradictory. How then can it be supposed to contribute to the harmonious self-expression of Reason? Put bluntly, the problem which Idealism has to face is that of showing how the 'spirit of Logic' can manifest itself in its own negation, logical contradiction. And this problem seems quite insoluble unless a meaning is given to Mind or Reason or Logic in the Absolute which is frankly discordant with the meaning that these terms possess in the analysis of finite cognitive experience: which would, of course, be tantamount to giving up the whole Idealist position.

But at this point a difficulty arises in connection with the distinction which, following Mr Joachim, we provisionally admitted between the two forms of Error. B's confident judgment, I have just been saying, turns out to be of the very type of the contradictory. 'But,' it might be rejoined, 'if you are right about the essence of contradiction, a fuller analysis of A's condition may show that you will have to say precisely the same thing about A. For if A is judging at all, he is claiming finality by that very act for what he asserts. The psychical condition of "doubt" does not imply that A is not claiming finality, but simply that that for which he claims finality is *something different*. A's judgment, made in the acute consciousness of his scientific limitations, may be expressed in some such way as this: "That the sun travels round the earth appears to me, in my present defective state of knowledge, to be the fact." Now there is still a certain claim to finality here. What happens is just that instead of final truth being claimed for the "sun-earth" connection, final truth is claimed for *another* connection. Instead of affirming as finally true that the sun travels round the earth, A is affirming as finally true that this sun-earth relation is an hypothesis provisionally entertained by him. But if this interpretation is admitted, then A's judgment seems to be just as good a self-contradiction as B's. In it, too, we have the claim to final truth which has been held to be the essence of contradiction.'

This criticism would, I think, be substantially just. I should accept without demur this revised version of the distinction between A's judgment and B's judgment. A's judgment does claim finality, and we must, on our previous reasoning, hold that it too is self-contradictory. But I want now to point out a very important distinction between the contradiction in A's judgment and that in B's. The connection of differences which A affirms, although not grounded in a way which offers a final satisfaction for thought, *is grounded in a way which thought can see to be final for thought*. It is a connection, that is, which can be observed to be definitely incapable of being more fully grounded without transcending the very conditions of experience itself. It is, in a word, an 'intellectually incorrigible' connection. And such a connection, even if formally contradictory, must clearly be accorded a quite different status from the type of connection affirmed by B, whose ground is not ultimate even for finite intelligence.

We are introduced here to a difficult problem, the relation

of the 'intellectually incorrigible' to 'ultimate Truth.' The chapter on 'Noumenal and Phenomenal Truth' will endeavour to make the issues clear and to offer a solution. At the present juncture I cannot attempt to do more than explain my reasons for holding that the connection affirmed in A's judgment is 'intellectually incorrigible.'

To see this most clearly, consider the different nature of the grounding in A's and B's judgment respectively. The ground of B's judgment, 'the sun travels round the earth,' is an objective system whose character is, not only at B's level of thinking, but at any level, inadequately comprehended. And this means that B's judgment must be recognised as indefinitely modifiable with the progressive deepening of the ground. But the ground of A's judgment is not an objective system capable of more and more complete articulation. A is affirming that this sun-earth relation appears to him, in his present defective state of knowledge, to be the fact. That is, what A affirms as final is just that he does really entertain a belief which he is conscious of entertaining. And the ground of this affirmation is none other than the testimony of the subject's own self-consciousness, which he can no more call in question significantly than he can dispute the actuality of experience itself. It is a ground which not only seems indisputable to A now, but must always continue to seem indisputable under the conditions of finite intelligence. There is accordingly no 'growing system' here whose development might be supposed to necessitate a modification of the connection of differences affirmed. We seem entitled to say, therefore, that the 'ground' here is one whose finality (since no one can ever suppose that he does not have an experience which his self-awareness tells him he has), for human experience, cannot be transcended.

I am not, be it noted, contending that the intellect is here confronted with differences connected in an intrinsically satisfying manner. On the contrary the intellect recognises that there is still here a problem. It does not understand this 'self-awareness' which seems to be a condition of experience, nor how it is related to the universe at large. But—and this is the point—it can see that while intellect remains itself it must accept self-awareness as a sheer *datum*. It can see that the process of deeper experience can never have the effect of throwing doubt upon that which is a condition even of the deeper experience itself. And this, although not ultimate Truth, is intellectual incorrigibility.

We are threatening to encroach, however, upon the matter of the chapter just referred to (Chapter III.) and must bring our present discussion to an end. Whatever one may have to say about the type of judgment illustrated by the case of A, no point, at all events, has been raised which places in jeopardy the contention that B's judgment cannot find a place within the Rational Absolute. Idealism, if it is to reconcile Error with its philosophy, must ignore just that aspect of Error which has been found to be its distinctive mark, its confident self-assertion. Dr Bosanquet ignores it, and it is thus that he is able to pronounce Error to be one in principle with Truth, differing from Truth only in 'systematic distinction and completeness.'[1] It is easy to solve the metaphysical problem of Error if we abstract from the very feature of it which sets us the problem. Whether or not it must remain for Idealism (as I hold) an insoluble problem, it may now be left to the reader to decide.

[1] *The Value and Destiny of the Individual*, p. 214.

CHAPTER II

THE SUPRA-RATIONAL ABSOLUTE AND ITS CRITICS

Section 1. Note on the Structure of the Total Argument

IN the preceding chapter I endeavoured to develop the epistemological argument for the 'Supra-rational' Reality. We shall still be concerned mainly with epistemological matters in this and the succeeding chapter. Before taking up the argument again, however, I should like to remind the reader of what was said in the Preface about the structure of the present study. I do not base my conviction that Reality is supra-rational solely (perhaps not even chiefly) upon the highly abstract and specialised considerations drawn from the analysis of knowledge. If there did not appear to me to be extremely cogent evidence in support of this position from other quarters, I confess that, even if unable to discern my error, I should entertain pretty strong suspicions that somewhere I had been guilty of fallacy. But the required confirmation does exist, and each of the later chapters will, in its own particular way, add its quota of support. In Chapters IV. and V. I shall take up the problem of freedom, and try to show that freedom, in a meaning of it which is compatible only with a non-intelligible Reality, is as indubitable a fact as anything in human experience. In Chapter VI. I shall present a similar argument with regard to the 'moral ought,' urging that moral obligation is also an indubitable fact of experience, and is likewise compatible only with a non-intelligible Reality. In Chapter VII. I shall consider the criterion of moral appraisement, and argue that the only criterion which is true to moral experience is one which presupposes the non-intelligible character of Reality. And in the final chapter I shall attempt to enlist the religious consciousness too in the service of our theory: arguing that certain constituents of religious experience commonly admitted to be fundamental to it show themselves on reflection to be in crass contradiction with one another save on the hypothesis that the Whole is supra-rational.

It may very well be, of course, that every one of these lines of argument is mistaken. But this brief explanation of my programme is inserted here because I should not wish to seem to be adopting a scepticism even more radical than Bradley's own—out-Heroding Herod, as it were—on the frail basis of a far from comprehensive epistemological discussion. I venture to hope that the reader who is acutely antipathetic to the point of view of the latter will consent to suspend judgment until he has traversed the remaining arguments.

In the present chapter I shall, in the first place, endeavour to bring out what precisely is implied in characterising Reality as 'supra-rational.' I shall then proceed to examine the applicability to our doctrine of the arguments most commonly levelled against metaphysical scepticism.

Section 2. The Absolute as 'Experience,' 'Self-consistent,' 'One,' and 'All-inclusive'

I wish first of all, then, to explain more adequately what I mean by calling Reality 'supra-rational.' I certainly do mean that it is in principle unknowable. Moreover, the whole value which the doctrine carries for subsequent philosophic construction depends, I believe, upon being in full earnest with this 'unknowability,' and not succumbing to the very present temptation to whittle it down into insignificance in order to save oneself from the supposed stigma of scepticism. But since there are certain characters which Bradley, even when speaking in apparently sceptical vein, deems it legitimate to ascribe to Reality, it will be well for us to examine at once the credentials of these characters. Can they, or any one of them, be ascribed with propriety to Reality, and if so, can their ascription be understood in a way which does not conflict with Reality's unknowability? The consideration of these questions will make it possible to define more adequately the view of Reality which the present work is concerned to maintain.

The most important by far of these characters, and the only one which will occupy us at length, is that denoted by the term 'experience.' That Reality, whatever else it is, is at least 'experience,' is an assertion which recurs with notable frequency throughout Bradley's writings. 'We perceive, on reflection,' says Bradley in one typical passage, 'that to be real, or even barely to exist, must be to fall within sentience.'[1] And again, developing the doctrine on the following page: 'Find any piece of existence, take up anything that anyone could possibly call a fact, or could in any sense assert to have being, and then judge if it does not consist in sentient experience. . . . When the experiment is made strictly, I can myself conceive of nothing else than the experienced. Anything, in no sense felt or perceived, becomes to me quite unmeaning. And . . . [thus] I am driven to the conclusion that for me experience is the same as reality. The fact that falls elsewhere . . . is a vicious abstraction whose existence is meaningless nonsense, and is therefore not possible.'[2] As Bradley later explains, of course, such statements must not be taken as meaning that facts are 'subjective states.' 'Subject' and 'object' are ideal distinctions made *within* the whole of sentient experience. Neither comes to us as an independent or primary reality. When we say that every fact consists in experience, we mean only that it is 'indissolubly one thing with sentience.' A reality apart from experience in this sense is, it is claimed, a sheer abstraction.

---

[1] *Appearance and Reality*, p. 144. [2] *Ibid.*, p. 145.

Now so far as Bradley's doctrine rests upon the kind of 'experiment' which is suggested in the latter of these passages, it seems to lie open to a fairly obvious objection derived from Bradley's own principles. For if the so-called facts of finite experience are as disparate from ultimate reality as the contrasted terms 'relational' and 'supra-relational' would seem to signify, then it is not at all evident what right Bradley has to appeal to a certain character, viz. sentient experience, in the 'facts' of finite experience, in order to substantiate the presence of a similar character in the one 'ultimate' fact, Reality itself. The application of 'ideal experiment' seems here out of place. It may very well be that while everything which finite mind, with its deficient equipment, can regard as 'fact' is charged with the character of 'experience,' *the* fact, genuine Reality, is not.

This particular line of argument, then, does not seem to me to be at all effective as a proof of the doctrine that 'experience' or 'sentience' must be ascribed to Reality. But, although it is the line of argument commonly adopted by Bradley [1] and evidently felt by him to be conclusive, it is not, I think, by any means the sole consideration which supported him in his exceedingly strong conviction. We have not so far judged it necessary to ask what exactly Bradley means by this 'sentient experience' which plays so ubiquitous a rôle. But when we do ask, we find that it possesses for Bradley certain characteristics which, from a new angle, lend distinct colour to the suggestion that Reality can significantly be said to be 'experience.' For sentient experience, so it appears, is capable of giving us an awareness of 'the many *in* the one'—even though it be at a pre-relational level. And so far as it does, it seems to resemble in formal structure the nature which we must suppose to belong to that ideal consummation of thought's aspirations in which thought and Reality are one and indistinguishable. The implication is that the 'lower' unity may

[1] Another good example occurs in *Appearance and Reality*, pp. 522-3.

be used as at least a 'clue' to the nature of the 'higher' unity. Bradley himself certainly takes this structural resemblance to afford a 'clue.' He expressly holds that it enables us to give some positive content to our notion of Reality's 'unity.'[1] And it is, I think, at least intelligible how on these premises Reality should be said to be 'of the nature of experience'—though, even granting the premises, the leap of faith required seems to me not inconsiderable.

To appraise with any justice the adequacy of this line of approach, however, it is needful to set out, in however condensed a form, certain of the central features in Bradley's doctrine of 'immediate' or 'sentient' experience.[2] Let me state the doctrine first of all without attempt at criticism.

Immediate experience, experience in which there is 'no distinction between my awareness and that of which it is aware'[3] is, Bradley holds, a quite obvious character of at least some of our mental states. Pleasure, pain, desire, volition—it is hopeless to maintain that of these we have no *direct* awareness. 'No perception of objects will exhaust the sense of a living emotion.'[4] But immediate experience is not confined to the phenomena of the emotional life. Careful analysis discloses, Bradley goes on, that it is a character of all of our mental states, cognitive as much as any other. Our experience can in no phase of it be reduced simply to 'consciousness'—if we mean by that the being of an object for a subject. 'Everything which is got out into the form of an object implies still the felt background against which the object comes, and, further, the whole experience of both feeling and object is a non-relational immediate felt unity.'[5]

---

[1] *Appearance and Reality*, p. 244.
[2] A very full and detailed statement and criticism of the doctrine will be found in Ward's article 'Bradley's Doctrine of Experience' (*Mind*, N.S., No. 133).
[3] *Essays on Truth and Reality*, p. 159.
[4] *Ibid.*, p. 159.   [5] *Ibid.*, p. 176.

It is this 'non-relational immediate felt unity' which specially concerns us here. The recognition of it Bradley considers to be of the first importance. The 'felt unity' environs, in a manner it includes, 'the entire relational consciousness.' 'It is the vital element within which every analysis still moves, while, and so far as, and however much, that analysis transcends immediacy.'[1] If we decline to recognise this unity given in feeling, Bradley insists, the continuity of our experience remains inexplicable. From the beginning of conscious life it is certain that everything that comes into the focus of thought out of the background of the felt is taken by us as continuous with what we have already got. Thinking starts not with a mere many, but with a many already taken to be somehow one. But since *thought* cannot be the source of a recognition of unity which *thought* itself presupposes, it is reasonable to infer that the unity is given in the immediate experience within which thinking falls: that thinking proceeds within, and responsive to the guidance of, a '*felt* totality.'[2]

Once granted this felt totality, Bradley's interpretation of the process of experience is able to proceed smoothly enough. In human experience we have, on the one hand, this unity given in feeling. But we have also, on the other hand, the mediate or relational consciousness, in which not unity but mutual externality, qualification from the outside, is characteristic. It may be that the earliest stage in the development

---

[1] *Essays on Truth and Reality*, p. 176.
[2] This is, *I think*, Bradley's main ground for holding that a 'felt totality' is the primary datum of experience. I do not find the argument anywhere stated with ideal clarity. But on the other hand I have said nothing which may not reasonably be read into many of the passages on 'immediate experience.' Perhaps the reader's attention might be directed especially to the 'Supplementary Note' appended to chap. vi. in the *Essays on Truth and Reality*. It is noteworthy that Bradley there introduces his doctrine of the 'felt totality' (p. 200) in express contrast with those doctrines which, holding that experience begins with a 'many,' are unable logically (as Bradley believes) to advance to the 'one.' The implication intended seems clearly to be that only by the admission of the 'felt totality' can you give any explanation of the recognised unity of experience.

of the individual and of the race was one in which experience was *merely* immediate, the relational consciousness being an outgrowth (the steps of which we can only conjecture) from the state of pure sentience.[1] But whether this be so or not, it is certain that 'mere' immediacy is now in fact transcended in our experience. Immediate experience has not vanished. But 'the fact remains that feeling, while it remains as a constant basis, nevertheless contains a world which in a sense goes beyond itself.'[2] And with this transcendence, we find, there comes also conflict. 'The felt content takes on a form which more and more goes beyond the essential character of feeling, *i.e.* direct and non-relational qualification. Distinction and separation into substantives and adjectives, terms and relations, alienate the content of immediate experience from the form of immediacy which still on its side persists.'[3] Thus, *feeling* reality as one, we yet find ourselves confronted in *thought* with a many. And this discordance arouses unrest, and provokes thought to a ceaseless endeavour to reconstitute the broken unity by seeking, in its own way, to resolve its ideal manifold into unity. But the breach is not thus to be healed. The 'way of ideas' is incapable in principle of restoring a unity such as we immediately experience. On the other hand, the breach declines to allow itself to be ignored. We cannot find satisfaction in the 'given felt unity,' for this embraces now a content in patent antagonism to its form. The unity which can alone bring repose must be one which somehow includes within it the sphere of 'terms and relations.' And thus there arises in us the conception of that which answers to the demand for theoretical satisfaction as being a unity which has the same *kind* of immediacy as that which we experience in feeling, but which is *supra*-relational, not *sub*- or *non*-relational.

These are briefly the points relevant to our purpose in Bradley's doctrine of immediate experience. It is pretty clear

[1] *Essays on Truth and Reality*, p. 173 ff.
[2] *Ibid.*, p. 190.   [3] *Ibid.*, p. 190, note.

how they bear upon the matter at issue. On this view we do already, in immediate experience, know what it is to apprehend 'the many in the one.' It is true that this 'felt unity,' the 'many felt in one'[1] as Bradley also calls it, cannot serve as the perfect experience of Reality. For the relational world must be conceived by thought to be included (as it is not here) within the unity of Reality. But it may be said to furnish us with a clue to the kind of experience that we want. We may suppose that the attainment of Reality would be for us 'something like' the felt unity of immediate experience. And with this, perhaps, it is not unnatural to claim that Reality is 'of the nature of (immediate) experience.'

Yet we must begin our criticism by pointing out that the 'leap of faith' earlier referred to is not to be disguised. Even if we grant Bradley's doctrine of the felt totality, it gives us no right to be certain that there is such resemblance between supra-relational immediate unity and sub-relational immediate unity as will warrant the ascription (by analogy) to the former of the term 'experience.' It should be clearly recognised that we are here, at best, in the region of highly precarious conjecture.

This criticism, however, I do not desire to stress; for the real criticism goes much farther back. It seems imperative to reject the basis of the analogy itself. In common with, I imagine, the large majority of Bradley's readers, I find myself quite unable to accept the view that in experience we start from (or, indeed, can even at any time possess) a 'felt unity,' a 'many felt in one.' One need by no means wish to dispute the view that 'feeling' is an essential element in all experience. Bradley seems to me entirely in the right in insisting that experience is never exhaustively described in terms of what

---

[1] *Essays on Truth and Reality*, p. 174. Ward (in the article referred to) substitutes 'as' for 'in' when quoting the passage containing these words. This wording somewhat sharpens the appearance of paradox in the doctrine, but Bradley could not, I think, demur to it as an expression of his meaning. Possibly in other contexts he has actually employed the expression.

is commonly meant by 'consciousness.' But that the feeling which is present can give us what is implied in the phrases 'felt totality,' 'felt unity,' etc., seems to me quite impossible.

Feeling may be *in* itself a unity, no doubt. But that is not to be a feeling *of* unity; and this is what is implied in the phrases just quoted, and in the argument as a whole. The whole point of the analogy is that in immediate feeling we are directly aware of a many as a one. But the difficulties in this view seem insuperable. How can feeling, as such, make us aware 'of' anything? Where there is, *ex hypothesi*, no distinction between the awareness and that of which it is aware, the objectivity implied by the word 'of' is incapable of justification. To be aware 'of,' or recognise an experience 'as,' something is possible only for a consciousness which distinguishes what is now before it from other aspects of its experience. Thus 'unity' has meaning for our apprehension only in distinction from, and relation to, 'plurality.' The appreciation or recognition of unity, in short, implies the activity of the mediating or 'relational' consciousness. There is no unity 'given' in feeling. Experience may start from the recognition of the One, but, if so, it can only be a One the purity of which is already 'vitiated' by the play of the relational consciousness.

The question of the source and nature of our recognition of the unity of the experienced world is extremely difficult. It seems to me that Bradley's doctrine is certainly right in what it denies. It denies that this unity can be established by thought. If thought started with the Many, it is argued, it never could proceed to the One. And this is, I think, true. In point of fact, unless the Many confronting thought were already recognised as somehow One, they could not even be apprehended as a Many. Manyness implies difference, and difference has no meaning for thought apart from a unity within which the differences fall. Cut out the recognition of unity and you find that you are left, not with many 'differents,' but with atomic unrelated particulars which simply fall apart.

It seems true enough, then, that the unity of our experienced world is not established by, but is presupposed in, thought.

But we are *not* entitled to conclude that because this unity is not established by thought it is therefore given in 'feeling.' That is to amend one error by making another no less fatal. We must be content with recognising, I think, that in our primary apprehension of Reality's unity both immediate and mediate factors are involved. Thinking presupposes that unity. And in this sense the unity is given, 'immediate.' But at once we have to add that to possess significance for us the unity thus 'given' must be distinguished from plurality, and thus 'interpreted' by thought. And in this sense the unity is 'mediate.' Reality comes to us neither as a merely 'felt' nor as a merely 'thought' unity. It is, perhaps, least misleading to say that its unity comes to us in an 'ideally interpreted feeling.' But if we use this expression we must keep clearly in mind that we do not *first* have a feeling, which we *then* proceed to interpret. Experience starts neither from the one nor the other, but from their concrete union.[1] And if this conclusion is sound in substance, I submit that no ground remains for holding that immediate experience, in the form in which it enters into our apprehension of unity, is capable of furnishing a clue to the perfect unity which we must postulate as the character of Reality.

I pass on to inquire concerning the further characters which Bradley ascribes to Reality, in what sense, if any, that ascription is legitimate. Here, however, there is less need for detailed discussion. In asserting Reality to be 'self-consistent,' 'one,' and 'all-inclusive,' Bradley shows himself, for the most part, well aware of the modifications needful in the metaphysical application of these conceptions. In the case of Reality's 'oneness' Bradley does, in my opinion, as has just been explained, attach a more positive significance to the conception

---

[1] Cp. Kemp Smith's *Commentary on Kant's Critique of Pure Reason*, p. xxxviii. (2nd edit.). 'Knowledge starts . . . self-consciousness.'

than the strict facts allow. But in the main (the chapter on 'Ultimate Doubts' makes this clear) he is fully alive to the inadequacy of each and all of these characters, even of 'unity.' Their application is, naturally, not taken to be meaningless. But Bradley would not, I think, dissent seriously from the view that the significance of their application lies rather in what they deny than in what they affirm. Let me say a word or two about each of them, indicating on the one hand their validity, and on the other hand their limitations.

First, then, as to 'self-consistency.' That Reality does not contradict itself, and therefore is self-consistent, is a presupposition of all thinking, and so far certain. But against this we have to remember that the ideal of self-consistency which operates in concrete thinking turns out to be defective—a mere 'phenomenal' transcript. When we say that Reality is self-consistent, therefore, we must guard ourselves against supposing that its self-consistency can be envisaged on the analogy of our positive 'systems of knowledge.' We do not know, even in principle, what is the character of that which satisfies the intellect, or is 'self-consistent.' The most that we can legitimately mean when we declare Reality to be self-consistent is, I think, that it does and must possess a character, whatever that character may be, which would satisfy in full the demands of the intellect.

Again, because we take Reality to be self-consistent, we have to reject the notion of a plurality of reals. For Pluralism, as we saw earlier, implies purely external relations, and these are self-contradictory. Thus we come to say that Reality is a 'single' system. And since, further, there is nothing which in any way is that can fail to belong to Reality, it is natural to go on to say that Reality is not only 'one' but 'all-inclusive.' But here once more we must beware. The unity that we ascribe to Reality cannot be adequate to Reality. It gets what meaning it has for us in being defined against plurality, belonging essentially, therefore, to a limited form of being. We have no positive idea of a unity adequate to Reality (although, as we have seen, Bradley is convinced that there is a 'felt unity' of immediate experience which 'serves to suggest to us the general idea of a total experience, where will and thought and feeling will all once more be one ').[1] And the spatial metaphor, 'all-inclusive,' is certainly not less inept. We have to recognise, I think, that each of these terms, in so far as its application is legitimate, is negative in import. When we affirm that Reality is 'one,' we reject the error that there is a plurality of reals. And when we add that it is 'all-inclusive,' we reject the error that there are such things as *mere* appearances, which are somehow isolated from the one Reality. There is a tendency, which may understandably be fostered by the doctrine that Reality is 'a single, all-inclusive system,' to picture Reality in terms of the most comprehensive unities we know in experience. But whatever we may say of the merely symbolical validity of the procedure—a matter that will engage our attention when we come to deal with religious experience—it must be pronounced to be, in any literal sense, illegitimate.

To sum up the results of this Section. We have seen that there is a valid significance in applying to Reality such terms as 'self-consistent,' 'one,' and 'all-inclusive,' but that it is a significance which does not prejudice the essential unknowability of the real. We have argued, on the other hand, that the term 'experience' is not applicable, or at least not with the positive significance which Bradley reads into it. I can imagine, however, here as in the other terms, a certain negative significance which does seem defensible. In saying that Reality is 'experience,' our primary intention might just be to reject the error of supposing that the real is crassly 'non-mental.' This would not be without value. Reality as supra-rational or supra-mental is, indeed, certainly not 'mental.' It possesses no assignable identity with what we can mean by 'mental.'

[1] *Appearance and Reality*, p. 160.

But, as against this, Reality is such that the mind would find in it its own full and final consummation. And, in these circumstances, to call it 'non-mental' is much more misleading than to call it 'mental.' Perhaps we can best express the situation by saying that whereas the ascription to Reality of 'self-consistency' calls attention to the fact that Reality must *satisfy* mind, the ascription of the term 'experience' calls attention to the fact that Reality must satisfy *mind*.

Section 3. *Criticisms of the Supra-rational Absolute.*
(a) *Indirect Criticisms*

I pass on now to the main task of the present chapter—the examination of some of the more formidable criticisms which have been levelled against the doctrine of the 'supra-rational' Reality. These criticisms may be conveniently grouped for purposes of discussion into two classes. There are, in the first place, the indirect criticisms which emanate from the counter-assertion that the primary certitude of all philosophy is that 'the real is the rational,' and that the business of philosophy consists not in debating a principle whose certainty may be apodeictically demonstrated, but rather in tracing its application to the various spheres of experience. And secondly, there are the direct criticisms which take up the notion of a 'supra-rational' Reality and profess to find in it a manifest self-contradiction. I shall deal with the former of these classes in the present section.

I need hardly say that the teaching which I have in mind here is that of the post-Kantian development of Idealism. It must have impressed itself upon all who are familiar with this body of thought how profound and relatively untroubled is the confidence of its exponents that at last philosophy has laid hold of the principle which is the one authentic key to the solution of all problems. However difficult may be its application in detail (and Idealists have not as a rule disguised that difficulty), still this principle—the 'Identity of Thought and Reality,' or the 'Rationality of the Real'—is absolutely compelled, so it is maintained, upon anyone who has understood the reorientation of the metaphysical problem which is necessitated by Kant's own development of it. Kant's postulation of an unknowable 'noumenal' reality behind the phenomena is based ultimately, it is held, upon a defective logic inherited from his Rationalist precursors. When we correct this logic, reinterpreting in terms of the true view of the nature and function of thought, the inference to the philosophy of Absolute Idealism is, it is claimed, irresistible.

What I want to suggest here is that the supposed necessity of the transition 'from Kant to Hegel' rests upon a fundamental fallacy: that while Idealism has been entirely in the right in insisting upon the revision of what it takes to be the Kantian view of 'pure thought,' it has gone hopelessly astray in supposing that the metaphysical corollary of this revision is the doctrine of the identity of Thought and Reality, and the consequent repudiation of the 'noumenal.'

Let me in a few words remind the reader of the substance of the Idealist's reinterpretation of the Kantian distinction of the noumenal from the phenomenal, as one finds it, for example, in Edward Caird's great work on Kant.

Influenced by his Rationalist upbringing, and by his unwavering faith in the infallibility of the traditional or formal logic, Kant developed his philosophy (it is maintained) on the assumption that 'pure' thought is an analytic unity, whose principle is bare self-identity. The ideal form of truth is 'A is A.' The mind cannot accept as theoretically satisfying, and as therefore adequately expressive of reality, any content which is not resoluble into this form. But if this be the ideal which thought demands, it is obvious that in the synthetic operations of the 'understanding' the mind is immersed in a process which never can lead to theoretical satisfaction or truth. That process may be necessary: it may be, as for Kant, the one way in which the mind can deal with the 'given manifold' which confronts it. If so, it will have a logic of its own which it will be imperative to study. But it will be an imperfect logic in that it deals with an imperfect expression of thought, a departure of thought from the purity of its inherent ideal. The syntheses of the understanding, then, can never produce truth. And the world which they reveal is one which, however systematically and elaborately presented, cannot be accepted by thought as the 'real' world. We must pronounce it to be a merely 'phenomenal' world, an appearance of that real world which the demand of thought posits but which remains ever impervious to the best efforts of thought to understand it. Reality, or the noumenal, is, at least theoretically, 'unknowable.'

But, the Idealist rejoins, this supposed gulf between the real world and the world disclosed by the understanding rests upon the doctrine that thought is an analytic unity,[1] and this doctrine is manifestly false. It is not merely in organising the world of sense experience that thought is unable to adopt the principle of bare self-identity. It never does, and never can, adopt it. For A is A—or that from which it ultimately derives, the 'I am I' which, Kant believes, expresses the unity of self-consciousness—shows itself on reflection not to stand for any movement of thought at all, but to be strictly meaningless. Differences are just as necessary to thinking as unity is. The principle which inspires thought is, we must say, not abstract identity, but identity in difference. Thought, in short, is essentially a *synthetic* unity. And once we have seen this, there is no longer any ground for supposing that the syntheses of the understanding are alien to thought's pure nature. On the contrary, they appear now as the advancing expression of thought's effort to realise adequately its own principle, identity or unity in difference. The consummation arrived at in the progress of the understanding, systematic

---

[1] The reader will remember that I am here only expounding—not defending—what I take to be Caird's interpretation of Kant. The accuracy of that interpretation is not at present in question.

unity of differences, is also the positive realisation of thought's own nature. Thus the articulation of an objective world and the articulation of thought's own nature proceed *pari passu*. The 'world' of the understanding is, accordingly, the revelation of truth and reality. We must still say, indeed, that in so far as thought's ideal is only imperfectly realised in this world, the real has not revealed itself in its final character. But interpreting the ideal of thought now as 'identity in difference,' we must see in the activity of the understanding the onward march of truth, and must substitute for the 'phenomenal' world of Kant a world in which ultimate reality progressively manifests itself according to the degree in which the ideal of 'system' or 'unity in difference' finds expression.

The Reality which thought posits and demands, then, is not 'unknowable.' For what thought thus demands is a character which in the developing syntheses of experience thought is progressively realising. The consummation of that development would be at once the realisation of the full nature of thought and the revelation of Reality. Thought and Reality are in the last resort one. And the thought that is one with Reality is not a thought divorced from the thought operative in our actual concrete experience, but simply the perfected development of that thought.

Now if this account has not been misleadingly brief, the point of the criticism to be here advanced will already be evident to the reader who has followed the contentions of the first chapter. I am entirely at one with the Idealist in insisting upon the substitution of 'identity in difference' for 'abstract self-identity' as the ideal of thought. But given this substitution, the Idealist supposes that there is now no barrier between the positive activity of thought, which consists in uniting differences, and the ideal of thought, which is unity or identity in difference. This assumption, so pregnant in metaphysical implications, it seems to me not possible to sustain. If I have been right, the manner in which thinking endeavours to unite differences is in principle incompatible with the ideal of unity *in* difference. In no thought-product can differences be united in the way in which they must be united in Reality. And the consequence is that Reality remains, as Kant held it to be, unknowable by thought: not, however, because thinking is unable to find expressed in its content the ideal of bare self-identity—the reason attributed to Kant—but because it cannot find expressed in its content the ideal of concrete unity in difference.

It follows that thought and Reality are not one, in any sense in which the term 'thought' can bear a significant meaning for finite experience. Thought's 'ideal' may be one with Reality.[1] But thought's 'ideal' is one thing, its *modus operandi* is another. And it is by the latter alone that we are able to attach positive significance to the term 'thought.' This suggests a further criticism (one to which Bradley has of course given classic expression) of the doctrine of the identity of thought and Reality. Thought, as we know it, is judgment, an active process. It rests upon the recognition of an 'other' over against thought, and its function consists in the attempt to banish this 'otherness' by resolving it into unity with itself. If no 'otherness' were recognised, no element antagonistic to thought's unity with itself, then no activity of thought could be stimulated. But the 'thought' that is supposed to be one with Reality, cannot, *ex hypothesi*, recognise anything beyond itself, any element of otherness. Such a 'thought' therefore will have lost the distinctive character by which we know thought in judgment or predication. This is the same as to say, with Bradley, that thought, if it were to attain its ideal, would 'commit suicide.' Seeking to banish 'otherness,' thought aims at a goal in which it would itself cease to be. And if this is so, if the consummation of thought's ideal, which alone gives us ultimate reality, is a whole in which thought no longer preserves any assignable identity of nature with thought

[1] In *one* sense of thought's 'ideal': see Chapter I., Section 4.

as we know it, then it cannot be proper to say, with Idealism, that thought is 'in principle' Reality, or that Reality and thought are 'ultimately' one.

Otherness is, in my judgment, as essential an element in the nature of thought as unity is. And its admission in this capacity is amply sufficient to disqualify thought from claiming the status of the one principle of Reality. The Idealist prefers, as a rule, for reasons into which we need not here enter, to use the terms 'mind' or 'self-consciousness' rather than 'thought' for the supposed supreme principle of Reality. But precisely the same objections seem to attach to these terms. Their meaning involves relation to an 'other': and for the one Reality there can be no 'other.'

This latter difficulty has not, of course, passed unnoticed among Idealists. Bosanquet in particular has made heroic efforts to meet it, and has argued with much ingenuity that 'otherness' is not really an 'essential' feature of self-consciousness. I cannot find his argument in the end convincing. But the importance of what it claims for a right decision on the question of the legitimacy of interpreting the Absolute by finite analogies is so apparent that it is desirable to devote some space to indicating its nature and the difficulties which seem to attach to it.

The gist of Bosanquet's argument is this.[1] Against the Idealist doctrine that in the self-conscious self we find a clue to the nature of ultimate reality, it is objected that the activity of selfhood is conditioned at every point by the recognition of an 'other' over against the self. But this objection, it is claimed, fails to take due note of our 'higher experiences.' It is in the higher experiences of the self that we are most likely to find its true nature revealing itself. And when we turn to these we find good reason to believe that the element of 'otherness' is a vanishing characteristic which becomes demonstrably less important as the self develops towards

[1] See especially Lecture VI. of *Principle of Individuality and Value.*

perfection. In these higher experiences the significant aspect is not 'self over against an other,' but 'self in other'; not discord, but unity. Take, for example, the mind's appreciation of great art—admittedly one of our 'higher' experiences. If we enter genuinely into the beauty of a noble picture, it is almost truer to say that we *are*, for the moment, the picture, than that we are spectators *of* it. We are scarcely conscious of our self as finite, as a self *over against* an 'other.' Unity is the dominating characteristic, 'otherness' all but negligible. And we shall find that the same thing is true (it is held) of the other experiences in which we suppose our self to be 'at its best.' Experience strongly suggests, therefore, that the importance of the element of 'otherness' in the life of the self decreases with the fuller realisation of selfhood. 'Otherness,' Bosanquet allows, never does completely vanish from the self as we know it. But its diminishing significance warrants the inference, it is claimed, that in perfectly rational selfhood 'otherness' will have altogether ceased to be. And if such an inference is sound, the chief objection to construing the Absolute (for which there can be no 'other') on the analogy of the self-conscious self is removed.

Now one might reply to this argument, in the first place, that even if it be granted that 'otherness' is a progressively less significant character in the development of selfhood, we are still not justified in inferring its complete negligibility in self or mind 'at its highest.' Bosanquet's admission that for finite mind, mind as we know it, 'otherness' never wholly vanishes, suggests that the inference is at least extremely bold. 'Mind as we know it' is, on the evidence offered, approaching asymptotically to a condition in which the aspect of 'unity' swallows up completely the aspect of 'otherness.' But it is difficult to see that an asymptotic approach warrants the belief that the thing concerned exhibits 'in its real nature' the condition of the ideal limit. Rather it would seem then to have passed into another nature. After all, though ·9

SUPRA-RATIONAL ABSOLUTE AND CRITICS

asymptotically approaches 1, we do not suppose that ·9 is 'at its highest' or 'in its real nature' 1.

I think, however, that criticism of Bosanquet's thesis may begin earlier, and assail the premises themselves. Is it so certain that our 'higher experiences' show a decreasing sense of 'otherness'? Does it not rather appear, when we look closer, that otherness and unity are complementary aspects of the life of mind, the one no less vital than the other? This seems to me to be the truer view. And to see that it is so, appeal may be made to that same sphere of artistic experience which was cited to support the contrary opinion. The kernel of the matter may be put in a question: 'Admitting that the self *in* other of artistic appreciation is one of our higher experiences, must we not yet say that a higher experience still is that in which we have come to realise that the admired work is (as every such work must be) an expression, however perfect, of a mere stage in the development of the self's full nature—a realisation in which we become conscious once more, therefore, of self *and* other?' An illustration should make the point plain enough. I shall name no special work of art, for in principle any work of art will do. No such work can fail to be inadequate in some measure to the fullness of spiritual growth. Its informing spirit, however lofty and enlightened, is inescapably limited by the cultural context of the age. And the discovery of that limitation, when it is discovered, is the rebirth of that self *and* other which, I am arguing, is as vital in the life of mind as 'self *in* other.'

Let us suppose, then, some person who in his callow youth has become acquainted with a great poem, a poem magnificent in the technique of expression but, perhaps on account of its relative antiquity, inspired by a *Weltanschauung* which harmonises only too well with the crude conceptions of its juvenile reader. Our youth finds in it that overwhelming emotional satisfaction which is only possible where concord between the spirit of author and reader permits of a true and deep marriage of minds. In this state of spiritual absorption the mind is in so intimate a union with its object that it will be quite true to say that our youth is hardly, if at all, conscious of his finitude, hardly conscious of an 'other' over against the self. Unity dominates otherness without question. But now let us go on to suppose that the same person returns to the poem perhaps twenty years later, a man of mature culture, who has probed far, with the help of all that is best in art, religion, and philosophy, into the depths of the problem of man and his place in the cosmos. The philosophy which inspires the poem, we may suppose, seems to him now to be shallow and misguided, belonging to a level of thought with which he was himself once content but which he has outgrown. He finds himself no longer able to merge his whole being in the poem. Its informing spirit he will feel to be definitely inadequate to the expression of his own spirit. By an effort of abstraction he will be able to place himself at the poet's standpoint and appreciate how perfect is the expression of the spiritual attitude. He will not be barred from a definite æsthetic enjoyment; but a part of himself, and that the profounder part, will remain without. No longer is the all-sufficing harmony, the complete unity of self with other, possible for him. The awareness of the spiritual limitation dwells with him as he reads, bringing acute consciousness of the 'other' which the artistic experience fails to include.

Now can we possibly maintain that the man who has come to recognise the spiritual inadequacy of a work (assuming, of course, that he has solid grounds for his attitude), and who consequently cannot banish the sense of the 'other' from the experience which it evokes, is at a lower level of experience than the boy who found in the work a complete expression of his soul, and in whose experience the sense of 'otherness' was consequently not present? There can surely be but one answer. All would agree that the self has genuinely grown, developed itself, in the intervening years. It is a 'higher' self in the second experience. And yet here, in opposition to what Bosanquet takes to be the rule, the higher experience shows increased and not diminished sense of 'otherness.'

It would be absurd to suggest, of course, that the exact opposite of what Bosanquet maintains is the truth, and that the sense of 'otherness' is the true mark of spiritual growth. Viewing the development of spiritual experience in the large, it is evident that the *next* higher stage after the disruption of a complacent unity, with its attendant discord, is the new synthesis which provides a temporary solution of the problem and brings a new sense of unity. But since such solutions must, in the very nature of finite life, be but temporary, the next higher stage again is the recognition of the achieved solution's inadequacy and the sense of 'otherness' once more. We have to recognise, I think, that *neither* aspect, neither unity nor otherness, can claim precedence over the other. They are rather complementary and alternating characteristics of the development of mind. There is a sense, indeed, in which unity or harmony is the 'ideal' of mind, and it is easy to construe this as meaning that unity is the essence or real nature of mind. But just because the ideal of unity is in principle unachievable by finite mind, the recognition of 'otherness,' which is inherent in the nature of self-transcending process, retains forever its essentiality for mind as we know it. The essence of the mind or self-conscious self, we must say, lies not in unity, but in the process of self-transcendence which aims at unity, a process in which sense of 'unity' and sense of 'otherness' are (to repeat the previous expressions) complementary and alternating characteristics.

It does seem to me of great importance that we should recognise clearly that the experience of unity is not *only* a symptom of the self's strength and value. It is *also* a symptom of the self's impotence and disvalue. For it denotes a failure on the part of the self so far to realise that its experience is not in fact harmonious, but is, as it must be, shot through with contradiction. The experience of unity is a symptom of the partial conquest of the 'other,' a guarantee of the substantial rightness of our direction. But just so long as we dwell in it we betray the limitations of our spiritual vision. The self which deludes itself into the belief that it has attained what it seeks, the self which acquiesces complacently in a supposed 'harmony,' gives us Error in the theoretical life and Immorality in the practical. Unconsciousness of 'otherness' is spiritual death, not realised selfhood.

I have appeared, perhaps, to elaborate unduly in these latter pages what may seem almost a digression from the main theme of the chapter. But the digression is more apparent than real. The question of the competence or incompetence of interpreting ultimate reality in terms derived from finite experience is fundamental to our thesis. I have been trying to show what seem to me the defects in Bosanquet's manner of meeting the objections against adopting for this purpose the category of self-consciousness. It is true, indeed, that Bosanquet does not go so far as to maintain that self-consciousness is a fully adequate category. But he does assert that we are entitled to take self-consciousness as a 'clue' to the nature of Reality, and speaks approvingly of 'a deeper conception of reality, framed at least on the analogy of self-consciousness.'[1] Or again he tells us that 'the absolute or infinite should present itself to us as more of the finite, or the finite at its best'[2] (adding, somewhat characteristically, as though this were the sole alternative, 'and not as its extinction'). But these more or less guarded expressions, 'clue' and 'analogy,' only serve to render the Idealism less clear-cut, without mitigating the fundamental difficulties. 'Clue' and 'analogy' imply an assignable identity of character between the terms of the comparison, else they are meaningless. And it is just this assignable identity of character which I hold to be lacking here. Self-consciousness is an experience which has inherent

[1] *Principle of Individuality and Value*, p. 222.   [2] *Ibid.*, p. 255.

in it the reference to an 'other' beyond itself. The Absolute is a unity in which no reference to an 'other' beyond itself can obtain. The 'clue' therefore is a false clue. If we insist upon using it, we perforce distort Reality. But, I agree, it is natural to insist upon using it so long as we retain our faith in the essential 'intelligibility' of Reality.

It would certainly be neither safe nor fair to adduce as weighty evidence for the incompetence of finite analogies the distressing embarrassments of the Idealist who ventures to close quarters with his Absolute and is obliged to offer a definite statement concerning the exalted mode of its activity. Yet, if an attempt were made to assemble any considerable number of these statements, I believe that the starkly paradoxical character of their language would astound Idealists themselves. The abiding value of Idealism—even of its Colossus, Hegel—is perhaps, after all, critical rather than constructive. The incompetence of categories such as Mechanism and Life to pose as ultimate principles of Reality is made out, as it seems to the present writer, with overwhelming force. But it does not follow that because the mind in its search for a true unity in difference is forced to pass beyond Mechanism, and beyond Life, the ultimate principle is therefore Mind or Spirit. It may be true that Mechanism has defects which Life has not, and that Life has defects which Mind has not; and again, that beyond Mind there is nothing higher that we can envisage. But this does not mean that Mind must be the ultimate principle, unless it is first presupposed that the ultimate principle is attainable by us. Where this presupposition is made it is, I think, entirely natural that in spite of the difficulties in the way of an even plausible presentation of the ultimate unity in terms of Mind, the actual adequacy of Mind to rank as the supreme principle should be taken to be virtually certain. But it may be that the difficulty of even plausible presentation is due just to the fact that no humanly accessible category, neither Mind nor any other, is adequate to the nature of the real—that every attempted presentation of the nature of the real is an attempt to express the inexpressible. Even Caird admits, when trying to expound the Hegelian doctrine of the Absolute, that Hegel 'seems to be breaking through the limits of language, by continual self-contradiction.'[1] It is, I presume to think, more than 'seeming.' 'The reality is the universal, which goes out of itself, particularises itself, opposes itself to itself, that it may reach the deepest and most comprehensive unity with itself.'[2] We know *why* Hegel used these terms. He has argued that we must think Reality as related and determined, but not as *externally* related and determined, and therefore, it must be, as *self*-related and *self*-determined. And this is one attempt among others to express the nature of a 'self-determined and self-related whole.' Yet such language conveys no real meaning. How can the whole go out of *itself*? *Mind* may, just because it is not the Whole, but the *Whole* cannot, because there is no place but itself to go to! Hegel is wanting to retain for his Absolute both relation and the integrity of perfect unity, and it cannot be done. Relation involves at least partial externality; and 'self-relation,' accordingly, if it is to be taken absolutely, remains merely a form of words. What meaning it has in its present context is solely negative, consisting in the implied denial that Reality is either externally related or relationless. The whole statement is strikingly reminiscent (to speak somewhat anachronistically) of the description in Bradley of the kind of thought which *could* be pronounced immune from contradiction—'a self-evident analysis and synthesis of the intellect itself by itself.' In each case there is an insistence by implication upon the removal of certain defects. But viewed as positive contributions to the interpretation of the character of ultimate reality they seem to mean (as Bradley without doubt was well aware) just nothing at all.

---

[1] *Hegel* (Blackwood's Philosophical Classics), p. 181.   [2] *loc. cit.*

In this last section I have been arguing, firstly, that the revision of the Kantian philosophy in the light of a truer conception of thought's ideal does not, as the Idealist contends, lead straight to the doctrine of the identity of Thought and Reality, but, on the contrary, leaves Reality 'unknowable' just as it was for Kant, although for different reasons: and secondly, that the Idealist's attempt to establish the claims of Mind to rank as the supreme principle of Reality by showing that the reference to an 'other' is not a fundamental characteristic of mind, must be adjudged to fail. The opposition of self and other, we have been maintaining, is not a diminishing factor in human experience, but rather ingredient in its very nature. The third, and last, Idealist position with which I wish to deal in this chapter concerns this opposition also, seeking to deny its ultimacy on somewhat different grounds from those already examined. Bosanquet's argument sought to show that we can in fact trace by observation a diminution of importance in the aspect of 'otherness,' as mind develops its true nature; which is taken to suggest that in the full reality of mind 'otherness,' as such, disappears. The present argument is more of the *a priori* variety. It asserts that whatever may be the difficulties in the way of envisaging the actual transcendence of this opposition, still it is absolutely certain on logical grounds that the opposition is transcended in the principle of self-consciousness. Let us see then what these grounds are.

The argument is a familiar one in the literature of Idealism. The significant thing about self-consciousness, it is pointed out, is that the self is here not merely opposed to an 'other,' but is *conscious* of itself as so opposed. And to be conscious of an opposition is in principle to transcend it. The apprehension of A as opposed to or distinct from, B, presupposes the apprehension of a unity within which the *distincta* fall. If we try to dispense with the apprehended unity of the terms, we find that they simply fall apart as unrelated atoms, and cannot possibly present themselves as opposed, or even different. Opposition is a relation, and relation is meaningless apart from unity. Thus we have to say that self-consciousness, in as much as it involves consciousness of the opposition of self and other, is possessed, in however inchoate and undeveloped a manner, of the unity within which the opposition falls. And this must mean that the opposition is not a *final* opposition for the self-conscious self. In self-consciousness the principle of reconciliation is present from the beginning. In the lower levels of experience it is there, as it were, only in the germ. But the course of experience is just the development of that germ. It is the process of rendering explicit what at first is merely implicit, viz. the unity underlying the opposition of self and other. No forced reading of actual experience is necessary to see that both in the theoretical field and in the practical the very essence of spiritual activity lies in the gradual overcoming of this opposition. In the self-consciousness which has fully realised itself the transcendence of the opposition will be complete. It follows that the claim of the category of self-consciousness to be adequate to ultimate reality is so far good, the duality of self and other being for self-consciousness a duality *in unity*.

Before proceeding to criticise this argument confirmation, and perhaps clarification, of the above statement of it may be offered in a citation from Edward Caird. The citation is characteristic, and has its fellow in a score of other passages in Idealist writers. '[Let us] consider,' says Caird, 'what the life of self-consciousness is. In the first place, self-consciousness presupposes consciousness—*i.e.* it is a consciousness of self in opposition, yet in relation, to a not-self. Yet in this distinction a higher unity is presupposed; for the self can be conscious of itself as so distinguished and related, only so far as it overreaches the distinction between itself and its object. Thus beneath the conscious duality of self and not-self there is an unconscious unity, which reveals itself in the fact that the whole life of an intelligence is an effort to overcome its own dualism—in *knowledge* to find itself, in *action* to realise itself, in an object or a world of objects, which at first presents itself as a stranger and even an enemy.'[1]

The argument is not, I think, unplausible. But it appears to me, nevertheless, to rest upon a demonstrable fallacy. It is true that in the apprehension of objects we cannot pass from the apprehension of A to the apprehension of B as different from A, save in virtue of the recognition that B belongs to one order with A. Every such passage to apprehended difference implies logically prior recognition of the unity within which the differences fall. But the point is that in the apprehension of the opposition of self and its object there is *no* such 'passage' from one term to the other. We do not first apprehend self, and then pass to the apprehension of an object-world as distinct from, and opposed to, the self. Nor do we start with the object-world, and later apprehend the self. If we proceeded in either of these ways, then admittedly the 'second' apprehension would rest on the prior recognition of a unity to which both terms belonged. But the facts are otherwise. For our apprehension of our 'self' belongs to a quite different category from our apprehension of successive 'objects.' It obviously does not come to us as a differentiation of an objective continuum. One of the most immovably fundamental things that we mean by our 'self' is that it is that to which an 'objective continuum' is presented. And this consideration puts us on the track of the right solution. The truth is that there is no 'passage' at all, but that to apprehend the self is *at the same time* to apprehend an object-world over against it, and that to apprehend an object-world (in its character as such) is *at the same time* to apprehend the self as that to which the object-world is present or presented. A 'self' which is not confronted with an object-world, and an 'object-world' which is not object for a self, are alike mere abstractions. Thus we do not, starting

[1] *Hegel* (Blackwood's Philosophical Classics), p. 182.

with one term, come to apprehend the second as opposed. The apprehension of the second as opposed is involved in the apprehension of the first. And if this is so, it is wrong to say that the second term must be recognised as belonging to one order with the first in order to be apprehended as opposed. No mediating condition is necessary, because the opposition of the second is given directly in the apprehension of the first.

The root error lies, then, in treating the consciousness of the unique opposition of self and object as though it were analogous to the consciousness of particular oppositions within the objective continuum. When we do justice to their distinctness, the necessity of postulating a logically prior recognition of the unity underlying the former opposites vanishes.

It is true, indeed, that the whole development of experience bears witness to the fact that the self does postulate an ultimate unity behind the opposition of self and not-self. But to postulate *that* the opposites are ultimately one is not necessarily to have even the germinal knowledge of *how* they are one. True, the fact of the process itself, with its continuous character, proves that the idea of *a* 'how' is operative. But it may not be, and in fact it is not, *the* 'how.' The adoption of a 'how,' prescribing a definitive line of advance, is a patent fact of experience. We must recognise that the self-conscious self has its own characteristic way of seeking to bring about the reconciliation of self and otherness. But neither on grounds of logic nor of observation is there reason to suppose that *its* way is *the* way, that the type of unity which it progressively seeks after is the type of unity which would be adequate to the final end in view.

Section 4. Criticisms of the Supra-rational Absolute.
(b) *Direct Criticisms*

We have devoted a good deal of space to that purely indirect criticism of the Supra-rational Absolute which is implied in the positive Idealist arguments for Mind as the ultimate principle of Reality. It will be remembered, however, that the philosophical position which I am trying to recommend in this study has been arrived at along a line of thought which is in its origin traditionally Idealist. The fact of this genealogy has seemed to make it desirable, if not indeed obligatory, to throw into relief the points of difference which compel me, in spite of an Idealist starting-point, to develop a metaphysical conclusion which is in somewhat drastic conflict with Idealism.

Let us turn now to criticisms of a more direct order. I have already hinted that in my opinion a good many of the current denunciations of the Bradleian Absolute would be not unjustly described as frivolous. Those with which I shall first deal can hardly fail, I think, to support that judgment in the mind of the impartial reader.

What, for example, are we to make of the criticism, all too typical, that Bradley's Absolute 'explains nothing'? Such an Absolute, it is urged, throws no light upon anything in the universe, and as such stands self-condemned as an essay in metaphysical theory. It is, as Signor Ruggiero (to the mortification of the present writer, who confesses the greatest admiration for Signor Ruggiero's historical judgments in general) has explicitly termed it, an 'absolute of straw.'[1]

The reply to this is, in the first place, that it is not true that the doctrine of the Supra-rational Absolute throws no light upon anything in the universe. It is surely an important contribution to our understanding of the universe to be led to see that the world which reveals itself through the intellect fails in principle to express the nature of the ultimately real. But, in the second place, if what the critic is desirous of insisting upon is that such an Absolute furnishes no insight into the final 'how' of things, then I should be ready to agree with him, but would beg to point out that this is not, in itself, a

---

[1] *Modern Philosophy*, p. 275 (English edition).

'criticism.' As it stands, it is a plain statement of fact. If it claims to be more, if it claims also to be a condemnation of the Bradleian Absolute, then that claim rests quite evidently on the assumption that an ultimate explanation of things is possible. But this assumption is precisely what it is the main business of Bradley's philosophy to disprove. In other words, the 'criticism' is just a particularly glaring instance of *petitio principii*.

Of a similar calibre is the contemptuous rejection of the 'unknowable' Absolute on the score that it is 'meaningless.' 'Meaningless' is a dangerous adjective, with boomerang potentialities which it is tempting to exploit. But (if one must take it seriously) *of course* the Supra-rational Absolute is 'meaningless,' if by that we mean that its positive nature is impenetrable by mind. And, equally of course, this is not an indictment of the doctrine in question, save on the assumption that the Absolute—Reality as a whole—is intelligible. Yet in no *other* way, so far as I can see, can the Supra-rational Absolute be held to be 'meaningless.' If the critic means only that the doctrine which maintains it contains no meaning for *him*, then there are more modest ways of expressing this situation than by the forthright declaration that the doctrine is 'meaningless.'

The next criticism with which we are to deal cannot, however, be dismissed in so summary a fashion. It can claim distinguished names among its advocates, notably that of Professor Pringle-Pattison. This criticism aims at the root of the Supra-rationalist philosophy, viz. its epistemology. It argues that it is only through the adoption of a false logic, the logic of abstract identity, that Bradley finds himself compelled to reject the world which the intelligence articulates, and compelled to erect as the ultimate reality this 'unknowable' Absolute. In Professor Pringle-Pattison's words, Bradley 'adopts this logic of abstract identity apparently without reserve, and because he finds it brings him to a deadlock he pronounces the actual world to be "unintelligible" . . . "self-contradictory" . . . "illusory."'[1]

With great respect for the author of this criticism, I must nevertheless deem it to rest upon a serious misunderstanding. Even on general grounds, indeed, a misunderstanding might be suspected. For Bradley has himself lashed most mercilessly, in season and out of season, the folly of a logic which would take 'A is A' as its ideal of truth. It is fair to say, I think, that there has been no philosopher of recent times who has been more urgent in driving home the lesson of Hegel, that differences apart from identity and identity apart from differences are the sheerest abstractions. It is at least exceedingly improbable that he should be himself a victim of the fallacy which he has so roundly denounced.

But apart from general probabilities, what do we in fact find to be the basis of Bradley's rejection of the world of the intellect? Bradley condemns as not giving ultimate reality all connections of differences by the intellect. This is agreed. But why? Is it because the ideal of the intellect is, in his view, abstract self-identity, which ideal is not satisfied in any such proposition? Not for a moment. A proposition of the form 'A is A' he would condemn even more vigorously, on the ground that it does not express a thought at all. Bradley condemns the connection of differences as carried out by the intellect only because, as he understands the matter, the intellect cannot connect differences *intrinsically*, but only through a partially external 'ground' which inevitably sets a fresh problem. Intellectual connections are thus incapable of achieving a genuine *unity in difference*, and it is for *this* reason that they are for Bradley metaphysically defective. To repeat, the fault is not that they do not realise a supposed ideal of abstract identity, but that they do not, and can not, realise the ideal of identity in difference. Bradley may of course be

[1] *Man's place in the Cosmos* (1st ed.), pp. 151-2.

wrong in this view. But until it is understood that this is his view, criticism is beside the mark.

I turn now to a criticism of a much more searching character, one which opens up a problem demanding careful investigation. The criticism appears in a good many forms, but their common essence may perhaps be stated thus. 'You hold,' it is said, 'that ultimate reality is unknowable. But if it is, what exactly is the basis of your judgment that the world of experience is not ultimately real? Surely that judgment implies that you are already in possession of the standard of the ultimately real? And if so, reality cannot be beyond knowledge.'

Now in principle the proper answer is, I think, clear enough, although it leaves undeniable difficulties awaiting solution. To condemn the world of experience, I should reply, it is not necessary that we should know what reality *is*. It is enough if we know what reality is *not*. If we know that reality *cannot* have a certain character K, and we discover, on examination, that the world disclosed by the intellect *does always necessarily have* the character K, then it follows logically that the latter world is not the real world. That is how the case stands with us here. We do not know what reality is. But we do know that it cannot have a character involving self-contradiction, which is the character we find inherent in the world of intellectual experience.

But this answer will not satisfy the critic as it stands. I am claiming that we have negative, but no positive, knowledge of the nature of reality. And this opens up the whole question of the possibility of a *merely* negative knowledge. It will obviously be imperative to offer defences against the familiar logical doctrine that 'every negative implies a positive.' If this doctrine holds good universally, then there must be some, and it is desirable to know precisely what, positive or affirmative meaning in our professedly merely negative proposition about the nature of reality: a proposition which, for shortness' sake, we may express in the form 'reality is not relational.'

There are, I think, two distinct lines along which this particular criticism may proceed. I shall deal with each in turn.

In the first place, it may be pointed out that all significant speech proceeds within a 'universe of discourse.' There is always a general theme or subject which determines the meaning of our particular proposition, whether affirmative or negative. Thus, *e.g.* when I say 'the heart of this flower is not yellow,' I am interested in the general question of the colour of the heart, and the significance of the proposition lies in its excluding yellow from the competing possibilities in the way of colour. The proposition could quite properly take the alternative form 'the heart of this flower is *a colour not-yellow.*' And so with all negation which has point at all. The exclusion of the particular character implies the affirmation that the thing is of the general character of which the particular character is an instance.

It is fairly evident, however, that the objection in this form may be repelled. I should agree without hesitation that thinking always proceeds within a universe of discourse. In the case of the proposition 'reality is not relational,' the special 'universe' is the metaphysical or ultimate characteristics of the real. But the question of whether or not the 'universe' in any given case prescribes a *significantly* positive content to negation depends entirely, I submit, upon the question of whether the character negated is a particular instance of a more general character which is *itself* significantly positive. Now in our present case the character negated is clearly not of this sort. It is itself of ultimate generality; or, to put it otherwise, that of which it (relationality) is an instance is just 'character-in-general.' The only positive form of which our proposition admits is 'Reality is of a character not-relational.' The element of affirmation which thus appears is obviously of no real moment—though it is quite enough to give our negation 'point.' It seems clear then that the dictum that 'every negative implies a positive' has, in this interpretation of it, no significant application to the case in hand.

The second form which the criticism may take concerns us more nearly. I may be reminded that, on my own showing, the intellect demands a 'ground' or 'rationale' for the connection of differences. Now this applies to negative judgments equally with affirmative judgments. The formula of the negative judgment is $A(x)$ is not B. But does not this recognition of a ground for the connection imply the apprehension of some *positive* character in A? It is true, of course, that if we are asked why A is not B, we may be in a position to reply, because A is not C, and not-C implies not-B. We should thus remain, so far, within the circle of mere negation. But evidently this is only to push the difficulty further back. We should now have to ask what it is in A that warrants our exclusion of C. Sooner or later, it would seem, a positive character in A must come to light. Must it not be so also with 'reality' in the judgment 'reality is not relational'?

I think I can show that, and why, the necessity does not exist in this particular case. Suppose I am asked on what ground I assert that 'reality is not relational.' I reply, in the first place, 'because reality is non-contradictory, and non-contradictory involves non-relational (in that, as we saw in Chapter I., it excludes the organisation of differences after the intellectual or relational pattern).' That is, my first reply takes the shape suggested in the preceding paragraph, 'A is not B because it is not C, and not-C involves not-B.' Now the next question, we agreed, would be, 'But on what grounds do you maintain that A is not C?' Very well, let us apply this to the case in hand. But when we do, we find that what we are asking for is just the ground for maintaining that reality is non-contradictory. In other words, we have got back to a connection concerning which it is absurd to ask for a 'ground.' We know that the apprehension of this connection must be immediate, since it is the logical antecedent of all mediating processes. Here, then, we have a negative judgment which requires no ground, and which does not, accordingly, imply the recognition of positive content in the subject which the apprehension of a ground would entail.

But does the term 'non-contradictory' not have itself a certain positive significance? Only in a purely *formal* sense. Formally we can give positive expression to it, as the 'self-consistent,' or as 'differences united in a way acceptable to the intellect.' But *concretely* we know only what is *not* self-consistent, differences united in a way *not* acceptable to the intellect. When we set ourselves to the criticism of experience, we find that the intellect rejects as not finally acceptable each and all of the connections of experience. And when we ask what it is that the intellect wants, what is the positive meaning of the 'non-contradictory,' we can find no answer in any actual experience, but only in the nature of the direction in which the intellect attempts to make progress. Employing that as our clue, we can see that the intellect wants a union of difference in which the principle of union is *internal* to the differences. And this may properly enough lead us to say that the non-contradictory is 'unity-in-difference.' But this is only a formal account, which receives no filling from experience. What unity in difference concretely means, we do not, and cannot, know.

The objection we have just been considering is the most important which has yet met us. Let me in one sentence sum up the answer that has been given to it, as follows: The judgment 'reality is not-relational' does not imply the apprehension of a positive content in reality, for the reason that it is the direct consequence of another negative judgment about reality ('reality is non-contradictory') which is by nature ungrounded, intuitive, or immediate.

And now I pass to the final criticism which I wish to notice in this section. The burden of my argument with respect to it will come at a later stage, but it seems advisable to state it in principle here. 'Do you realise,' the critic may ask us, 'that your Supra-rational Absolute flies right in the face of man's most deep-seated convictions as to the *orderly* character of the universe. The "orderliness" of Reality is a veritable postulate of significant human experience. But your Absolute rejects all that man can possibly mean by "order." It is unintelligible, so far as our finite intelligence is concerned. And such a "cosmos" is surely perilously near to a "chaos."'

Now, with respect to the alleged postulate of the orderliness of reality, I do of course agree that the intellect assumes the self-consistency of reality, and in this sense its 'orderliness.' But the point of the critic's remonstrance is that this order must be an 'intelligible' order, or it loses all significance for us. Here I do most emphatically join issue. Paradoxical as the contention may at first sight appear, I am prepared to argue that it is only if the 'order' postulated by the intellect be interpreted as an order *not* intelligible that Reality can in the end be legitimately taken as 'cosmos' rather than 'chaos.' For—and here lies the crux of the matter—man is a conative as well as a cognitive being, and *qua* conative he *must* (as I shall later try to show) believe in his own personal freedom, *must, i.e.* recognise that there is in reality that which is incompatible with the logical continuity of an 'intelligible order.' This conviction of free initiative, I shall try to prove in Chapters IV.–V., is not something which gives way in the individual before the dissolving force of analysis. It is something inherent in self-conscious experience, ineradicable, not even subject to modification by the individual's possible intellectual assent to the philosophy of Absolute Idealism. But if this be so, what must be the straits of the man whose philosophy tells him that it is a postulate of the intellect that reality is an 'intelligible' order, and whose every significant act of will bids him deny this postulate? Surely this civil strife of the faculties, this warring in the very seat of the soul, may well reduce the hapless spectator of it to a sceptical despair? It is to the man who holds that the 'order' postulated by the intellect is 'intelligible order' that Reality should in truth appear as 'chaos.' For us it is still legitimately a 'cosmos'; for the practical postulate of personal freedom finds no contradiction in the theoretical postulate of an orderly reality, when once we frankly acknowledge that the order, or consistency, or harmony of Reality is incapable of interpretation in terms of intellectual categories. The 'heresy' of Suprarationalism is not an enemy of the values. Properly understood it is their most potent guardian.

CHAPTER III

NOUMENAL AND PHENOMENAL TRUTH

Section 1. Absolute Idealism's Rejection of Correspondence Notion of Truth

IN this chapter I purpose to consider how the view of Reality that has been expounded reacts upon the general theory of Truth, with special reference to a fundamental distinction which arises naturally out of our discussions—the distinction between Ultimate or Noumenal Truth, the kind of satisfaction which the intellect ideally wants, and what may be called (with the misgivings proper to so ambiguous a term) Phenomenal Truth, the kind of satisfaction at which in practice the intellect can alone significantly aim. The import of this distinction will best emerge if we turn our attention first of all to the doctrine of Truth sponsored by Absolute Idealism, observing carefully the points at which our own different metaphysical position compels modification.

For Absolute Idealism, Reality is a systematic whole, intelligibly continuous throughout. And just because it is intelligibly continuous throughout, there can be no barrier opposed in principle [1] to the effort of the intellect to apprehend it as it is. Since, again, there is thus absolutely no aspect of Reality which must perforce remain an 'other' over against thought, the proper goal and culmination of the thought-process, which is also the attainment of Truth, must be envisaged

---

[1] One is tempted to stress the qualification 'in principle'; for there would seem to be still some who would impute to Idealism the overweening claim that the finite intelligence can *in fact* comprehend the universe in its totality.

NOUMENAL AND PHENOMENAL TRUTH 83

as a state in which the distinction of thought from Reality ceases to be. For so long as any such distinction remains, Reality is presenting an aspect of otherness or opposition to thought, and so far fails to be 'intelligible throughout' for the thinking subject. Truth, therefore, is to be found only in that thought which has become identical with Reality. And hence Idealists tend to speak almost indifferently of Truth *or* Reality. Such distinction as may be allowed is at most one of aspect. Truth is the character of 'the one significant whole.' When understood in its full and proper nature it is not, we are told, an attribute of judgments 'about' Reality, but just that perfect systematic coherence which is the character of Reality itself.

Thus it is that it comes to be maintained in the Idealist theory of Truth, that Coherence is not merely the test or criterion of Truth, but also its essence, meaning, or nature. And Idealism, I think, is bound to hold this. Given its premises as to the nature of Reality, the steps to the conclusion seem fully logical. The Idealist grants, of course, that his conclusion wears a paradoxical air. When we speak of the proposition 'Charles I. died on the scaffold' as a 'true' proposition, we certainly do not usually mean by its being 'true' that it is marked by systematic coherence. We mean, to use a rough expression at present, that what is affirmed corresponds with what did really take place. But this, the Idealist urges, is merely the illusion characteristic of an inadequate stage of thought's development. It is inevitable at the level at which there still remains an opposition between knowing mind and object to be known. But he has shown (he will proceed to tell us) that the search for truth at this dualistic level is not finally satisfied at this level, but attains what it aims at only in an experience in which the dualism breaks down in that fully coherent whole which is Truth and Reality in one. This Truth is, no doubt, Ideal Truth, never to be completely attained by man. But it is none the less the *real* nature of the Truth which you seek after in ordinary experience, the logical culmination of that search and strictly continuous with it. It expresses what you would attain were your search deepened and expanded to its ideal completion. Accordingly, while your view of Truth as 'correspondence' with Reality is natural at a certain level, you are bound to admit that at that level at which Truth 'comes into its own,' fulfilling its proper nature, there is nothing 'outside' for Truth to correspond with. Truth in its real meaning is one with Reality itself, and 'correspondence,' as an ultimate theory of its nature, must be frankly abandoned.

Now if 'one-ness with Reality' is indeed the logical termination of the advance of the intellect—a consummation genuinely continuous with the process—then there does seem to me no option but to reject outright the Correspondence view of the meaning of Truth. That view will not hold good of Truth even at the human level. For if Reality is intelligibly continuous, there is no room for any distinction of principle between 'human truth' and 'ultimate truth.' The one flows directly into the other.

Section 2. *Supra-rationalist Modification of this Rejection. Noumenal (or Ideal) Truth and Phenomenal Truth*

Nevertheless, I do not think that the Correspondence theory is to be so easily dismissed. The view of the relation of thought and reality outlined in the previous chapters is, in spite of obvious affinities, divergent from the doctrine of Absolute Idealism in respects which affect profoundly the problem of Truth. We shall find, I think, that the readjustment to which we are compelled affords at least a qualified vindication of the Correspondence view of the meaning, though certainly not of the criterion, of Truth. Let us see how this is so.

The essence of the matter is as follows. I should agree with the contention of Idealism that the demand of the intellect for

NOUMENAL AND PHENOMENAL TRUTH

satisfaction is not to be met short of the Whole, and that in the Whole the distinction of thought and Reality ceases to be. And there is no particular objection to entitling this perfected attainment 'Ideal Truth.' But, in opposition to Idealism, we found it necessary, in Chapter I., to say that this Whole in which the intellect would find its final satisfaction is 'supra-rational.' It is in principle inaccessible to the finite intellect. 'Ideal Truth,' then, is supra-rational, in principle inaccessible to the finite intellect. It follows that the Truth which we have called 'Ideal' Truth cannot be said to be in any proper sense *continuous* with that Truth which has significance for the processes of finite thinking. For this reason it cannot be legitimate to point to the character of 'Ideal Truth' (which suffers nothing outside of itself), and to say that this is what is 'really,' or 'in the end,' meant when people talk about Truth. We could say this only if our finite efforts after Truth developed progressively towards 'Ideal Truth'—which they do not. In the absence of this continuity we have to agree, I think, that Ideal Truth is not merely a 'higher' Truth than that which the finite mind in practice means by Truth (although it assuredly is this) but also, in an understandable sense, a 'different' Truth.

The consequences of this admission, as concerns the status of 'Correspondence,' are most important. We may still justly join issue with those who say that 'Correspondence' is the last word about Truth, pointing out to them that the final satisfaction of the intellect, 'Ideal Truth,' must be envisaged as an experience in which thought and reality are no longer disunited. But we must at once go on to admit that Ideal Truth is not continuous with what Truth concretely means for the intellect, and that its nature cannot therefore be rightfully taken as merely expressing 'better' (*i.e.* in a more developed form) the meaning which Truth has at the level of operative thinking. Hence we shall be led to assign to the Correspondence view at least a qualified validity. If it is indeed the case that the intellect, in pursuing Truth along the sole path that is open to it, is debarred in principle from attaining that Ideal Truth in which 'Correspondence' loses its meaning, then we do have to recognise in 'Correspondence' a meaning which is ultimate for positive, concrete thinking.

It is necessary that we should be quite clear about the precise character of this concession which, as I understand it, must be made to the Correspondence notion; and I may venture briefly to re-state what is central.

If the Ideal Truth which, in common with Absolute Idealism, I hold to be one with Reality itself (and therefore to exclude 'Correspondence' from its meaning) is rightly to be regarded as a strict *development* of our search after Truth in ordinary experience, then it is necessary to say that 'correspondence with reality' represents a view of the nature of Truth which attaches to an inferior level of thought's development, and must be superseded by the Coherence Notion. This is the state of the case as it appears to Absolute Idealism, for which 'Ideal Truth' is a coherent system continuous with the systems of our finite knowledge. If, on the other hand, 'Ideal Truth' does not possess this continuity, if the intellect's search after Truth proceeds along lines which do not, and cannot, lead to 'Ideal Truth' (the view maintained in these pages), then the case is radically altered. There is no longer any point in holding that the nature found in 'Ideal Truth' is the 'proper' nature of the Truth sought in ordinary experience. In *one* sense of course it is, *but not in any sense which would compel us to abandon 'Correspondence' as what Truth must concretely mean for intellect.* For in holding that this 'Ideal Truth' is supra-rational, we are thereby admitting that what we may call 'Phenomenal Truth' cannot with positive significance be transcended by the intellect. We are admitting that for finite beings the level at which thinking seems to be over against a world to be thought about—the level of the Correspondence view—is an ultimate level for positive concrete thinking.

Within certain limits, then, the Correspondence view of the meaning of Truth is for us legitimised. Correspondence is not the *ultimate* meaning of Truth. For we are able, by a critical analysis of the intellect's demands, to see that what would finally satisfy the intellect, and be therefore Truth in its fullest sense, is a whole which cannot suffer the diremption which a Correspondence theory demands. On the other hand, since this Ideal Truth (or, as we may also call it from a slightly different viewpoint, 'Noumenal' Truth) is not a continuous development of the intellectual process, we may justly say that what Truth means as a conception with positive significance for intellectual operations is unaffected by the transcendental deduction of Ideal Truth. Truth from the point of view of significant positive thinking will retain a meaning reconcilable with common usage of the word, such as the correspondence of the thought *which* we think with the reality *about* which we think. As long as there exists the dualism between knowing mind and a reality to be known, it is at least extremely hard *not* to mean by Truth 'correspondence.' As Mr Joachim[1] puts it: 'Within such a sphere, "truth" inevitably implies two factors; and so long as the duality is maintained, some form of the correspondence notion is the only possible theory of truth.' And I have been consistently urging, of course, that the transcendence of the duality in 'Ideal Truth' is a condition to which the finite intellect is inherently incapable of even approximating.

The Correspondence theory of the nature of Truth has, of course, weighty objections to encounter beyond those which arise from the metaphysic of Absolute Idealism. In adopting it (in qualified form) as the outcome of the present argument, it is necessary to remind the reader of the limitations already acknowledged (in the Preface) to pertain to the epistemological part of this work. Thus the Correspondence theory presupposes that there is an 'ideal intermediary' in knowing.

[1] *The Nature of Truth*, p. 119.

But the postulation of an ideal intermediary could be ultimately justified only after detailed examination of a controversial literature so vast and so various that to begin to consider it in the scope possible here would be worse than useless. I propose, therefore, merely to offer a very few observations of a general nature on this issue before passing on to develop the significance, and defend the implications, of the view of Truth for which the way has been prepared in the preceding pages.

But first of all let me say this. At least a great deal of the dissatisfaction that is felt towards the Correspondence view is due to the obvious difficulties to which it leads in connection with the *criterion* of Truth. If that which we directly cognise is always an ideal intermediary, how, it is naturally asked, can we ever know when 'ideas' do correspond with reality? This is a problem which will engage us in a later section, and in its Supra-rationalist setting it will not, I venture to predict, prove wholly intractable. The present problem of the *meaning* of Truth should not be prejudiced by assuming its insolubility.

Apart from difficulties over the criterion, however, the main criticism centres upon the validity of postulating an ideal intermediary at all. Why not admit that reality can be apprehended 'face to face,' in which case truth will not imply 'correspondence,' but will just be the property belonging to cognitions which apprehend reality in and as itself?

Now there are a good many arguments which the Idealist could offer against the doctrine of 'direct apprehension' of reality. One obvious line to take would base itself upon the thesis maintained in part of our first chapter, to the effect that all our 'objects' involve differents connected in a way that is self-contradictory. If they do, they cannot be 'real,' whatever else they may be.[1] But it seems possible to take lower

---

[1] It is noteworthy how seldom the champions of 'face to face' apprehension of reality take serious account of this objection—perhaps ultimately the most damaging of all.

NOUMENAL AND PHENOMENAL TRUTH

ground than this and still conduct a fairly successful action. It may perhaps not be wholly wasted space to say a few words upon a more elementary argument which seems to me still to carry weight.

How do we first come by our notion of a realm of 'ideal contents' or 'ideal meanings'—instead of 'reality'—as the immediate object of the mind when it thinks? The fundamental condition is, I think, our becoming explicitly aware of self-contradiction in our experience. Prior to that we have no suspicion of apprehending anything *other* than reality, although it seems true also that we are not then consciously apprehending the real as 'real.' But when we become conscious of erroneous apprehension, we become conscious *ipso facto* that here at least our immediate object of apprehension is not reality. But we do apprehend *something*—a content of definite character. What is the status of the content, since it certainly has not the status of the real? It assuredly has some sort of being. But since its claim to any being, now that its 'objective' reality is denied, seems to rest upon its existence as the content of our thinking, it seems natural, if not inevitable, to go on to say that it has 'ideal' being. It is an 'ideal content' or 'ideal meaning.' The immediate object of erroneous apprehension at any rate, therefore, seems to exist in an ideal medium.[1]

But having got so far, it is very difficult to draw a line here [2] and leave the immediate objects of our other apprehensions where they were. Once the conception of an occasional ideal intermediary is attained, the felt identity of character in the relation of all contents of apprehension to the apprehending mind presses for the recognition of ideal status in *all* content. This universal extension is not, indeed, formally inevitable.

[1] The hypothesis of a realm of 'subsistence,' advanced with a view to securing a 'non-mental' home for the immediate object of erroneous apprehension (and for certain other inconvenient phenomena), seems to raise at least as many difficulties as it removes.

[2] The difficulty of according a 'realist' status to the immediate object of memory-judgment (even where supposedly veridical) may also be expected to suggest itself at an early stage.

It is conceivable that the mind may pass abruptly from the apprehension of ideal meaning to the apprehension of the real itself, without any kind of recognisable alteration in the subjective characteristics of the experience. But in view of the indubitable felt continuity, the onus of proof at least seems to rest upon those who would insist upon the different status of different contents.

Before passing from these matters, there is a point which it is perhaps advisable to refer to. The term 'idea' is, as everyone knows, highly ambiguous, and it would be possible to interpret the Correspondence view of the meaning of Truth, when stated shortly as the correspondence of 'ideas' with reality, in a way which makes it clearly nonsensical. Apart from colloquial usages, the term 'idea' may stand for two very different meanings. It may signify a particular psychical existent or mental state, an event in the life-story of an individual mind. Or it may signify the meaning that is apprehended through the mental state—the so-called 'ideal content.' It is in the latter signification, of course, that the term is used in the above statement of the Correspondence view. When I say that the claim to truth in the knowledge-situation is the claim that an 'idea' corresponds with reality, I certainly do not mean that it is claimed that a particular mental state corresponds with reality, but that it is claimed that the meaning apprehended in that mental state so corresponds.

These cursory remarks must, I fear, suffice. I am going to take it that Truth, at the level at which it has positive significance for finite intellects—Phenomenal Truth, as we have called it, in distinction from Noumenal or Ideal Truth—means the correspondence of ideas with reality. But what exactly does 'the correspondence of ideas with reality' mean? To answer that is to answer the question of the criterion of (Phenomenal) Truth, and to this problem we may now turn our attention.

Section 3. The Criterion of Phenomenal Truth
(a) *Correspondence*

Our problem is, by what test are we to appraise the adequacy or inadequacy of our ideas to represent the reality which, at the phenomenological level, is taken as confronting us? Is it possible, for example, to hold that Correspondence is the 'test' as well as the 'meaning' of Truth? that to know whether we have got Truth we have to compare what is affirmed in the judgment with a 'reality' somehow independently given? The objections to such a view are very numerous and very obvious, and it is really abundantly clear that Correspondence cannot be the 'test.' But since it would be overbold to suppose that this theory is, even yet, without disciples, and since, further, one does often in practice seem to oneself to be applying the 'Correspondence test,' it will be well to open with some observations upon it. To do so will at least serve to prepare the ground for a more satisfactory theory.

Let us take, then, the kind of instance in which we are accustomed to imagine ourselves to be testing a truth by its 'correspondence' with 'fact,' and let us see what it is exactly that we are doing. Suppose that Smith says to us 'This is a stone pillar,' and that we, regarding the pillar closely and possibly feeling its texture with the hand, think or say, 'Yes, that is true, for the "facts" bear it out. Smith's judgment corresponds with the fact.' Now do we really here compare Smith's judgment with what is just 'fact'?

For the sake of precision we must allude first of all to an elementary point which has to be borne in mind, on whatever view one holds of the test of truth, with reference to the appraisement of the judgments of other persons. Smith's judgment is not, strictly speaking, one of the terms in our comparison. We do not compare Smith's judgment, for the simple reason that we cannot know it. The verbal expression of Smith's judgment in the proposition is what we know, and this is only an indication, capable of all degrees of inexactitude, of the real inner nature of what is being affirmed. What we do compare with the so-called 'fact' is the meaning which the verbal expression of Smith's judgment provokes us to affirm, a meaning which we assume to be identical in all relevant particulars with Smith's meaning. It is quite clear that this assumption is, at least sometimes, profoundly mistaken. The sage may signify assent to the fool's declaration that 'all is vanity,' because the meaning these words stimulate him to affirm is in accord (as he thinks) with 'fact.' But if the sage were cognisant of the actual thought in the fool's mind he would in all probability tell the fool that he was talking nonsense. The assumption, then, that the judgment of another can be one term in our comparison is never strictly true, and is often false in a way which promotes serious fallacies.

This consideration, however, is relatively unimportant. It is the other term of the comparison that is our chief concern. What is the status of this 'fact' with which we suppose the judgment to correspond? And let us henceforth assume, to avoid the difficulties indicated in the last paragraph, that it is our own judgment, not another person's, that we are trying to appraise. The presupposition of the theory is that the 'fact' is a fragment of reality itself, a transcript of the objective world unmodified by any subjective influences. But analysis of the 'fact' very soon discloses to us that such 'facts' are nothing but creatures of theory. A fact exists *for us* only in the medium of judgment, and judgment is not a transparent window but a subjective function of an exceedingly complex nature. Activities of distinguishing and relating in terms of certain categorial characters are involved in the apprehension of even the meanest 'fact.' And the arguments which have from ancient times been led to establish this are not overthrown by being ignored. If you choose to neglect this subjective aspect of our 'facts,' what you are left with is not a 'given reality' but a particularly vicious abstraction. It is

NOUMENAL AND PHENOMENAL TRUTH

inexcusable to assume that that which results only in connection with a complex process is itself indifferent to the fact of the process.[1]

Of course, to 'recognise' this subjective aspect must not be taken to mean that we can straightway pronounce the fact as apprehended to be in disagreement with the fact as it is in the real order—the 'epistemological object' (to use Dr Broad's terminology) in disagreement with the 'ontological object.' That is a matter which can only be settled by further investigation. But what it does mean is that in our so-called 'Correspondence test' we are not comparing a judgment with some directly given reality, but simply with another judgment: with another judgment, which, for reasons not yet specified, we take to correspond with the objective reality and to be therefore 'true.'

As these last words indicate, what the Correspondence theory does is merely to throw the problem of the test of Truth back a stage. The 'fact' with which the judgment is to correspond turns out to be itself a judgment, and 'Correspondence' tells us nothing as to how we are to know when the latter judgment represents reality—when it is, in short, 'true.' It is evident, then, that in order to apply the Correspondence test with any effect we must already be in possession of some independent criterion of the 'true' judgment.

The fundamental vice of the Correspondence test is thus that its application really presupposes some other criterion. We may easily see that this is so even in regard to that class of instances which may fairly be said to represent the stronghold of the Correspondence theory—propositions in which something is predicted which is, apparently, borne out by the subsequent 'facts.' Brown says to us 'There will be a thunderstorm to-night.' If (to use the ordinary way of speech) 'a thunderstorm does in fact occur,' we naturally tend to say that Brown's judgment is proved true by the event. It accords

[1] Cp. Bradley, *Appearance and Reality*, pp. 27-8.

with 'fact.' But what, again, is the 'event' or 'fact'? In so far as I can use it as a term in my comparison, it is just a judgment of whose veridical character I entertain no misgivings. What happens is that I compare Brown's judgment (in the measure in which I apprehend it) with the judgment which I find myself making with considerable conviction (and suppose other persons similarly situated to find themselves making with like conviction) 'to-night' with respect to the climatic conditions. And the truth of this latter judgment, the genuineness of *its* correspondence with reality, is clearly something that demands its own independent justification.

'But,' common sense may retort, 'surely such objections are purely academic? We shall admit, if you like, that the "fact" of the thunderstorm is a fact for us only through judgment. But this judgment (and many another of kindred nature) is one which we find forced upon us by reality itself, not a "construct" of our own. It is a judgment which, as you know very well, everyone, yourself included, would make in the given conditions, and there would be universal agreement that anyone who refused his assent to it was out of his mind—or at any rate out of his "senses." There is surely nothing outrageous, therefore, in speaking of the thunderstorm as an "objective fact."'

This response would mean, of course, the frank abandonment of Correspondence as an ultimate test: and it has the merit of permitting us to see the type of test which often underlies the ostensible adherence to Correspondence. The correspondence alleged is now granted to be one of judgment with judgment, and in assuming that the correspondence gives truth, it is assumed that the second judgment is true for reasons other than correspondence. What are these reasons? In point of fact, two distinct criteria are suggested by the statement made. And neither of them will bear a moment's scrutiny.

The sense of passivity, which is first suggested, is almost valueless. It is easy to show that there has gone to the making of a judgment such as 'this is a thunderstorm' not even a little, but a very great deal of, 'construction,' even although the judging mind may appear to itself now to be purely receptive. And at any rate, it would be an exceedingly odd reading of experience which could find evidence for the view that the judgments in which we are relatively passive are in general the judgments in which we are most likely to be stating the truth about reality.

As to the second criterion suggested—that a judgment is true in so far as all normal people (whatever 'normal' means) would make substantially the same judgment under substantially the same conditions—is Truth then to be ascertained by a mere counting of heads? If Truth is as difficult of attainment as has usually been supposed to be the case, then it may very well be that, at the present elementary level of our information about the physical world, we are one and all hopelessly wrong in what we mean to ascribe to Reality when we affirm, *e.g.* that a thunderstorm is taking place. What is actually going on in Reality when we make the judgment is in all probability something of quite undreamt-of complexity, something which, could we envisage it, we should declare to be not in the least like the meaning which we intended to assert in the judgment. And in this connection we may note a point which will have to receive fuller treatment later. What even the scientist (let alone Omniscience) means when he says that a thunderstorm is taking place has probably, in spite of the identity of verbal expression, far greater divergence from, than resemblance to, the meaning of the plain man: which further illustrates the hopelessness of appealing to the unanimous consent of mankind to support the veridical character of the common-sense judgment of 'fact.'

It is not disputed, of course, that in our everyday practice we are as a rule content to take the consensus of opinion of normal persons as sufficient warrant for the truth of perceived 'facts.' This is no doubt the case, but it merely illustrates the disparity of logic and life. About the only way in which there seems even a remote possibility of evading the difficulties that have been raised would be to take new ground and boldly contend that the deliverances of normal perception are not so much a *test* of fact as what is actually *meant* by fact. When we say 'there will be a thunderstorm to-night,' what we mean (on this view) is that to-night all normal persons in the vicinity who observe the weather conditions will pronounce that a thunderstorm is taking place. Such a view would escape the difficulty of having to show what ground there is for supposing normal perception to be in accord with reality, although not the difficulties connected with the actual variations within so-called 'normal perception.' But it has more than enough difficulties of its own, without our borrowing from those common to it with other theories. Above all, it clearly implies a new interpretation of the *meaning* of Truth. Truth on this view does not mean correspondence with the real order of things. It means merely correspondence with certain propositions about that order. But it is vain thus to try to eject from the conception of Truth its fundamental reference to the 'real' order of things. The defect in this view is really of a piece with that which the Idealist theory of Truth exhibits, viz. conflict with what, in the persisting subject-object duality of experience, it seems inevitable for us to mean by Truth. It is surely a confusion to suppose that a person predicting a thunderstorm to-night means *merely* that to-night a certain judgment will be made upon the weather by all normal and suitably situated persons. He may *also* mean this, but what he means primarily is that physical reality will undergo a certain determinate modification. And it is only because he means this latter that it is possible for him also to mean the former.

Section 4. *The Criterion of Phenomenal Truth*
(b) *Rational Coherence*

It will not repay us, I think, to dwell further upon the Correspondence theory of the criterion of Truth. I pass on to explain what has seemed to me to be, on the whole, the most satisfactory view. This view includes elements both of the Intuitionalist and of the Coherence theory—with Coherence as the dominant element. Coherence, I shall argue, is not the *sole* test. There are certain well-defined cognitive situations in which an immediate certainty (I am speaking, be it remembered, at the Phenomenological level) would seem to be procurable. But, in the main, Coherence is the test; and since I do not suppose myself able to add much that is of value to the explanations and vindications of this test to be found at large in Idealist writings,[1] I shall say little more about it than is required to make clear the manner of its application to the present metaphysic.

What is to be maintained, then, is that the truth of a judgment is to be tested by its capacity for harmonising with all the other judgments which we make about reality. (The necessary reservations just alluded to will be dealt with later.) On the whole, the orthodox Idealist justification of this test does not suffer alteration or diminution of force on account of the different metaphysic that is adopted in this work. The difference lies rather in what it is that is supposed to be thus tested. It is not, for my view, 'Noumenal' Truth that is here being tested. The test of Noumenal Truth has already been considered in Chapter I. and found to lie beyond the grasp of intellectual process. The intellect can attach no positive significance, paradoxical as it may appear, to that which would alone satisfy its demands. Here we are to discuss rather the test which is proper to intellect in its positive

[1] Among such discussions, chaps. vii. and viii. of Bradley's *Essays in Truth and Reality* seem to the present writer especially worthy of attention.

processes. It is then only Phenomenal Truth of which I am claiming that Coherence is the test—or at any rate the main test. And if this admission should seem seriously to derogate from the importance of the inquiry, it is well to remember that Phenomenal Truth is just another name for that which Truth concretely means for human beings. Philosophy itself (if I am right) can aim no higher than this. The intellectually *satisfactory* is an impossible ideal. The intellectually *incorrigible* is the best to which thinking can aspire. In investigating the conditions of intellectual incorrigibility we are investigating the conditions of what may fairly be called final truth for human beings. And this can hardly be esteemed a trivial matter.

This being understood, then, we may proceed to show the manner in which the Coherence test connects with our doctrine. Phenomenal Truth means, we have taken it, the correspondence of our judgments with the objective reality about which we judge. Now if we are to possess any criterion for determining when we have achieved correspondence, it is obvious that we must know something already of the character of this objective reality—while, on the other hand, the something that we know must not be such as to render the process of thinking itself otiose. Do we know anything of this kind? Yes, one thing we do know 'beyond a peradventure.' We do know that the real is 'self-consistent.' We know this, because the presupposition of it is immanent in the nature of all thinking. We cannot question it, because even a significant question assumes it. We may fairly be said then to 'know' that objective reality is non-contradictory, or self-consistent.

Now to be non-contradictory, we saw, means to be a unity of differences in which the differences are in no sense external to the unity. And this character, we also saw, attaches only to a type of whole to which the intellect can legitimately assign no positive meaning. That, however, is beside the point from the Phenomenological point of view. For the intellect does *in fact* assign a positive meaning to a non-contradictory system, even if it is a meaning which is ultimately indefensible. Reality it rightly pronounces to be self-consistent, and, placing its own interpretation upon the nature of self-consistency, it proceeds, in order to bring about the correspondence of its ideal world with the real world, to endeavour to achieve a fully harmonious body of judgment. The fact that it seeks to secure harmony by uniting differences through a 'ground' which is perforce partially external to the differences—by a method, therefore, which is strictly self-stultifying—matters not at all from our present point of view. What matters is that it does adopt a characteristic method, that it does mean something to itself by 'non-contradiction' or 'self-consistency.' And its 'test of truth' is just what it means by self-consistency. A judgment to be true must unite differences consistently. If it does not, it does not represent ideally the real world, which we *know* to be self-consistent.

Our operative test of Truth, then, is coherent system; even if, in seeking after such system, we have to interpret it in a way which debars it from ever being truly systematic—a true unity in difference. We may ask now what is to be said of the possibility of completely satisfying the Coherence test, and of thereby assuring ourselves of the correspondence of our ideas with objective reality. The question, however, in a manner answers itself. Coherence is our test, but if coherence were an ideal capable of self-completion we should not have required to reject it as metaphysically unsound. And since I can thus never make my cognitive experience fully answer to my test, I can never be sure that any judgment does represent the aspect of the real order which it tries to represent. On the other hand, by the very character of the test it will be natural to claim greater certainty for our judgments the more fully they are developed along the path which is taken to lead to perfect system; and that means in practice, the more comprehensive and internally harmonious is the unity or system which furnishes the ground of the connection of differences. But complete certainty is plainly an idle dream. I may, for example, be comparatively sure that a certain chemically defined substance acts as a corrosive force upon certain metals. I may have pushed my researches into 'grounding' both deep and wide, and seen that if this judgment is false then a great part of my ideally constructed physical world falls to the ground. But both in depth and in width, both intensively and extensively, it is evident that an indefinite amount of potential data remains unascertained. There is no question then of having here, or anywhere, a fully self-contained system. The insight into an absolutely necessary connection which could come only from a system that is self-complete is forever denied us. We cannot say, therefore, with legitimate assurance that any connection, even if supported by a system which is relatively both expansive and internally harmonious, corresponds with what obtains in the real order. At no stage in finite experience can the Coherence test be applied in a way which excludes grounds for doubt.

There can be no absolute certainty, then, in terms of the Coherence test, although an intelligible meaning can be attached to the phrase 'degrees of certainty.' No intelligible meaning can, I think, be attached to the phrase 'degrees of Truth.' It is easy to understand how we can have 'degrees of Truth' if Coherence is not only the 'test' but the 'nature' of Truth. Degrees of coherence or system would then be, quite directly, 'degrees of Truth.' But if Coherence is only the test of Truth, and the nature of Truth is correspondence with Reality, the matter is otherwise. Truth becomes primarily a matter of 'yes' or 'no.' No doubt there is a sense in which we can speak of an ideal representation corresponding 'more' or 'less' closely with the reality. But even so, we could not possibly hold that 'degrees of coherence' show a constant proportion to 'degrees of correspondence.' On the contrary, the course of experience teaches us that often, with the advent of a single fresh item of relevant information, a judgment supported by a high degree of coherence has to be modified in a way which leads to a most radical revision of the mental 'picture' of the real event. The degree of correspondence attaching to the former judgment bore no kind of proportion, we have to say, to its high degree of coherence.

The constant probability, therefore, of having to revise one's mental picture of any reality must be accepted even at the Phenomenological level; with certain reservations, again, shortly to be discussed. 'Hard facts' are just mental pictures which the pressure of experience has not as yet obliged us to modify (though it may well be that it ought to have obliged us). It is sometimes maintained, indeed, that the development of science does not really tend to overturn the ordinary perceptive judgments of daily experience—'the sun is shining,' and so on— but merely places these judgments in a wider orbit of explanatory connection. The scientist, it is said, may make many *other* judgments when he attends to the phenomena in question, but he *also* makes the common-sense judgment 'the sun is shining.' Such propositions, it is supposed, have so far resisted modification, and there is no reason to expect that further scientific development will be any more disastrous in its effect. But this view, I think, rests on misunderstanding. What the astronomer is concretely meaning when he judges that the sun is shining is something which bears very little resemblance indeed to the meaning of the plain man. Without venturing upon a description of what the astronomer's mental picture is, it is safe to say that it is not the picture of a yellow ball shooting out light very much as a gun shoots out bullets. The plain man's picture is not as a rule a great deal more refined than this. And the astronomer would certainly say that it is a sheer distortion of the reality. When we attend, therefore, to the inner meaning of the judgment, to what is really being affirmed, it seems plain that even from the Phenomenological point of view we must agree that a constant process of modification of our ideal representation of reality is inevitable.

At the same time I am convinced that it is possible, and that it is one of the defects in the usual statement of the Coherence theory, to push too far this doctrine of the judgment's susceptibility to modification. Consider again the simple perceptive judgment 'the sun is shining.' When we make this judgment we are ordinarily aware of certain feelings—*e.g.* the feeling of warmth—and in so far as we affirm, *i.e.* make the judgment, that we are 'enjoying' such feelings, what we affirm does not seem to be open to modification after the manner of the content of the 'objective' judgment. And, in certain conditions, our apprehension of 'yellowness' and 'brightness' in this situation will fall under the same category. For in so far as we affirm only that we have or enjoy a certain sensum, and do not assign to it an objective interpretation, our affirmation seems to rest on unchallengeable ground. Of course we do, as a rule, affirm much more. We do, as a rule, affirm that yellowness and brightness belong to the spherical object overhead, not just that we 'enjoy' certain sensa. And at this point —where the judgment refers to 'objective' reality not to subjective feelings—criticism of the judgment's validity may begin at once. But it seems to me of the first importance to see that, with respect to subjective feelings, the person feeling is the ultimate authority as to what is felt. A feeling which he is definitely conscious of enjoying is a feeling which no amount of science or philosophy will ever be able to persuade him that he did not enjoy. This does not imply that every man is an infallible introspective psychologist. Without doubt practice, and knowing what to look for, are indispensable for the accurate observation of our subjective sensations. But the point is that the task of the psychologist in this connection is no more than to use every artifice to induce the integrity of a pure remembrance, unclouded by presuppositions. The ultimate authority is the experiencing subject himself. His testimony, once the way is cleared for its untrammelled deliverance, must be acknowledged to be final. If he insists that he experienced a sensation of yellow, then it is entirely *ultra vires* for the psychologist (as indeed he well knows) to tell him that he believes this only because of his ignorance of psychology.[1] In short, we do have here, in these judgments which report our own subjective sensations, assertions not legitimately modifiable by the progress of science, assertions which may therefore reasonably claim to be 'intellectually incorrigible.'

Section 5. The Criterion of Phenomenal Truth
(c) *Immediate Apprehension*

We must, however, go into this matter much more deeply. For, as the reader will have gathered, we have come now upon the reservations which must be made to the doctrine that, at the Phenomenological level, rational coherence is the test of Truth. We seem, in the above discussion, to have struck contact with a class of judgments whose 'Phenomenal' Truth, *i.e.* whose intellectual incorrigibility, is directly apprehended. Here the attempt to support the connection affirmed by grounding it within a system would be quite irrelevant, for the connection carries its warrant with it. We have now got before us, in fact, a very similar type of case to that which occupied our attention in the concluding Section of Chapter I, and whose status in the realm of Truth we were not then adequately equipped to determine. The subject of experience, we saw there, not only apprehends objects and events, but is aware of himself as apprehending. It seems probable that this self-awareness is, in its degree, a constant factor in experience. But whether this be so or not, it is certain that the subject *can* be aware of himself as judging or believing something (or again of feelings and sensations). We have to ask what exactly

---

[1] The phenomena of 'colour-blindness' are irrelevant. The person who sees 'green' when normal people see 'red' *does* see green. His subjective experience is, so far, what he says it is.

is the difference of principle in these 'reflex' judgments (if we may use this term for the judgments guaranteed by self-awareness) which renders them, apparently, exempt from the Coherence test of Truth. Can valid grounds be produced for assigning to them an infallibility which is denied to the ordinary run of judgments?

Let us note carefully the special peculiarity of these judgments. Their characteristic is that they do not involve anything that can fairly be called 'interpretative' activity. The activity of attention is required to bring them into due relief, but the business of this activity is simply to make explicit what is assumed to be there already implicitly, without transformation or addition. Anything more than this defeats the very purpose of attention. Undoubtedly interpretative activity is involved in the *objective* judgment—'the sun is a yellow ball, etc.'—but the rightness or wrongness of the interpretation there is absolutely irrelevant to the validity of my judgment that I entertain a belief that the sun is a yellow ball. So far as the 'reflex judgment' is concerned, there is no evidence of 'interpretation,' and it is because there is no interpretation present that we find that the fuller development of the cognitive life brings with it not the faintest obligation to modify the assertion made in the reflex judgment. Fuller experience may force me to modify my view of the nature of the sun. I may cease to believe that it is a yellow ball, just as I have ceased to believe that it travels round the earth. But this will not cast one atom of doubt on the fact that I *once did believe* the sun to be a yellow ball, and to travel round the earth. Judgments of particular objective fact are one and all modifiable, because they are one and all interpretations of the relations of differences within a system, and because this system, which determines the relations of the differences, is subject to an indefinite amount of growth and revision with advancing experience. But in the reflex judgment there is no 'system' impregnating, and furnishing ground for the connection of, the differences. We make the judgment, connect the differences, not through a ground that itself demands a further ground, but *immediately*. There is indeed a 'ground,' if we like to use it so, in the fact of self-awareness itself. This is what warrants the connection we affirm. But—and here is the crucial point—self-awareness is a ground which the mind must realise that it is absolutely meaningless to impugn. For we can see clearly that as long as human experience remains human experience, there is no sort of means *but* self-awareness of ascertaining the nature of our own experiencing—nothing, therefore, which could ever bring its authority into question. The recognition of the veridical character of self-awareness seems to be an irremovable element of human experience, offering us a 'ground' which we may seek to transcend only by seeking to transcend the conditions of our own finitude.

Any theory of Truth which cannot admit the intellectual incorrigibility of these reflex judgments stands, I think, self-condemned. It will certainly not be able to produce any instance in which a judgment guaranteed by self-awareness suffers modification with advancing experience. To take an example which has often, and with justice, been cited against the Coherence doctrine [1]—the experience of pain. I may find out all kinds of things subsequently about the nature and conditions of pain, but absolutely nothing which will induce me to suppose that I did not in fact have precisely the feeling with which my self-awareness acquainted me.

The Coherence theory in its orthodox statement, however, refuses to exempt any class of judgment from its test of 'harmonious system.' And it is worth bearing in mind that the connection of that theory with Idealist metaphysics makes such a view inevitable. For, to Idealism, Reality is intelligible throughout. Everything, therefore, is capable of being

---

[1] As in Professor Stout's article, 'Bradley on Truth and Falsity,' in *Mind*, N.S., No. 133 (p. 52).

'understood,' even an apparent condition of finite experience like 'self-awareness.' The Idealist, accordingly, is forbidden by his doctrine to say 'I know I have a feeling of pain because my self-awareness acquaints me with it.' For to him 'self-awareness' cannot be an *ultimate* ground. He is obliged to push on his researches and ask how and why self-awareness guarantees the connection here affirmed. He is obliged to seek to understand the nature of finite self-awareness—ultimately, I suppose, 'in the light of the Whole.' It is an advantage of the theory of Truth which issues from Supra-rationalist metaphysics that it eliminates some very absurd inquiries.

Section 6. Phenomenal Truth, as the Intellectually Incorrigible, contrasted with Noumenal Truth, as the Intellectually Satisfactory

These reflex judgments are then, in our view, intellectually incorrigible, finally valid for human experience, and as such must be pronounced to possess unqualified 'Phenomenal' truth. But we have to see now that it is definitely only at the Phenomenological level that their truth can be asserted. They do not possess 'Noumenal' or 'Ultimate' truth. They are intellectually *incorrigible*, but not intellectually *satisfactory*. If we had to allow to them the latter character, then of course the epistemological argument for the supra-rational character of the real would collapse. We should be admitting that we were mistaken in holding that the intellect is incapable of reaching satisfaction in any union of differents. Here would be a plain instance to the contrary, the acceptance of the authority of self-awareness as a completely satisfactory bond of union.

But the all-important distinction must be observed between a bond of union which satisfies because it is intrinsically satisfactory, and one which satisfies only because we see that under the conditions of finite life we cannot hope to transcend it. This is the key to the right appreciation of the status of the 'truths' guaranteed by self-awareness. These are intellectually satisfactory *only* in the latter sense. When we regard them, we see that to question them is absurd from the point of view of finite experience, since even the questioning mind itself cannot free itself from the recognition of the authority of self-awareness. It is right and proper, therefore, for finite mind to accept as final these pronouncements which it has no power ever to transcend. But to accept a connection because it is seen to be untranscendible by finite mind is one thing. It is quite another thing to accept a connection because it is seen to be intrinsically satisfying, genuinely self-explanatory. The latter is the kind of connection that the intellect demands for the ultimately real—a unity in difference, in which the differences are intrinsic to the unity and the unity is itself wholly bound up with the differences. Only then does there cease to be any *possible* question—as distinct from any *answerable* question—as to how or why. But, most emphatically, we do not have this intrinsic satisfactoriness in the case before us. We do not understand the meaning and status of self-awareness in the scheme of things, nor, therefore, how it is connected with the connection which it professes to warrant. We have to accept self-awareness as an intellectual surd, an irreducible 'fact' for us, no doubt, but, just because irreducible, a sheer mystery. And how can we say that complete intellectual satisfaction is achieved in a complex which has its roots in sheer mystery? I am not saying, it must be remembered, that there is here the sort of intellectual dissatisfaction which stimulates further inquiry. Rather the reverse. The Idealist has already been criticised for supposing that any fruitful inquiry can be made by finite mind into the questions that remain. But I am insisting that however keenly we may be aware that a connection guaranteed by self-awareness is not transcendible by finite mind, there does still remain a question which we realise we should have to answer if we were to *understand* the connection, make it fully intelligible—'how is finite self-awareness related to the universe at large, the scheme of things as a whole?' If we admit that the intellect will accept as real only what is self-consistent, then we must allow that until such a question is answered we do not 'know' reality.

What we get then in these reflex judgments is the intellectually incorrigible, not (strictly) the intellectually satisfactory; final Phenomenal Truth, not final Noumenal Truth. We get Truth in so far as Truth possesses positive significance for finite beings, although not the Truth which would reveal the ultimate nature of Reality. This Phenomenal Truth is, on my view, as already observed, the highest at which philosophy can aim. But it is by no means confined, as we shall see, to such relatively trivial aspects of experience as we have so far dealt with. I shall try to show in later chapters that a similar 'intellectual incorrigibility' attaches to the belief in personal freedom, and again to the belief in moral values. These too, I shall argue, are judgments which are bound up with the very nature of finite experience, judgments which are certainly not self-explanatory, but which are nevertheless incapable of significant question under the conditions which govern human nature.

Section 7. Status of 'Geometrical Truths' in Idealism and Supra-rationalism Respectively

It would be ridiculous in a work of this sort, which cannot claim to do more than break the ground for further research, to attempt to set forth anything like an inventory of 'final phenomenal truths': or, again, to attempt to deal in detail with more than a very small number of them. Most of the 'truths' which seem to me to have a reasonable chance of being thus established could not be treated in a manner calculated to carry any conviction without embarking upon a lengthy specialised inquiry into the respective fields of experience to which they refer. I propose to conclude this chapter, nevertheless, by saying something about the reaction of the general doctrine I am maintaining upon one group of propositions which are of peculiar interest for the theory of Truth —the group, namely, pertaining to the science of geometry. The apparent certainty of geometrical 'truths' has always been a sore stumbling-block for the Coherence theory of the test of Truth. To insist that propositions of the nature 'the three angles of a triangle are equal to two right angles' express only 'partial truth,' has been a paradox which it has proved hard for the Idealist to sustain. On the presupposition as to the nature of the mind's apprehension of space which the Idealist customarily adopts, I believe that it is impossible to sustain it. On the other hand, the Idealist doctrine does, I think, emphasise one side of the truth with just as much propriety as the critics of it emphasise the other. The correct solution is not visible until we make the distinction which has been the main theme of the present chapter, the distinction between Phenomenal Truth and Ideal or Noumenal Truth. In the following pages I shall try to show that, if we accept the Idealist presuppositions above referred to, our proper course is to deny, with Idealism, that geometry can attain Noumenal Truth, but to admit with the critics of Idealism that it can attain intellectual incorrigibility. Final Phenomenal Truth is open to geometry.

The presuppositions in question are that the apprehension of space is the logical (though certainly not the psychological) *prius* of our apprehension of objects, and that the space so apprehended is Euclidean space, a homogeneous, tridimensional continuum. I do not propose to offer a defence of these assumptions, highly disputable though they be. Those who are unable to accept them may be requested to neglect this brief discussion, or else to regard it merely in the light of an illustration of the principle upon which Phenomenal is distinguished from Noumenal Truth.

Let us suppose, then, that these presuppositions are conceded. What I wish to maintain is that such a judgment as 'two straight lines cannot enclose a space' enjoys final Phenomenal Truth: and that in general, with respect to the science to which this judgment belongs, final Phenomenal Truth is everywhere possible.

It is easiest to demonstrate this if (as in the analogous argument above) we contrast the judgment here in question with the ordinary judgment of particular objective fact, whose capacity for attaining final truth is denied. What is the relevant difference? In both cases we have the connection of differences through a 'ground.' The apprehended nature of space is the ground of the judgment 'two straight lines cannot enclose a space,' just as much as the apprehended nature of material objects is the ground of judgments in physical science. But—and here is the point—in the spatial judgment the ground is present in its final form from the beginning. What we are 'given,' as simple brute fact which we cannot question (this is the obvious consequence of its *a priori* character), is space as a homogeneous, tridimensional continuum, and a judgment such as that which we are considering simply reads off such implications of the construction we make as are determined by the known character of this 'given.' It is the ground (here the apprehended nature of space) which prescribes the specific connections which we affirm in all judgments. But in this instance, since the ground is not liable to revision, or even question, by the intellect, the connection it prescribes is (if we have read the implication aright) not liable to question either. In judgments in physical science the grounds obviously possess a quite different status. They are, and must ever remain, hypotheses, not datal facts. They are susceptible of indefinite modification from the increase of our experience of the physical world, both intensive and extensive. And with these alterations in the apprehended grounds there must alter concurrently the meaning of the connections which they warrant. But the child who sees —not *says* but *sees*—that 'two straight lines cannot enclose a space' has precisely the same logical warrant for his assertion as has the most accomplished mathematician. And that warrant is infallible, not a questionable hypothesis, but a self-complete datum. Here, accordingly, there is no infinite process imposed upon the mind before it may justly claim finality. We have the ground in what must remain for us its final form from the beginning. Neither advancing spatial knowledge nor developing objective knowledge can—if space, as defined, is indeed the logical *prius* of our apprehension of objects—impose upon it the slightest modification. We can make our assertion, therefore, knowing that no accretion of experience attainable by the human mind will have any power to overturn it.

It is the failure to distinguish the intellectual incorrigibility of the ground in geometrical reasoning from the admittedly developing character of the grounds in our reasonings upon physical things which vitiates the treatment of geometrical truth by most Idealist writers. These writers are accustomed to treat a proposition like 'two straight lines cannot enclose a space' as though it fluctuated in logical stability according to the more or less developed nature of the ground. The proposition is supposed to be in this respect precisely the same in principle as such a proposition as 'water freezes at 32° Fahrenheit.' The meaning of the latter proposition, it is argued (as I think, justly), is conditioned and even constituted by the 'appercipient background' of the judging mind, and this background is of a very much higher calibre in the case of the scientist than in the case of the plain man. What the scientist asserts and what the plain man asserts in the verbally identical propositions are very different things, and the scientist's more systematic assertion must be adjudged, by the Coherence test of Truth, the more true. Now this is probably very right and proper where the 'backgrounds' are physical hypotheses. It is mere perversion of the facts where the background is the *given* nature of space. The proposition 'two straight lines cannot enclose a space' does without doubt depend vitally upon the nature of the system which prescribes the connection. But the point is that this system *in so far as relevant* is precisely the same for the tyro as for the most accomplished geometrician. The development in our knowledge of spatial inter-relations does not add one iota of cogency to the ground of this proposition. It would be interesting to know if the Idealist can produce any geometrician who has felt it to be otherwise.

The fundamental point is, in a word, that in geometrical judgments we have all the relevant data before us from the start; in so far at least as such data are procurable under the conditions of finite mind. The qualification denoted in the last clause, however, is essential. We know how we have to *think* space. And we know how, thinking space thus, we have to think the mutual connection of constructions made within it. But we do not *understand* space. We have not the least conception of its place in the economy of the Whole, and there are even excellent reasons for believing that in the manner that we think it, and must think it, it cannot ultimately be. Our 'ground,' therefore, is once more (as in the case of 'self-awareness') a sheer mystery, even though it be intellectually incorrigible. And if this is so, it becomes nonsense to suppose that in spatial judgments we are asserting ultimate truth. A connection of differences cannot be self-consistent, intrinsically satisfying, where the ground is related to the rest of our experienced world in a way that is not intelligible to us, as is the case with space. The Idealist is right, therefore, in denying Truth in the fullest sense to these judgments. But since they may reasonably be pronounced 'intellectually incorrigible,' it only promotes misunderstanding to treat them as though they possessed no higher status than patently modifiable judgments in other spheres. They should be recognised as 'ultimate' for finite mind: or, to use the terminology of this chapter, 'final phenomenal truths.'

CHAPTER IV

MORAL FREEDOM (I)

Section 1. *Introductory*

As has often enough been remarked, there is a curious paradox attending the problem of freedom, which lends to all argument about it a certain air of unreality. For whatever be the outcome of theory, it seems just not possible to engage in practice without believing that one is free; and free even in the so-called 'popular' or 'vulgar' sense of being the arbiter between genuinely open possibilities. The Determinist philosopher may in his philosophising convince himself that a freedom of 'open possibilities' is sheer illusion, hopelessly untenable in theory, and even (perhaps) seriously mischievous in practice. He may sincerely believe that there is not one major proposition in the whole field of philosophy upon which confidence is more amply justified than that which affirms the irrefragable causal continuity of all things within the universe. And yet—paradox of paradoxes!—in the very next deliberate act of will that he performs he gives the lie to his own considered doctrine by tacitly, but insistently, claiming personal exemption from the universal order. For no amount of sophistication, it would seem, can rid a man of what Sidgwick has called 'the immediate affirmation of consciousness in the moment of deliberate action.'[1] Illusory this affirmation of freedom may be, but it bears all the marks of being an 'illusion' which philosophy itself is powerless to eradicate, an 'illusion' inexpugnable from the experience of a self-conscious conative being.

[1] *Methods of Ethics* (6th ed.), p. 65.

That this deliverance of the practical consciousness is not illusory but veridical will be the thesis of this and the following chapter. And although I cannot yet define with precision the nature and scope of the freedom which I wish to defend, this much may be said at once. It is in all essential respects the freedom believed in by the plain man.[1] I am prepared to maintain the literal truth of such asseverations as that of the plain man who, having (as we say) given way to temptation, obstinately refuses the asylum of convenient psychologies and philosophies and insists that he is rightly to be blamed, for 'he could have acted otherwise.' Nor do I mean merely that he 'could have acted otherwise,' if his 'character' had been different; but, quite simply, that character and circumstances being what they were, the agent could nevertheless have willed the believed higher course. Naturally, it will be no part of my purpose to deny that formed character has a potent bearing upon the direction of the will in conduct. No sane philosophy can thus turn its back upon obvious facts. I shall attempt later to indicate what exactly I take this influence to be. But, I shall urge, it is of fundamental importance to recognise that man is ever more than his formed character at any moment. Formed character is an abstraction from personality—the latter involving, as indeed its most distinctive feature, the constant potency of creative activity. A being who could not express himself save in the response of his formed character to the given situation would not be a 'person,' but just a spiritual corpse.

[1] One naturally feels a good deal of diffidence in setting out to recommend a doctrine of free will of a type adherence to which appears to be almost universally regarded as a sure mark of philosophic immaturity. The Idealist tradition in philosophy, no less than the Materialist, has been active in pouring contempt and ridicule upon a freedom of 'open possibilities.' For Spinoza, the vulgar conception of freedom 'provokes either laughter or disgust' (*Ethics*, ii. 35, Schol.). And Bradley has roundly declared that 'no philosopher who respects himself can be called on any longer to treat it seriously' (*Appearance and Reality*, p. 435, note). I can here only register, leaving to the text to justify, my firm conviction that it is entirely possible to appreciate the reasons underlying the prevailing disparagement, and at the same time to reject these reasons as utterly inadequate.

There is no experience, perhaps, in which man's sense of spiritual livingness is so keen as where he is engaged in combating this 'formed character,' which from an abstractly psychological point of view is sometimes mistaken for his intrinsic self. It is precisely because man is, and knows himself to be, something more than the complex of habits, tendencies, sentiments, etc., which he might enumerate in giving a so-called 'psychological' account of himself, that he finds himself able at once to deny that his choice is adequately explained as issuing from his formed character, and at the same time to insist that it does, nevertheless, issue from his *self*.

Shortly I shall proceed to the elaboration of this view, and to its defence against the manifold objections which any such view almost automatically evokes in the mind of the philosopher. In the Section which now follows, however, I propose to make some comments upon the Idealist doctrine of freedom. And that for two reasons. Firstly, because the adoption in the present work of the general standpoint and starting-point of the Idealist philosophy makes it desirable to show how this important Idealist doctrine is affected when we substitute, as we are now obliged to do, the Supra-rational for the Rational Absolute; and secondly, because it is extremely important to see clearly at once that the type of freedom which Idealism undertakes to defend has nothing whatever to do with that freedom which constitutes the traditional problem of philosophy —in which connection I hope to show that the freedom which is the perennial subject of human interest is precisely that which I am endeavouring to vindicate in this and the succeeding chapter.

Section 2. *Criticism of the Idealist Doctrine of Freedom*

The negative side of the Idealist doctrine need not detain us. It consists in the denial that human conduct is subject to 'natural' causation. Its classical statement in T. H. Green's *Prolegomena to Ethics* is doubtless familiar to all. The nerve of the argument is, it will be remembered, that 'motives,' the determinants of human conduct, cannot rightly be interpreted as 'natural events' (as mere physical wants, *e.g.* may be) in that they imply for their possibility the constitutive activity of the 'non-natural' principle of 'self-consciousness.'

It seems evident, however, that even if so much were granted, a good deal more is necessary before human freedom is established as a significant reality. In fact it is, I think, fair to say that Idealism's real problem of freedom only now begins. For the Idealist has got to explain to us how we are to conceive the relation of the constitutive activity of finite subjects to the constitutive activity of the one Absolute Mind or Spirit. The finite spirit may not be determined as 'natural' objects are determined. But it is extremely hard to see how, consistently with Rational Monism, it can be conceived as other than a channel through which the Absolute Spirit pours its being. The Idealist can certainly have no commerce with such views of freedom as that adumbrated in the above section, views which postulate a break in the rational continuity of things. These are ruled out *ab initio*, as 'sins against the Holy Ghost of Logic' (to borrow Professor Sorley's apt phrase). How then is the freedom of finite persons to be saved? This brings us to Idealism's positive doctrine.

So far as I understand it, the orthodox Idealist answer is in essentials that of Spinoza. It may be briefly outlined as follows. Everything that is issues by rational necessity from the nature of the Whole, Supreme Mind. But man, *qua* mind, is in a position of peculiar privilege. For, *qua* mind, he *is* the Whole in principle. The Supreme Mind is the full consummation of the mind which is present, in germinal form, in every rational being. Accordingly the progressive development of mind or rational personality, as it grows in complexity of systematic organisation towards its ideal of fully concrete unity, must be regarded as a process in which man articulates, in advancing degrees of adequacy, the nature of the Whole

MORAL FREEDOM

itself. Hence follow the most important consequences. Our actions all flow from the nature of the Whole, without doubt. But in the degree in which our personalities are rationally organised, and therefore express the nature of the Whole, they must be held to flow from *our* nature also. And so far we shall be *self*-determined or 'free.' Or (to follow more closely the language of Spinoza) so far as our action can be understood by reference to our own nature alone, thus far we are its 'adequate cause,' or genuinely 'active.' In a word, while no man is wholly free, every man is free in 'degree,' according to the measure in which he articulates in his own personality the systematic unity of the Whole.

Now this doctrine—whether or not we call it a doctrine of 'freedom'—does, I think, follow logically enough from the Idealist presupposition of the ultimate identity of Mind and Reality. It possesses a similar status to the doctrine of 'Degrees of Truth and Reality,' of which, indeed, it is little more than an application. But it will be evident at once to the reader that if the Bradleian supra-rational Absolute be accepted in place of the Idealist rational Absolute, the doctrine loses all significance. From the Supra-rationalist standpoint there can be no principle available for determining the degree in which finite mind manifests the character of ultimate reality. A doctrine which presumes to tell us what freedom is, and how far it extends, 'in the light of the Whole,' is on Supra-rationalist principles the merest verbiage.

It follows, however, that the doctrine of freedom which the present work will seek to maintain must itself be less than ultimate. Actually, no more will be claimed for it than that it expresses 'final Phenomenal Truth.' But on this two remarks fall to be made.

Phenomenal Truth is, when viewed in contrast with Noumenal Truth, 'illusion.' But it is not *mere* illusion. It is necessary to distinguish between 'illusions' which are removable by the advance of experience, and 'illusions' which are not thus removable, because rooted in the nature of experience itself: or, otherwise expressed, between 'intellectually corrigible' and 'intellectually incorrigible' illusions. Only the former class does it seem fitting to regard as illusions in a seriously dyslogistic sense, 'mere' illusions. And it is to the latter class, I shall argue, that the 'freedom' here to be defended belongs. I shall try to show that it is something the assertion of which is ineradicably bound up with the nature of human experience. And if the objection is still made that, even granting these premises, yet a doctrine of freedom which makes of it a 'necessary illusion' cannot be held of much account, since the knowledge we have *that* freedom is ultimately illusory is amply sufficient, even without the knowledge *how*, to deprive it of all moral import, the answer is, I think, obvious enough. The objection rests on the false assumption that to have knowledge that, for an ultimate vision, man is not 'free,' is equivalent to having knowledge that, for an ultimate vision, man is 'determined.' But the latter does not follow from the former in the very least. If we keep consistently to the conception of ultimate Reality as 'supra-rational,' it is evident that the same reasons which compel us to say that 'freedom' (as man must conceive it) is illusory, compel us also to say that 'determination' (as man must conceive it) is illusory. It is absolutely vital to keep in mind that the 'ultimate' point of view gives no *positive* information. 'Ultimately not-free' does *not* entitle us to say 'ultimately determined.'

My argument for Libertarianism as against Determinism will not then seek to show any more, in the last resort, than that freedom is a 'necessary' illusion. Even if the conviction of freedom be proved to be an ineradicable element in human experience, it must still be admitted to be in a sense 'illusion' (since, to give only one reason, the concept of freedom with which we work carries an inherent reference to an objective world so characterised that its ultimate reality cannot be accepted). But on the other hand I shall try to show that Determinism is an illusion not merely 'in the last resort' or 'metaphysically,' but also from the standpoint of *human* experience. It is Determinism, not Libertarianism, that is the 'mere' illusion, the illusion corrigible by fuller thinking. That, at least, is the case which we shall endeavour to make good in the sequel.

And the second remark is this. It is not all loss that one should be debarred by one's metaphysical doctrine from attempting a 'metaphysical' justification of freedom. On the contrary it may be urged—and the argument seems to me unanswerable—that for those who believe that the Whole is intelligible, and that therefore an ultimate or metaphysical justification is obligatory, no justification of *freedom* is or can be possible: or, at any rate no justification of the kind of freedom which is a postulate of the moral life. The burden of the 'coherent Whole' lies like a dead-weight upon all endeavours after a metaphysical justification of freedom. When 'the shouting and the tumult die' the simple question is put, 'Could any man, on your theory, have acted otherwise than he in fact did'? And to this question only one answer is possible on the doctrine of an intelligible Whole, an answer which to the plain man means the straight denial of freedom. Only where the oppressive 'sense of the Whole' is absent can it be said that the problem of freedom has life and meaning. For a Rationalist metaphysic the solution—an adverse one—is strictly speaking pre-determined.

This brings us to a topic, however, upon which somewhat ampler discussion is necessary. I hold not only that the Idealist doctrine of freedom is false as a statement of fact (resting as it does upon a false metaphysic), but also that it is utterly irrelevant if offered as a contribution to the problem of *freedom*. The freedom which Idealism defends is not the freedom about which the plain man is concerned, and (if this should seem to the reader more important) is not the freedom which constitutes the traditional problem of philosophy. That problem arose in the interest of moral responsibility. It is the freedom necessary to vindicate moral responsibility that has been for so many centuries a main battle-ground of the philosophers and the theologians. And this freedom the Idealist doctrine not merely fails to defend, but, by the very character of the freedom for which it argues, must be held by implication to repudiate.

For what is the freedom that is required to validate moral responsibility? There is surely no great mystery about it, if only we are prepared to approach with open minds. Limiting our considerations, for simplicity's sake, to responsibility for wrong-doing, it is quite evident that the passing of moral censure upon a person, in implying the belief that the person *ought* to have acted otherwise than he in fact did, implies also the belief that the person *could* have acted otherwise than he in fact did. It is possible, indeed, that the 'judger' may have cause to believe that the person has so habituated himself to the form of conduct in question that he is now virtually incapable of acting otherwise. But if he does so believe, he yet only passes censure upon the person because he assumes that such a state of affairs has been brought about by *past* acts of will which 'could have been otherwise.'

This is not a matter, however, upon which elaborate argument is really in place. Other conditions there are, of course, implied in the conception of moral responsibility—conditions, e.g. such as Bradley has set forth in the first chapter of *Ethical Studies*. But that the condition just stated is also indispensable (although not included in Bradley's list) it is only possible to deny if one is also prepared to deny that the moral 'ought' has meaning without the assumption of a 'can.' Blame and praise are alike utterly pointless if we believe that the person could not have acted otherwise than he did. In other words, the conception of moral responsibility loses all significance unless it can be maintained that there is in rational beings a real capacity for alternative action.[1]

Now the freedom for which Idealism contends is certainly not a freedom which involves a capacity for alternative action. It is not even neutral with respect to it, for it is inextricably bound up with a metaphysic for which any such capacity is unthinkable. Ought it not then to be acknowledged frankly that Idealism's 'freedom,' instead of vindicating moral responsibility (as we not unnaturally expect of a philosophy which professes to champion 'freedom'), is definitely inconsistent with it? It would at least minister to clarity of discussion if Idealists would emulate the candour of Spinoza, and avow openly that on their view moral praise and blame should be replaced by mere congratulation and condolence.

[1] I am aware, of course, that a number of attempts have been made, in recent ethical literature especially, to justify the union of moral responsibility with Determinism. But I must frankly confess that the arguments advanced appear to me to be so obviously of the nature of special pleading that to traverse them in detail is mere waste of time and labour. One can understand, and in a measure sympathise with, the attitude of mind in which these attempts originate. As a rule they are due to the writer's natural reluctance to admit that moral responsibility is a mere fiction, working along with his firm conviction that a freedom of 'open possibilities' has long been proved to belong to the realm of mere mythology. But however keenly one may *desire* to dissever moral responsibility from a freedom of this suspect type, their indissoluble connectedness really seems to be one of the few perspicuously plain truths of human experience. To be morally responsible means, I suppose we can all agree, to be the legitimate object of moral praise and blame. But to impute praise or blame to a person if you know that that person could not possibly have done otherwise (whether in his present act or in those of his previous acts which condition the present act), is a proceeding which so flagrantly violates the fundamental nature of our moral consciousness that not even the authority of many of its champions should prevent us from calling it nonsensical. The common practice of moral judgment in mankind generally, wherever that judgment is critical and considered and not, as so often, thoughtless and all but mechanical, is flatly inconsistent with it. One could, of course, select examples from the hasty and semi-automatic 'moral judgments' passed in everyday experience which might seem to lend to it a certain plausibility. But from this field one could select examples which would support almost any doctrine. Reflective moral judgment, the judgment that is deliberately concerned to judge justly, is the only kind of judgment which really counts in this matter.

It is, of course, easy to understand the reluctance of Idealists to admit the incompatibility of their doctrine with moral responsibility. No philosopher wishes to find himself obliged to defy the postulates of so apparently fundamental an aspect of experience as the moral consciousness. Some Idealists, as for example Bosanquet, have sought very strenuously indeed to rebut explicitly the suspicion of a-moralism, but the result (as I venture to think others beside the present writer must have felt) is a little bewildering. In the very midst of metaphysical argument which seems to imply beyond question that the moral point of view is merely secondary and subordinate, we are suddenly confronted by passages whose one aim seems to be to allay the apprehensions of the jealous guardian of morals. When Bosanquet assures us, for example, that 'there is no meaning in applying to him [a moral agent] any "must" or "cannot help it" except in the sense that everything is what it is,'[1] he is obviously hoping to persuade the reader that his doctrine is in reality morally innocuous. But how can the reader fail to recall that the whole burthen of Bosanquet's tale is that 'everything is what it is' *in virtue of its rational coherence with the entire system of reality?* And a 'must' or 'cannot help it' which means *this* is so far from being morally innocuous that it must be said to imply the sheer denial of all significance to the sphere of morals.

It is, I think, not altogether easy to determine what Bosanquet's thoughts really are on this matter. A somewhat less ambiguous expression of his view occurs, however, in a passage just subsequent to that already cited. There, in reference to his well-known doctrine that freedom in its true meaning is in the last resort one with rationality, he tells us that all that this doctrine does 'is to supplement the strictly moral attitude "it is I, and I only, who have to act; it is I who determine what is to happen, and in determining it I am good or bad," *an attitude which cannot exist* per se, *nor be pushed to the bitter*

[1] *Principle of Individuality and Value*, p. 355.

end.[1] When we couple this with the further statement that our assumption of absolute freedom is 'quite right and true in view of a moral decision to be made'[2] but (as is implied) metaphysically invalid, we can see fairly clearly what Bosanquet's attitude is. He is very loth indeed to condemn unreservedly the moral point of view. But he cannot disguise from himself that on his own principles this point of view will not bear ultimate scrutiny. The *philosophic* point of view entails for Bosanquet what he euphemistically calls a 'supplementation' of the moral point of view. 'Annihilation' is the word which a good many readers will regard as more fitting. Even the plain man, with all his undoubted talent for harbouring contradictions without unrest, will be a little suspicious of the value of a 'moral' postulate which is 'metaphysical' moonshine.

It is an ungrateful task to have to dwell further upon what to myself seems so incontrovertible a fact as the incompatibility of Absolute Idealism with moral responsibility. But there are one or two arguments adduced by Idealists which seem to have exercised a good deal of influence in the way of disguising the true position, and some reference to these appears to be unavoidable.

One line of argument, which has on occasion been utilised by ethically interested Determinists as well as by the Idealist is as follows. 'Is it not apparent,' it is asked, 'that observation of the actual facts of experience reveals no slackening of moral effort on the part of those who subscribe to our doctrine of freedom (or determinism)? Many of the greatest figures of history, and especially of religious history, have explicitly adopted a view of this type, and yet it would be grotesque to accuse at least the majority of these persons of failing to honour the voice of Duty either in precept or in practice. How are we to interpret this save as meaning that a

[1] *Principle of Individuality and Value*, p. 355 (italics mine).
[2] *Ibid.*, p. 353.

denial of the freedom of "alternatives" is not felt to invalidate moral responsibility?'

Now as to the facts here alleged there is, I think, no serious dispute. Intellectual conviction of the systematic or determined character of the universe, even where it takes the uncompromising form of the theological doctrine of Predestination, does not, or does not conspicuously, extinguish the fire of moral aspiration. But why is this? Must we accept the somewhat paradoxical interpretation which the Determinist suggests? Or is there not a far simpler interpretation to our hand in the phenomenon to which we drew attention at the beginning of the present chapter? Is the reason, in short, not just that by the very constitution of our nature it is a psychological impossibility to engage in willing at all without spontaneously claiming for oneself the 'freedom' which one's explicit theory may deny? If such a claim does indeed force itself upon man throughout his practical endeavours, then little wonder if his philosophical or theological dogma, unable to find a footing in the foreground of his consciousness, is almost wholly inoperative. This explanation is surely at least a possible one, and it seems distinctly preferable to supposing that rational beings subscribe with open eyes to so manifest a self-contradiction as the union of moral responsibility with Determinism.

But more. The theoretical conviction of universal necessitation is *not* in truth wholly inoperative. In respect of the wider purposes of life, as when men and nations, taking long views, plan their future, the insidious influence of Determinism is unmistakable. What, for example, of the proverbial 'apathy of the East?' And this phenomenon, be it noted, is entirely consistent with the explanation of the partial impotence of Determinism upon conduct offered in the preceding paragraph. Where it is a case of the 'duties nearest to hand,' our immediate practical concerns, the deliverance of the volitional consciousness pushes Determinist theory into the background.

MORAL FREEDOM

But where it is a matter of planning for the distant future, the claims of 'theory' are not directly opposed, and consequently are not eclipsed, by the claims of the volitional consciousness, and Determinism forthwith assumes its baneful sway.

One further influence which has done much to obscure the real divergence between what the Idealist calls 'freedom' and the freedom in which the plain man is interested, must be adverted to before concluding this section. This influence is the ambiguity of the term 'freedom' in our actual common speech. There is *one* meaning of freedom in our common speech with which the Idealist doctrine is undoubtedly able to effect a rapprochement. It is characteristic of the Idealist doctrine to hold that freedom is a matter of 'degree,' being present in more or less fullness according (in part at least) to the intellectual enlightenment of the person concerned. Now there is much in our ordinary language which the Idealist can cite by way of testimony to the propriety of such an interpretation of freedom. We do all speak of the 'circumscribed' lives of the uneducated, and of the increasing 'freedom' or 'emancipation' which follows in the train of knowledge. The ordinary man is ready to recognise that the slum-dweller who may not be able to read or write is 'limited' by his ignorance, is debarred from enjoyment of a thousand activities which lie open to his more favoured brother. Furthermore, there is the obvious truth that the uneducated man, in that he has accepted his working ideas and ideals more or less uncritically, is a 'bondsman' to the forces of his environment in a sense which does not apply in comparable measure to the sage who permits no belief to gain an entry which does not approve itself before the bar of his own reason. All this is matter of general agreement: and it means that there is at least some currently employed sense of the word 'freedom' in which it is, as the Idealist tells us, a question of 'degree.' But will this entitle the Idealist to claim that his doctrine of freedom is not, after all, really different from that which the plain man means by freedom, and not, accordingly, incompatible with what the plain man means by moral responsibility?

It seems eminently clear that it will not. The freedom which depends upon enlightenment is one type of freedom, without doubt. But no one should be in the slightest danger of confusing this type of freedom with the freedom which is the presupposition of moral responsibility. So sharply distinguished are they in the ordinary man's mind that he would be conscious of no incongruity whatever in admitting that he enjoys only an insignificant measure of the freedom of 'enlightenment,' at the same time as he vigorously insists upon his absolute 'moral' freedom. The moral freedom, the freedom which is presupposed in all moral praise or blame, consists not in the possession of a comprehensive range of possible ends, nor in the extent to which rational reflection is responsible for the adoption of these ends, but solely in the capacity (of which every agent seems to himself to be directly aware) of identifying himself in act with *any one* of such ends as do present themselves before him in conative situations. If he does really possess this capacity, then (certain further simple conditions being fulfilled) he recognises that he may properly incur censure for identifying himself with an end which he knew, or believed, to be evil. But if he lacks this capacity, then emphatically *not*. Moral judgment, he will tell us—and who, that is not out to save a theory, will contradict him?—is, in the absence of such a capacity, the hollowest of mockeries.

The freedom of enlightenment is, in its different degrees, an acknowledged fact. Concerning it, there is no 'problem' of freedom at all. That in itself should be enough to make it evident that such is not the freedom about whose reality and unreality men have contended so long and so bitterly. What man has always been vitally concerned to know is whether sober and impersonal examination of the facts forces us to conclude, as it is claimed, that all of our acts—so-called 'good' and so-called 'bad' acts alike—'could not have been otherwise than they were': or whether, perhaps, the 'nobler hypothesis' suggested by the testimony of our practical consciousness may not, after all, be capable of support on purely rational principles. This is the real 'problem of freedom,' for it is the problem upon whose settlement the tremendous issue of man's moral responsibility finally turns. To pretend that any positive support is lent to 'moral responsibility' by the demonstration that man possesses, in various degrees, the freedom of enlightenment, is either a disingenuous evasion of the issue, or an unwitting exploitation of the ambiguities of language.

At least the general character of the freedom I am to defend is now obvious enough, and its cardinal importance to human interests is, I hope, equally obvious. Roughly speaking, what I shall try to show is that the apparent testimony of the practical consciousness as to the reality of 'open possibilities' is no illusion, but veridical. Without further preamble let us address ourselves to this task.[1]

[1] Before finally taking leave of the Idealist theory, I should like to emphasise—what the purpose of this section has tended to obscure—my substantial agreement with a very great deal of what Idealist moral philosophers have written on the topic of human freedom. While I absolutely decline to allow that the 'freedom' with which they are chiefly concerned is rightly to be called 'real' freedom (with the implication that the freedom of 'open possibilities' is not freedom at all, or at best quite unimportant), there seems to me no ground for denying that it is a 'real' *kind* of freedom. To a self conscious of its potentialities of self-development, conscious of an 'ideal' self which is at the same time its most 'real' self, all obstacles to that development—ignorance, prejudices, tyrannical passions, etc.—are bound to present themselves as restrictions upon its *self*, 'shackles' which must be thrown off if 'freedom' is to be gained. Thus all advances in self-development, all advances towards realisation of the 'true self,' may fairly enough be said to be advances in the self's 'freedom.' Moreover, the Idealist is obviously right in urging that this freedom, the freedom which is one with self-expansion and self-realisation, is antithetic not to 'submission to law,' but to arbitrariness and caprice. The art of living has, in all of its branches and as a whole, its own inviolable laws. Only by recognition of, and willing submission to, these laws is any full measure of this freedom attainable. All this is, I think, true, and, as developed in the writings of Idealists from Plato onwards, fertile in valuable ethical implications. What I reject is simply the underlying assumption that the traditional 'problem of freedom' finds here a satisfactory solution. That problem, as I understand it, remains exactly where it was.

Section 3. Conditions of Problem Surveyed and Method of Argument Determined

Even the more confident advocates of Determinism are, as a rule, prepared to admit that the 'immediate affirmation of consciousness at the moment of deliberate action' does constitute a real difficulty.[1] For this 'practical conviction' of freedom is, to all appearances, inexpugnable from human nature. Moreover, although it is spoken of as a 'practical' conviction, which suggests a distinction from 'theoretical' convictions, it is quite evident that the distinction must not be interpreted as meaning that the 'practical' conviction does not claim to be *true*. It assuredly does claim 'truth.' That it is practical does not mean that it is pragmatical—claiming only to be 'useful.' If we oppose it to 'theoretical' conviction, it can only be on the ground of the peculiarly intimate relation which it bears, both as to stimulus and as to content, to the conative side of our experience.

But the Determinist is apt to retort, *prima facie* with a good deal of justice, that the difficulties in the way of *accepting* this immediate affirmation of consciousness are incomparably greater. Against its implicit claim that there are genuinely open possibilities, that there is no irrevocable causal continuity, a formidable array of objections can readily be marshalled. We must defer detail meantime. But, to speak generally, we have got to recognise (1) that for many metaphysicians the 'intelligibility of reality' has the force of an *a priori* postulate of thought; (2) that the achievements of science have rendered the hypotheses of causal continuity almost unassailable in respect of those material processes which are, by reason of their

---

[1] I am speaking, of course, only of philosophical Determinists. The difficulty may not be felt by the purely 'scientific' Determinist—the kind of person who is blind even to the possibility of any revelations of the nature of man which do not appear through the channels of natural science. But Determinists of this class have no claim to be listened to in a philosophical discussion.

relative simplicity, most readily susceptible of accurate observation and crucial experiment;[1] which suggests the natural enough inference that it is only the greater intricacy of the factors involved which obstructs the discovery of irrevocable law in those highly complex material processes into which the human organism enters, and which constitute the material expression of 'conduct'; (3) that even in this latter field, the field of 'conduct,' at least a beginning seems to have been made (the Behaviourist would, of course, couch his claim in much less modest phraseology) towards the discovery of explanatory 'laws'; (4) that we do in our everyday experience take it for granted (with apparent success) that we can predict, in at least rough, approximate fashion, the reactions to given circumstances of those whose 'characters' we most fully know; (5) that even with respect to our own actions, it is only an extremely small minority, viz. deliberate volitions, that we feel any disposition to deny to be causally continuous with the past; (6) that the very conception of a 'free act' is fraught with grave difficulties, since it is by no means obvious how an act which the agent's 'character' does not determine in relation to the circumstances can be said to be the agent's *own* act at all. The cumulative force of these objections can scarcely be denied to be very considerable. And what is there really, it may be asked, to set on the other side? What is there to support the

[1] I wish to take no advantage of the 'principle of indeterminacy' recently introduced into scientific thought. It cannot be said to have yet attained a secure place in the storehouse of accredited scientific truth. Many eminent scientists are disposed to regard it as standing for no more than a confession of temporary ignorance. In any case, the advocate of free-will has (as such) no need to recognise a principle of the sort in inorganic nature (his preference would even be, I think, for the reverse), although he must, I think, affirm its validity for the human organism. Not that indeterminacy in the human organism would be *equivalent* to 'free will.' It might mean mere 'chance'—a totally different conception. It is really astounding to find it seriously suggested by contemporary scientific publicists that the alleged indeterminacy of the inorganic world itself is of the nature of 'free will'! One would have thought that it required no special discipline in psychology to recognise that it is necessary to have a will before one can have a free will.

'immediate affirmation of consciousness' that we can interrupt the causal sequence? Is there, *e.g.* the slightest indication from experience that we ever actually *realise* this capacity which we are supposed to possess, by the performance of an act which cannot reasonably be interpreted as the 'reaction of character to circumstances'? If not, if the immediate affirmation of consciousness merely stands alone, like some *Athanasius contra mundum*, little wonder, it may be said, that even temperate thinkers are disposed to urge that the conviction of freedom must yield to *force majeure*.

Now I might reply, indeed, that a conviction admittedly 'inexpugnable' can never 'yield': or, more precisely, that as against an 'inexpugnable' conviction there can be no *force majeure*. Counter considerations here can never produce more than a 'balance' of opposite forces. But that point I do not wish to press. I wish, rather, to work towards my positive argument for freedom by taking up the challenge to the Libertarian contained in the question just posed. 'Is there any evidence from experience of actual *realisation* of the supposed capacity of the will to interrupt the causal continuity of things?' It is not, of course, absolutely essential for the Libertarian to show that there is. It would not even, in strict logic, destroy the claim to freedom if (*per impossibile*) it could be decisively established that in no past act has there been divergence from the order which would be followed if causal continuity were a fact. For it is the capacity to choose between open possibilities that is at issue, and the interpretation would still remain abstractly possible that man has always (as the champion of freedom agrees that he has often) elected freely to follow that line of action which accords with the 'course of nature.'[1] But, admittedly, no one would be likely to put much credence in so forced an interpretation. It will obviously support in the most important way the conviction that man has the power to

---

[1] This point will be elaborated later in discussing the self's adoption in willing of ' the line of least resistance.'

interrupt the causal order, if we can find evidence that man actually does in fact interrupt that order.

And this evidence *can* be found. It stares one in the face, if one looks for it in the place where by the nature of the case it is alone possible for it to appear. By the external observation of conduct no break in causal continuity could be satisfactorily established, even if it existed. Any appearance of discontinuity could always be taken as signifying merely an inadequate understanding of the agent's character: the more readily since (as we shall see later) there will never be, even if freedom is a fact, *crass* discontinuity between character and act. There is one way, and one way only, in which the disruption of causal continuity between character and act could make itself decisively known. That is through the subject's own immediate experience of himself in acting.

And if we look here, I venture to affirm, we do find all the evidence of a positive character which can legitimately be demanded in the present issue. Everyone knows what it is to have the experience referred to as an 'effortful act of will.' If we scrutinise that experience with care, we shall see that part and parcel of it is an indefeasible certitude that herein I am creating a definite rupture in the causal continuity of past and present. There is inherent in it, we shall also see, a like indefeasible certitude that I 'need not' be creating this rupture, that I could be acting otherwise, that there were genuinely 'open possibilities' before me at the moment of volition. The experience of effortful willing carries with it, in short, both the claim to freedom, and the claim to be here and now utilising our freedom to interrupt that causal continuity which the Determinist holds to be all-pervading.

For this reason the experience of effortful willing may be said to furnish an even more striking assurance of the reality of our freedom than does the 'immediate affirmation of consciousness at the moment of deliberate action.' I propose, therefore, to give to it, in preference, the central place in the development of my positive argument for freedom. It will be necessary, first of all, to analyse the experience with some care. I shall endeavour to bring out its uniqueness of nature by distinguishing it off from certain other experiences with which it is liable, more or less, to be confused, and then to elicit from it the precise purport of the claims in the way of freedom which it seems, in virtue of its uniqueness, spontaneously and necessarily to evoke in the subject of it. When the work of analysis is completed, we can pass on to consider the crucial question of the ultimate credentials of these claims.

We may begin, then, by distinguishing the effortful act of will from the 'impulsive' act. Over this distinction, however, there is no need to linger. Simply *qua* act of will, the effortful act is different from any impulsive act. Any experience which we are prepared to recognise as 'willing' involves, as the impulsive act does not, the self's conscious adoption of the 'end' as *its* end—or, as it is sometimes expressed, the self's active identification of itself with the 'end,' or 'object.'

But, in the second place, the effort of the effortful act is not just the activity inherent in willing as such. The latter, the conscious identification of the self with an end, is something which does not admit of 'more' or 'less,' whereas we clearly speak of 'more' and 'less' effortful acts of will. Indeed, many acts of will we take to be, in this regard, quite effort*less*. This is most conspicuously evident in situations of so-called 'moral temptation.' In such situations we have before our minds a course of action which we believe to be bad, but which we at the same time feel to be the course to which our existing conative tendencies *per se* incline us; to be, in short, 'in the line of least resistance.' Now we may deliberately choose, or will, this end: and if we do, we certainly do not regard ourselves as having made 'too little' effort, but just as having made *no* effort at all. We have, as it were, deliberately allowed the 'natural man' in us to take his course. In a true sense, the so-called 'line of least resistance' in conative situations is a

MORAL FREEDOM 133

line of *no* resistance. It follows that the effort which we mean when we speak of an effortful act of will is something quite distinct from the activity which distinguishes willing from impulsive action, and which belongs to all willing.

And for this reason I am not sure that the term commonly used for this effort, viz. '*effort of will*,' is a very happy one. It is apt to suggest that effortful willing involves only a more intense form of the activity which is proper to willing as such. I should for myself prefer the term 'moral effort,' for the reason especially that such a title draws attention to the fact that effort is felt to be called forth and to be made always in the interests of a believed 'higher' end, which stands in contrast with a believed 'lower' end which is in the 'line of least resistance.' Indeed, what other incentive to effort *could* there be? What could induce anyone to act in the line of greater resistance, *i.e.* in opposition to the end towards which he is conscious of being most strongly inclined, except that this course is regarded as being somehow objectively 'better'? It is true, indeed, that the end to which effort is directed may be, though a felt 'higher,' yet a merely 'egoistic' end. And accordingly those who accept, as I do not, the Crocean distinction of Economic from Moral Value will dissent from the term 'moral effort,' as implying an improper restriction if intended to cover *all* effortful acts of will. As I cannot here debate either this, or certain kindred issues,[1] I shall not therefore press the nomenclature I prefer, and shall continue to adopt the traditional usage. I am concerned at present only to make the point that effort is felt to be always in the interests of a believed higher against a believed lower. Its function has the appearance of being, to use a common expression, to reinforce a believed higher but felt weaker desire against a believed lower but felt stronger desire. Or, as we might put it on the assumption of the restriction of effort to the 'morally' higher, the *raison*

[1] On the relation of Egoism and Moral Value see, however, Chapter VI., Section 6.

d'être of effort of will seems to be to make moral achievement possible by enabling the self to transcend the *status quo* of its existing conative tendencies in the direction of its ideal.

Again, we distinguish quite clearly the effort of the effortful act of will from either *physical* effort or *intellectual* effort. Effort of will bears no intrinsic relation whatever to the physical or intellectual effort that may be involved in the course which we will. Often the end recognised as in the line of least resistance, and thus calling for no effort of will, is one which is also recognised as involving intense physical effort; and, on the other hand, the end which *is* felt to demand effort of will may be perfect physical immobility. Similarly in the case of intellectual effort. Situations arise in which one is aware that one would like to continue to pursue some scientific train of thought, that the bias of one's existent conative tendencies inclines one to a course involving considerable output of intellectual energy, but that one ought, in the special circumstances, to make the effort to relax. Indeed, great effort of will may be felt to be involved in a course which is almost void of either physical or intellectual energy; as presumably, for example, in the early stages of certain ascetic disciplines of the East, before practice has made effortlessly perfect the achievement of the desired quiescence of mind and body.

Once more, we distinguish quite clearly the effort of effortful willing from the energy which belongs to our impulsive nature. If, *e.g.* we experience, as we often do, the uprising of a powerful impulse within us, and proceed to align ourselves in will with the course to which the impulse inclines, the felt presence of the impulsive energy certainly does not cause us to regard the act as a case of the 'effortful act of will.' On the contrary, the more powerful the impulse, the more likely is it that the end to which it inclines us will be felt to be the course which is in the line of least resistance, and as such the course the willing of which is effortless. In fact, in the extreme cases, where the impulse has such strength as to dominate our whole mental being, as, *e.g.* where we are in the grip of some over-mastering terror which impels us to blind and headlong flight, we have an experience which we should probably cite as the exemplar, not of effortful activity, but of complete passivity. We speak in such cases of having *lost* control of ourselves, of being subject to the governance of animal instinct.

The experience of effort of will, then, seems to be quite distinct from the experience of physical or intellectual effort, or of impulsive energy, or even of the activity involved in willing as such. Careful introspection will, I think, leave no serious doubts on the necessity of making these distinctions. We have now to attend to certain 'affirmations' which appear to be inherently bound up with this experience in virtue of its uniqueness. First of all, with respect to the source of the effort. The effortful act is felt as issuing from the self, and yet not from the self regarded as just the unity of its existing conative tendencies. And when I say that it is so 'felt,' I mean that this is the ideal interpretation directly and inevitably dictated by the experience when we attend to it with the question as to 'source' in our minds. It is evident enough that the effort is felt as made by the 'self.' The self takes credit for making it, and condemns itself in so far as the effort made is insufficient. But it is equally evident that the effort is felt not to be determined by the self's existent conative dispositions (or, as we may call it, its 'character as so far formed'). For the course which this latter dictates is, *ex hypothesi*, the course in 'the line of least resistance,' the adoption of which is felt to be effort*less*. The effort is felt, then, as self-determined, and yet as not determined by the self's character as so far formed, not, *i.e.*, causally continuous with the self's *past*. We may think this a paradox, although I shall later argue that it is a paradox only for a falsely abstract and external way of regarding the self; but the present point is just that it is the immediate report of the experience itself.

But not only is there implicit in the effortful act of will this absolute assurance that the self here and now originates the effort: there is also absolute assurance that the self could refrain from making the effort, and again (if the circumstances happen to be such as to permit of the question significantly arising) could be making a greater effort, or a less effort, with corresponding differences of the concrete act of will in each case. Naturally I do not mean that the agent explicitly asserts as he acts, 'this which I am doing I could forbear to do, etc.'; but I do mean this, that once the question is put to the agent after an act experienced as effortful, 'could you have acted otherwise than you did?', the revival of the experience in imagination absolutely *compels* an affirmative answer in the terms I have indicated. It is an answer which we are *obliged* to return by the very nature of the experience itself.

And with this we come upon the full-blown claim to that kind of freedom which, I have insisted, is a condition of moral responsibility. We have the claim that there are genuinely open possibilities lying before the self; that in situations of moral temptation, where there is a presented contrast between the end of duty and the end of inclination, it lies wholly and solely with the self here and now whether or not, or how far, it makes the effort to rise to duty. Nothing, be it noted, is claimed which is inconsistent with the obvious fact of the powerful influence of the self's past character upon the act of will regarded in its total nature. So far as the claim to freedom here made is concerned, the self's character perfectly well may, as it in fact obviously enough does, prescribe the nature of the alternatives presented, determine the extent of the gulf which in any instance separates the end of duty from the end of inclination, and settle therefore how great is the effort required to 'rise to duty.' All that is claimed (and it is important to bear this in mind in view of the chimerical versions of freewill which the less scrupulous opponents of Libertarianism delight to assail) is that whether or not, or how far, this effort is made, lies solely with the self here and now.

In so far as the foregoing analysis is sound, we have in the effortful act of will an experience of ourselves of a unique kind which is such as by its very nature to oblige the subject of it to affirm his own freedom, in the sense of freedom just explained. Our task now is to come to some decision upon the ultimate credentials of this affirmation or claim.

But it is of quite cardinal importance, I think, to see clearly at the beginning that an inquiry into the credentials of this affirmation of freedom is not so much an inquiry into the reasons for *believing*, as an inquiry into the reasons for *disbelieving*. The question to be asked is 'Why should we *not* accept the validity of the affirmation with as much complaisance as we accept the validity of any other affirmation which we find ourselves *obliged* to make?' Here is an affirmation which comes to us bearing an authority far more profound than that of well-authenticated scientific laws, an authority, indeed, strictly comparable to that of syllogistic inference. For our nature *compels* us to judge thus, it would seem. As such, this affirmation cannot be legitimately required to furnish positive grounds for believing, but only to dispose satisfactorily of the reasons presented for disbelieving.

To this way of posing the problem it is no answer at all to urge that a mere 'feeling in our minds' is far too frail a basis to serve as the sole positive support of a claim of such far-reaching significance. The adoption of this attitude is not uncommon. But it betrays a serious misunderstanding of the conditions of solution of the problem of freedom. The sole positive evidence that ever *could* be adduced for free will must from the nature of the case be of the type of 'immediate experience' or 'feeling.'[1] I do not mean, of course, that a fully cogent argument for freedom can be developed without

---

[1] If, at least, we except the 'ethical argument for freedom.' This argument is, I think, of very real importance, but it depends for its force upon the validity of certain postulates which require independent discussion. At the present stage of the argument it must be discounted. See, however, Chapter VI., Section 7.

any reference to other aspects of reality. This is not so. If the argument is to convince, we must be able to show, for example, that freedom is consistent with the actual observed facts of personal behaviour. But the point is that such references can never have more than a *negative* import. No interpretation of the observed facts of behaviour, nor *a fortiori* of the observed facts of organic and inorganic nature, could ever furnish us with a positive indication of freedom. The investigation of these phenomena might, indeed, assist the Libertarian's case if it happened to suggest a strong probability for the hypothesis that causal continuity is not universal. But, at the very best, we could clearly infer from this only that the observed facts are *compatible with* freedom, not that they *require* freedom. The facts, as so envisaged, would be just as compatible with the hypothesis of the intervention of mere 'chance,' as with the hypothesis that rational beings have this originative power which we call freedom. And as we shall see later, freedom as experienced (and there is no other way of understanding what it means) is apprehended as being quite as sharply opposed to 'chance' or 'capricious intervention,' as it is to 'causal continuity.'

There is, then, nothing in observed objective facts, whatever be the result of their examination, which could establish positively, nay, nor even suggest, the reality of personal freedom. Were it not for immediate experience man would never so much as harbour a suspicion that he is a free agent. For this reason the defender of freedom is bound to rest his case ultimately upon such experience, trying as best he may to establish its credentials. But, for the same reason, it is obviously illegitimate for the Determinist to seek to discredit his opponent on the ground that the latter's case hangs in the end on nothing more substantial than a 'mere feeling.' It *does* so hang, but this is not a defect. It is due to the very nature of that which is being defended. If there *is* freedom, then it is on this basis, and on no other, that it can be known to be. To demand of the defender of freedom that he should cease to rest his case upon a 'mere feeling' and conduct his argument more tangibly in the 'scientific' region of observed facts, is just to invite him to abandon his thesis altogether.

The Determinist, on the other hand, may properly enough rest his case, in large part, upon consideration of the observed objective facts. These facts, although they can on no interpretation positively point to freedom, may on one interpretation positively point to the rejection of freedom. If we find that the facts, wherever investigated, cannot reasonably be construed to be other than subject to all-pervasive causal law, then of course there is no room for the hypothesis of personal freedom in the sense that is here in question. The Determinist is, in principle, able to develop a strong argument irrespective of what he may also have to say in criticism of such experiences as that of 'effortful' willing.

Nevertheless the Determinist who appreciates his problem is likely to give a good deal of labour to disturbing the credentials of the 'feeling' of freedom, and that for two reasons.

(1) It is not really possible, at the present stage of knowledge at any rate, to maintain seriously that the observed facts of human conduct *demand* the hypothesis of all-pervasive causal continuity. The argument for irrevocable causal law in this sphere draws a good deal of its strength from mere analogy with the sphere of material processes—an analogy which perhaps appears more and more venturesome the more closely we attend to the differences in kind between the material and the mental. It is true, of course, that observation of conduct itself points indubitably to at least a measure of intelligible continuity. The possibility of at least approximate prediction in the sphere of conduct is established beyond reasonable doubt, and implies intelligible continuity of some sort. But no responsible Libertarian really wishes to deny this. He knows that if his 'freedom' is to be one which he can make any show of defending at all, it must be one which is

consistent with a distinct measure of continuity. For my own part, I shall consider it an obligation to make clear that the freedom which I defend does not jeopardise in the smallest degree such measure of continuity in conduct as is definitely established from the observed facts.

Those Determinists, of course, who do not admit the existence of a 'mind' as distinct from a 'body' at all, or again, those who, while admitting the existence of mind, deny that it has any efficacy in bringing about the changes which comprise human behaviour, will not be affected by the questionable character of the analogy of mind with matter. The analogy, for them, is of one set of material processes with another set. They do not bring 'mind' into the argument. But in adopting this position they do not strengthen, but immeasurably weaken, the demonstrable case for determinism in human behaviour. For it is not now permitted to them to take any account of the undoubtedly impressive evidence for causal continuity referred to in the preceding paragraph, viz. that furnished by the relative constancy observable in the relation between 'character' and 'conduct.' The Behaviouristic Determinist is only entitled to assert intelligible continuity if he can show constant relations between the material processes of the body and the material processes which constitute conduct. It is safe to say that he is very much further off from his goal than the 'spiritual' Determinist is from his. A beginning has been made, let us admit, with the 'conditioned reflex' and its allies. But it is the merest beginning. So far as the present writer has been able to discern, explanation by the 'conditioned reflex' has not yet extended, in actual practice, beyond certain extremely simple types of experience, in respect of which the defender of freedom would not be in the least perturbed at having to admit that he is essentially 'inactive.' The speculative jump required to extend the principle to cover the whole gamut of human behaviour may fairly be described as prodigious.

(2) Even if the Determinist does succeed in assuring himself that the observed facts demand a deterministic explanation, nevertheless this assurance will not of itself be effectual in silencing the contrary testimony of his practical consciousness. And since the practical consciousness is as integral a part of himself as the theoretical, his soul will become the seat of an unresolved dualism which, to him as a philosopher, cannot be other than embarrassing. With one side of his nature he will find himself denying freedom, while with another side asserting it. In such a situation it is impossible that he should be confident of the validity of either pronouncement, or expect others, similarly circumstanced, to be persuaded by his arguments. It will behove him, therefore, if he is to attain to a satisfying Determinism, to expose the illusoriness of the common testimony of the practical consciousness—an end which can only be achieved if, by an analysis of the experience which underlies it, he is able to show that what seems to be a spontaneous and necessary interpretation is really an understandable misinterpretation, the confusion in which, once brought to light, we may guard ourselves from repeating. Only by a demonstration along these lines could the dualism be resolved in favour of Determinism.

It is for the Determinist, then, a matter of vital importance to 'explain away' the 'practical' certitude of freedom, to show that the experience underlying it does not really compel the affirmation which it seems to compel. And it is even more vital for the Libertarian to repel such attempts. For if he cannot maintain his case here, there is nothing else, we repeat, to which he can appeal for positive support. In fairness to the Libertarian, however, it must again be emphasised that his obligation is rather to rebut contrary arguments than to initiate a positive argument. The onus of proof lies upon the Determinist. For it cannot be denied that everyone knows what is meant when we speak of putting forth an 'effort of will' and acting against what is felt to be the 'line of least resistance,' and it is certain that the universal interpretation which such experiences evoke, apart from theory, is 'libertarian.' If the Determinist's arguments do not succeed in disturbing the natural interpretation, the Libertarian position may fairly be said to stand: always providing, however, that the Libertarian is able to show also that the freedom which he asserts is incompatible neither with observed facts nor with any well-authenticated metaphysical postulate.

Section 4. *Criticism of Attempts to 'Explain away' the Sense of Effortful Activity*

In pursuance of the duties thus imposed upon the Libertarian, let us now consider the validity of the attempts that have been made to discredit the experience of 'effortful' activity.

The first thing that strikes one, however, is the surprising paucity of direct criticism on the primary point at issue in recent psychological literature. 'Surprising' we say, for the fashionable psychology of the day is nothing if not anti-Libertarian. Most commonly, the sole moving forces of conduct are supposed to be the group of (more or less numerous) instincts which form the hereditary endowment of human nature, and each of which possesses a definitive quota of impulsive energy. All human action is, in the last analysis, a resultant of the interplay of these primitive forces. It is agreed, of course, that the original ends often undergo much elaboration and refinement in the process of experience, so that frequently a good deal of skill is required to penetrate their disguise. But it is vigorously denied that any force other than that belonging to the primitive impulses has any efficacy in human affairs. Now this is the sheer negation of freedom. It seems reasonable, therefore, to expect that the writers who so confidently discourse in this manner would pause for a moment to explain away the type of experience which, in the interpretation it naturally or commonly evokes, runs directly counter to the Determinist's hypothesis: explain away, that is, the so-called experience of 'activity.'

'But' (perhaps our psychologist will reply) 'we do not want to deny the reality of "activity." On the contrary, we are talking of "activities" all the time. Our psychology is dynamic through and through. Is the "activity" of which you speak anything other than the "psychic energy" of which we speak, and which we assign to the instincts? Is your "experience of activity" not just the awareness accompanying the kinetic expression of such psychic energy—which awareness could no doubt easily enough generate in the agent the libertarian illusion that one "could have acted otherwise than one did." If it is anything else than this, then we do not find any trace of it in our experience, and, to be frank, do not believe that it exists.'

Should the psychologist reply in this wise, then we must be equally frank, and point out to him that his failure to recognise any awareness of activity other than the awareness of impulsive energies is due simply to a defect in introspective analysis. There is an all-important difference, which he has not appreciated, between the self's awareness of itself as a *scene* of activities, and its awareness of itself as *active*, let alone *effortfully active*. Consciousness of impulsive energy can give us awareness of activity only in the former of these meanings. When we are conscious merely of a strong impulse urging us in some specific direction, we are conscious of *an activity going on in us* (ourselves as a 'scene of activity'), not of *ourselves as active*. Even more markedly, when we are conscious of the presence in us of 'conflicting' impulses, urging us in mutually incompatible directions, the self appears to itself as a mere 'scene of activity.' There is all the difference in the world between such experiences and that type of experience illustrated by the successful issue of a moral conflict, in which the self seems to itself to be declining to accept the 'line of least resistance'—which is just that direction which action would take if left solely to the interplay of the impulsive energies—and by 'effort of will' to be identifying itself with that harder course which it believes to be right. In the latter we have a self conscious not of activities going on in it, but of itself as active.

The two kinds of experience are quite radically distinct. We must be on our guard against any interpretation which should admit, and yet unduly minimise, the difference. It might be suggested, for example, that the difference is just that, in the case of experience of self-activity proper, we are conscious of the operation of an energy which (for some reason) we identify in a special way with the 'self.' But this is not sufficient. It is impossible to reconstitute the genuine experience of activity in these terms. The experience described might give us the self aware of itself as *displaying* energy, but not the self aware of itself as *creating* energy, and this is what we at least seem to have in the characteristic experience of activity. The self would still be for itself (on the interpretation suggested) a mere 'scene of activity' rather than itself active. We should keep before us, if we are to judge aright in this matter, that most striking example of the experience of self-activity—the 'hard choice' in which we seem to ourselves to be reinforcing the 'weaker but higher' desire by an 'effort of will.' In such experiences we are sure that we 'could have acted otherwise.' And the indispensable condition of such assurance is the consciousness of ourselves as *creating* the energy in question. The consciousness of ourselves as merely *displaying* energy could not possibly induce in us the conviction of freedom in the sense of a capacity for alternative action. Yet the consciousness of 'displaying' energy is all that there could be if the energy is of the nature of impulsive energy, even if the impulse or complex of impulses concerned happen to be regarded by the self as somehow pre-eminently 'representative' of the self.

We dwell on this matter, because it is really not possible

for the problem which the experience of activity sets, or should set, for the Determinist, to be understood by anyone who has not distinguished quite clearly this experience from the experience in which we are aware merely of activities going on in us. The latter experience offers no difficulties to a Determinist theory. But it is certainly not the experience to which people refer when they reject Determinism on the ground of an alleged 'immediate experience of activity.' It is, strictly speaking, no more an experience of activity than is the state of the overtaxed brain-worker who, on retiring to rest, is unable to sleep on account of the phantasmagoria of ideas that wildly and confusedly keep rushing into his mind. Here is a scene of 'activities,' if you will. But it is the very antithesis of the experience which any sensible person would select as an experience of 'self-activity.'

Not all the 'instinct psychologists,' however, have been oblivious of the fact that there is something in the experience described as 'acting against the line of least resistance' that, on their principles, needs explaining—or explaining away. McDougall is one honourable exception whose name will occur to the mind at once in this connection. McDougall devotes the better part of a long chapter (Chapter IX.) in his *Social Psychology* to the attempt to discover what is really happening when, as we say, we reinforce the weaker impulse by an 'effort of will.' This is indeed matter for gratitude. And although I am unable to believe that his analysis, in spite of much that is ingenious and instructive, succeeds in avoiding the difficulties which seem to me inherent in his presuppositions, it will be worth our while to consider its main points in brief compass. It is perhaps as plausible an attempt as any in the literature of this school to show that the type of experience upon which the Libertarian rests most of his case does not, when properly interpreted, imply any 'incalculable factor.'

McDougall begins, it will be remembered, from William James's familiar statement of the situation. In certain cases of moral conflict the effort of the will appears to come in 'to determine the victory to the side of the weaker impulse.' But McDougall is not prepared to say with James that with this 'effort of the will' we come up against an 'ultimate and insoluble problem.' That, as he believes, is a conclusion which will make any genuine 'science of society' impossible. 'Some attempt must therefore be made to show that the effort of volition . . . involves no new principles of activity and energy, but only a more subtle and complex interplay of those impulses which actuate all animal behaviour and in which the ultimate mystery of mind and life resides.'[1] His task will be, as he further expresses it, to find in our mental constitution (and in accordance with the straightforward principles already established) 'the source of that influx of energy which seems to play the decisive rôle in volition.'[2]

There follows now a short discussion of the different types of conational process, with a view to bringing out the specific characteristic of 'volition.' The general conclusion which emerges is that the differentia of volition is the introduction of the idea of 'self.' 'In the typical case of volition a man's self, in some peculiarly intimate sense of the word "self," is thrown upon the side of the motive that is made to prevail.'[3]

The important thing, however, is to show in what precise way the 'idea of self' functions in volition. His conclusion so far, McDougal thinks, is approved by many psychologists, notably by Stout and Bradley, both of whom make self-consciousness of the essence of volition. But these writers have not succeeded in making quite clear, he thinks, just *how* self-consciousness plays its rôle.[4]

It may be worth while to pause at this point, however, to notice what seems to be a misunderstanding in McDougall's references to Stout and Bradley. Stout and Bradley, when they speak of self-consciousness as a condition of 'volition,' are not

---

[1] *Social Psychology*, p. 200 (20th edition).
[2] *Ibid.*, p. 203.   [3] *Ibid.*, p. 212.   [4] *Ibid.*

thinking (as I understand them) only of what they would call the 'special' case of volition in which we seem by 'effort of will' to act in the line of greatest resistance. They are aiming at an account of volition in general, applicable to bad volitions just as much as to good volitions—to the deliberate adoption of the end of the 'lower but stronger' impulse, as well as to the deliberate rejection of it in favour of the end of the 'higher but weaker' impulse. Thus when Bradley approves the 'obscure dictum' that 'in volition we identify the *self* with the end of the action' (I quote McDougall's expressions), he is not thinking of the differentia of 'good, hard choices' from 'bad, easy choices,' but just of the differentia of willed action in general from impulsive action. McDougall does not appear to recognise that this is so. The assumption underlying his suggestion of defect in Stout's and Bradley's treatment is obviously that they are engaged in trying to explain what *he* is here going to explain better, namely, 'action in the line of greatest resistance.' If, as seems pretty evident, they are not, then the implied criticism of them for not showing how exactly self-consciousness enters into the 'hard choice' loses all point.

While rejecting McDougall's claim to be advancing upon Stout and Bradley, let us go on to see, however, the solution which he offers to his own problem. How exactly does the idea of self function in making possible 'action in the line of greatest resistance'? McDougall's answer is as follows. The mere *idea* of self can do nothing. But round the idea of self there has gathered, in the experience of everyone, that system of emotional and conative dispositions which we call a sentiment, and in this 'self-regarding sentiment' our solution is to be found. In McDougall's own words—'*The conations, the desires and aversions, arising within this self-regarding sentiment are the motive forces which, adding themselves to the weaker ideal motive in the case of moral effort, enable it to win the mastery over some stronger, coarser desire of our primitive animal nature and to banish from consciousness the idea of the end of this desire.'* [1]

McDougall now proceeds to illustrate his thesis by pointing out how in specific instances the 'impulses excited within the system of the self-regarding sentiment' carry out their work of reinforcement. But we need not follow him into his detailed application—fortunately, since we could hardly avoid the discussion of certain incidental difficulties which are not germane to our immediate purpose. The principle of McDougall's solution is before us, and the principle of my criticism can be expressed in direct relation to it.

But first let me make all proper concessions. There *are* cases, many cases, in which a 'higher' desire, which would not be effective *per se* against a 'lower' desire, passes into action as the direct result of its reinforcement by an 'impulse excited within the system of the self-regarding sentiment.' A man whose inclination to spend the evening in the tavern tippling with his cronies is a good deal stronger, as it stands, than his inclination to please his wife by spending the evening at home, may call to mind the social disapproval which the former course will evoke, and the aversion which he feels to such disapproval of himself may easily be powerful enough—without our requiring to assume the introduction of any unique force like 'will-effort' or 'will-energy'—to give the victory to the latter course. Or again—to take now a motive more closely approximating to McDougall's 'higher plane' of conduct—most men have, by the time of their maturity, formulated for themselves some kind of 'ideal character' representing what in their reflective moments they feel that they really most want to be. Now every man wishes to appear well to himself. But he cannot appear well to himself if he sees himself behaving in a way that conflicts with his chosen ideal. He therefore feels an aversion to having to think of himself as so behaving—as disloyal, idle, etc. And the

[1] *Social Psychology*, p. 213.

MORAL FREEDOM

weight of such aversion, if introduced into a practical situation such as that above depicted, may be quite sufficient, simply as aversion, to tip the scale once more in favour of what would otherwise be the weaker impulse.

It seems to me, then, very probable that the sentiment organised round the idea of the self does, as claimed, furnish impulses which will in many cases so reinforce what would be by itself the 'weaker' impulse as to make that impulse effective. With this, as a mere statement of fact, I have no disposition to quarrel. But what I do most emphatically contest is McDougall's further and central contention that this is an account of what happens in those conations in which we seem to ourselves to be making an effort of will, and, in virtue of it, 'acting in the line of greatest resistance.' It is that type of experience which McDougall has set out to explain. But so far as the present writer can see, the type of experience which conforms to the conditions which McDougall has described could not possibly carry with it for the agent the appearance of effort of will or 'acting in the line of greatest resistance' at all.

How could it? Let us look carefully at McDougall's account of what happens. We have in the first place a weaker impulse, a, opposed to a stronger impulse, b. As things stand, action towards the end of a (which end we may symbolise as α) would be, and would so appear to the agent, 'action in the line of greatest resistance.' But, McDougall maintains, if the impulsive constituents of the situation remained thus, action would never in fact be directed to α. Such action is made possible only by the accession of a new impulse s (excited within the self-regarding sentiment) which ranges itself on the side of a, and is of sufficient strength to make $a+s$ stronger than b. Action directed to α thus becomes *now* 'action in the line of *least* resistance.' And what the reader of McDougall must want to know, and what, so far as I can see, finds absolutely no explanation in McDougall's pages, is *why it does not also appear to be so to the agent.* If it does so appear, if the action does under the new conditions present itself as frankly 'action in the line of *least* resistance,' then we have here no explanation whatever of that which McDougall proposed to explain—action which seems to the agent to be in the line of greatest resistance. And if it does not so appear, one would, I repeat, very much like to know why. It would only be possible that it should not so appear, I think, if we could assume that the agent is unconscious of the contribution made to the balance of power by the new impulse *s*. But this would be to assume in the teeth of the evidence. There is no more reason why we should suppose ourselves unconscious of accession of impulsive strength from an impulse which happens to be connected with the self-regarding sentiment, than in the case of any other kind of impulse.

To put the matter in a nutshell. McDougall's explanation of action which appears to be in the line of greatest resistance is that it is really action in the line of least resistance. But he altogether fails to show how the factors which make it action in the line of least resistance do not *also* make it *appear* as action in the line of least resistance.

I am compelled therefore to conclude that McDougall has offered no plausible explanation of the experience which he set out to explain. There are conative experiences, we have admitted, which correspond to the conditions which he describes. But they are not, and could not be, experiences in which we appear to ourselves to be putting forth an 'effort of will,' and 'acting in the line of greatest resistance.' And so long as one confines one's explanatory hypothesis, as McDougall does, to the interplay of impulsive energies, no tenable explanation of such experiences, I venture to think, ever will be forthcoming.

On the whole (although I have to confess what may be serious limitations in my knowledge of the relevant literature) the older psychologists seem to me to have been more discriminating in their criticisms of activity. They did keep pretty clearly before them the fundamental requirements of any successful attempt to 'explain away' the experience of activity. What requires to be done is to analyse the so-called experience of activity in such a way as to make clear (1) that its constituents involve no factor of a unique kind such as could warrant the assumption that here a unique type of force is operative, and (2) why it is that the assemblage of these constituents does in fact give rise in the subject to the supposition that a unique type of force is operative. Both of these conditions seem to have been kept clearly in view by psychologists like Münsterberg.[1] They are kept clearly in view also, I think, by Bradley, whose inveterate hostility to the concept of 'activity' is very well known. Bradley's analysis of the 'experience of activity' (so-called) is intended, it is true, to refer to self-activity in general, or at least to voluntary activity in general, and does not distinguish off the 'effortful' variety for special treatment. But it is made plain by many remarks that he takes the alleged ultimacy of the experience of effortful activity to be disproved at the same time—as just a rather egregious example of what is in principle the same nonsense. I think it will be profitable, therefore, if we consider, by way of complement to the explanation of the 'new' psychologists, the explanation of the experience of activity which is offered for our acceptance by Bradley in *Appearance and Reality*.

There is, Bradley tells us, 'no original experience of anything like activity.'[2] It is a 'secondary product, the origin of which is far from mysterious.'[3] When we make 'a serious attempt to decompose it,[4]' we find that 'the perception of activity comes from the expansion of the self against the not-self, this expansion arising from the self.'[5] What this statement means may best be seen by reminding ourselves of the psychological nature of

[1] See Professor A. S. Pringle-Pattison's essay ' The " New " Psychology and Automatism' in the volume entitled *Man's Place in the Cosmos*.
[2] *Appearance and Reality*, p. 116. [3] *Ibid.*
[4] *Ibid.* [5] *Ibid.*, p. 96.

desire. The essence of desire for an object is 'the feeling of our affirmation in the idea of something not ourself, felt against the feeling of ourself as, without the object, void and negated.'[1] It follows that if the idea in question finds realisation, the tension is released, and we are conscious of self-expansion; just as, on the other hand, we are conscious of repression and contraction of the self if the idea is prevented from finding realisation. But, Bradley adds, the 'mere expansion, of course, would not be felt as activity, and *its origination from within the self is of the essence of the matter.*'[2]

Some explanatory comments now follow in the text. In the first place Bradley warns the reader against confusing the self-expansion just referred to with 'the enlargement of the self in the sense of the whole individual.'[3] It is only the 'enlargement of the self' in relation to that particular change in the not-self in which it feels itself, in desire, ideally affirmed. Such enlargement is quite compatible with what, from a general point of view, is a 'narrowing.' Thus even where we desire self-destruction, the activity towards it, since it consists in the removing of something felt, in the desire, as repressive of the self, is so far an expansion or enlargement. And it is felt definitely as self-expansion (not just the expansion of a *part* of the self) because the self naturally identifies itself with that part of itself which for the time occupies the foreground. The idea whose actualisation, in Bradley's account, brings with it the sense of self-expansion (the idea of the desired change) 'not only is felt to be a part of that self which is opposed to the not-self—it is felt also to be the main feature and the prominent element there.'[4] 'We may say, generally, the self here *is* that in which it feels its chief interest.'[5]

The second comment is mainly concerned with those cases of

---

[1] *Ethical Studies* (2nd ed.), p. 68. I have cited this passage, in preference to any in the discussion of self-activity in *Appearance and Reality*, as being more convenient for a condensed account of Bradley's view.
[2] *Appearance and Reality*, pp. 96–7 (italics mine).
[3] *Ibid.*, p. 97. [4] *Ibid.*, p. 95. [5] *Ibid.*, p. 97.

MORAL FREEDOM 153

the perception of activity which appear to resist the application of Bradley's principle of explanation in that no 'idea' of the desired change seems to be present. The solution offered is that the requisite idea is present implicitly though not explicitly, and an account is given of the process involved. The notes added to the later edition of *Appearance and Reality* defend the use made of the distinction between implicit and explicit ideas, and the argument as a whole seems to me to be valid, at least in the sense that the account of perception of activity with 'implicit' ideas is no *more* difficult to accept than the account of it with 'explicit' ideas.

Finally, Bradley explains a little more fully what he means by insisting that activity is experienced only if the 'expansion' is apprehended as originating 'from within the self.' If I may venture to substitute an illustration for the symbols which Bradley uses, the point may be made out as follows. Suppose I want to get hold of an apple that is just out of my normal reach. With my arm outstretched I am about to jump up to grasp it, when the branch suddenly dips in the wind and deposits the apple in my hand. With this fulfilment of my desire I experience, doubtless, an *expansion* of my self against the not-self. But I do not experience an *activity* of my self. If, on the other hand, I get hold of the apple only through jumping towards it, or perhaps rising on tiptoe, I am conscious not merely of self-expansion, but (according to Bradley) of self-activity. And what makes the difference is that whereas in the former case my self-expansion (in the realisation of the desire) is not apprehended as 'originating from within my self' —it comes about through a 'chance' event in the external world—in the latter case it *is* so apprehended. In this latter case I experience an expansion of the self which I feel to arise from the self. And with this I do get the full perception of activity.

This I believe to be a fair account of Bradley's theory. But surely it will not do? So far as I can see, his 'explanation' will not explain *any* experience of self-activity, much less the experience of the effortful act of will which is our especial concern. When we look closely at the condition stressed by Bradley, that the self-expansion must be felt as 'originating from within the self,' we see that this phrase is really a way of begging the whole issue. 'Felt as originating from within the self' may mean here, broadly, either of two things. Either it means that we connect our felt self-expansion with our self simply as 'effect' with 'proximate cause.' Or it means that we connect our felt self-expansion with our self as the effect of a *first* cause, of a genuine origination—in short, as the effect of an *act*. On the former of these meanings it seems impossible that we should experience 'self-activity' at all. For in apprehending the self as 'cause,' we are apprehending it also as 'effect' of previous causes. It is just one 'link' in the causal chain. There is nothing here to generate the consciousness of self-*activity*. On the latter of these meanings we *should* experience self-activity—but just because that experience is already presupposed in the experience that is supposed to generate it. What could be meant by saying that the self-expansion is felt as originating from within the self, as an effect of self as *first* cause, save that in that experience we are conscious of self-*activity*? In no other way, so far as I can see, than by having the experience of activity in originating the self-expansion could we ever come to connect the self-expansion with the self as effect with *first* cause. On this meaning, therefore, the explanation of the experience of activity proceeds in terms of that which is to be explained, and must be rejected.

On neither interpretation, then, as it seems to me, of the phrase 'felt as originating from within the self' do we get an explanation of the experience of activity. On the one interpretation Bradley's conditions seem plainly incapable of generating the experience. On the other interpretation the experience itself is covertly introduced into the conditions. It is perhaps superfluous, therefore, to go on to consider the competence of the proposed explanation to cover the experience of effortful activity. But it may be pointed out that the description 'a felt expansion of the self, felt as originating from within the self' is just as applicable to those volitions in which we deliberately follow the 'line of least resistance,' and which are therefore experienced as effortless, as it is to effortful volitions. The description thus fails to lay hold of the specific essence of the experience of effortful activity, and cannot (apart from the earlier difficulties) be accepted as its ultimate analysis.[1]

It is a duty, I suppose, to add something at this point about the bodily sensations which for many writers are so important a factor in our experience of activity. 'Feelings of innervation' in the old sense have long been discarded. But it is still maintained, with a good deal of probability, that in every experience of so-called 'effort of will' there are present a number of bodily sensations—muscular contractions, tensions in the head, and so on—varying according to the specific nature of the act, but possibly with a nucleus common to all; and maintained, with a good deal less probability, that these bodily sensations are the very core of our experience of activity. Can we, perhaps, by making due use of these sensations, supplement Bradley's account of the perception of activity in a way which will make it fully satisfactory? One great difficulty in that account was, we saw, the insufficient specification of

[1] I ought not, perhaps, to have omitted to draw attention to one further item in Bradley's analysis—the 'wavering' and 'oscillation' in the felt self-expansion which he alludes to at the bottom of p. 99, and which he regards—I think—as ingredient in all experience of activity. But it seems fairly obvious that the root difficulty is not mitigated by the insertion of this condition. Plainly the experience of 'wavering' and 'oscillation' cannot be identified with the experience of 'struggle,' though Bradley almost seems to suggest such an identification in the passage just referred to. We may perfectly well have these characteristics in the 'effortless' volition in which we seem to ourselves to be merely following out the bias of our desires. Nothing is likelier than that we should, in the course of such volitions, be subjected to repeated 'checks' through adverse conditions: and the self-expansion will then be felt as a 'wavering' one. We are brought by this supplementation no whit nearer to the specific essence of the experience of activity.

the phrase 'originating from within the self.' Suppose that, to the account of the perception of activity as 'the experience of a self-expansion apprehended as originating from within the self,' we add the rider that the 'self' must be at the same time sentient of a peculiar set of bodily feelings. Will this elaboration bring us any nearer to the truth?

I do not think that it will, no matter what varieties of bodily feeling the psychologist may choose to select. One's own introspective report is, no doubt, an unconvincing basis for argument, but I certainly do find it impossible, for my own part, to make the conditions as given exhaustively cover that which I experience in an 'effort of will.' When I imagine a typical effort of will, and then seek to reconstitute it in terms of the above analysis, I do find, indeed, all of the said elements present, even certain bodily feelings, but I find also something more. And that 'something more' is neither of the nature of bodily feelings nor ideal changes, but something *sui generis*—something which is incapable of description in terms which belong to other forms of experience, and which has on that account deservedly been accorded a name of its own, 'activity,' or 'effort' of will. This, of course, is the introspective result which would be expected if the experience *is* irreducible. And the critic will no doubt be ready with his taunt that the introspection is doctored to suit the thesis, or is, at the least, unconsciously biassed by the thesis. But I would, with all respect, invite the critic to consider carefully whether the boot is not on the other leg: whether when he 'looks into his own breast' and finds in the experience in question nothing but a complex of feelings and ideas of well-authenticated types, he is not really failing to find anything other than these because he is looking only *for* these. The good psychologist, like any other good scientist, is by nature sceptical of the mysterious, the 'unconnected.' His impulse is towards simplification by the establishment of unity in the differences. But it is an impulse which, if uncritically indulged, leads on occasion to a simplification which is in fact a falsification. And when the psychologist reports to us that he finds nothing unique in the experience of activity, I think that it has so led.

This line of defence is not, I grant, very satisfying by itself. But it becomes very much more cogent—conclusive, as I think—when we add to it considerations drawn from a slightly different point of view. As was remarked at an earlier stage, the critic who seeks to resolve the experience of activity into a complex of elements which give no justification for the assumption of a unique originative force, is under an obligation to make at least plausible the generation from the experience as he has analysed it of the 'illusion' of freedom which the subject of the experience does have. If the critic cannot do this, then it may fairly be retorted that his analysis is inadequate to the facts. Now I submit that this 'illusion' is not made one whit more understandable by any bodily feelings one may care to introduce into one's description. The experience of activity in a typical effort of will is ideally interpreted by the subject as signifying the introduction of a unique originative force which he exerts against the line of least resistance, and which need not have been exerted by him at all. How could bodily feelings of whatever sort possibly help to evoke such a conception? The ideal interpretation which the subject of feelings of muscular contractions, kephalic tensions, etc., naturally places upon these experiences, merely as such, is surely just that certain processes or activities are going on in certain bodily areas, and exciting appropriate psychical changes. Why should it be otherwise? The particular feelings which the critic adduces are identical in kind with innumerable other feelings which are admitted to receive from the subject of them just some such simple interpretation as this. There seems no reason to posit an exception in this particular case, save that a preconceived theory demands it. Yet if these feelings do receive from the subject of them a 'normal' interpretation, it seems impossible to understand how they should contribute in the smallest degree to the 'illusion' of unique originative force. The respective 'ideal interpretations' are as disparate as could be.

Section 5. *Recapitulation of General Argument*

Much yet remains to be said before it will be possible to feel any solid justification for inviting the reader's assent to my view upon this thorniest problem of philosophy. But at the stage we have reached it seems well to pause for a moment to recapitulate in outline the main argument of the chapter.

The belief in freedom, in the sense at present roughly designated as the capacity for alternative action, rests ultimately, we saw, not only for the plain man but also for the philosopher, upon the interpretation evoked by a certain feeling or immediate experience. There is (apart, it will be remembered, from the possibility of an ethical argument) no other positive basis for the conviction of freedom. The most significant feeling in this regard is the so-called feeling of 'activity' or 'effort of will.' Everyone knows the type of experience which is denoted by these terms, and it is, I think, undeniable that the 'ideal interpretation' which such experience naturally evokes in the subject is a libertarian one. The Libertarian, I argued, has got to defend the view that this interpretation is really, as it seems to be, compelled by the experience: and he ought also to satisfy the critic that what the interpretation affirms is not inconsistent with well-accredited observation in the sphere of conduct. The Determinist's obligation to investigate the experience of activity is not so immediately obvious. He can make a case of sorts by developing the scientific or philosophic arguments for the 'universal reign of law.' But to rest in this position—to refrain from any attempt to show that the libertarian interpretation of the experience of activity is *not* compelled by the experience—is, apart from other objections, to acquiesce in a possible dualism between the practical and theoretical consciousness which, so long as it remains, must reflect back doubt upon the adequacy of the determinist hypothesis. It is logically imperative upon the Determinist, therefore, if he is to make his case fully cogent, to show that the so-called experience of activity does not really mean what it seems to mean: to show that the supposedly necessary interpretation which it evokes is really a misinterpretation. The condition of his showing this is that he should be able to resolve the experience in question, without remainder, into such a set of elements as clearly do not, reflectively considered, carry with them libertarian implications: and also—and this is necessary if only to confirm the veridical character of his analysis—to make it clear how an experience so constituted does generate the 'libertarian illusion.' In the later Sections of this chapter we have considered some typical attempts to 'explain away' the experience of activity along these lines, and have reached the conclusion that so far at least as these attacks are concerned, the experience must stand.

In the next chapter I shall turn to considerations of a different order. The rebuttal of the *metaphysical* objections to a freedom of the kind which I defend is implicit in the matter of the earlier chapters. Not only, we have seen, is there no metaphysical necessity to believe in a rationally continuous universe. There is actually a metaphysical necessity to deny a rationally continuous universe. But there are a host of further difficulties—some serious, others, I am bound to think, frivolous—commonly alleged. Most of them are psychological in character. In course of dealing with them (as I now propose to do) I shall endeavour to render determinate what has up till now been deliberately left general, the concept of 'will-effort' or 'will-energy.'

CHAPTER V

MORAL FREEDOM (II)

Section 1. Defence against 'Caprice' Criticism.

I WISH to begin this set of defences and explanations by considering what may be called the 'Caprice' criticism. This lethal weapon of assault is in such high favour among Determinists that if (as I believe) our armour is invulnerable against it, it will be desirable to make this clear at the earliest possible opportunity.

The essence of the Caprice criticism can be stated quite shortly and simply. 'The Libertarian alleges,' we are told, 'a type of willing whose peculiarity is that it is not, or not completely, determined by the character of the agent (in relation to his circumstances). But in what sense is an act which does not issue from the character of the agent the agent's *own* act? Surely it cannot be understood as *his* act at all. It must rather be ascribed to the intervention of some external agency. But to be at the mercy of this foreign power, to have a "freedom" in which we have no possibility of knowing what act will issue from us next, is not to have freedom at all. It is to be in the direst bondage. It substitutes for control exercised by the self's own inherent nature, control exercised *ab extra*. This is the extremest form of slavery. And so far from validating moral responsibility—the professed aim of the Libertarian's misguided efforts—it clearly destroys the notion of responsibility altogether. For how can the self be held accountable for that which, *ex hypothesi*, does not issue from its own nature? And finally, apart altogether from its utter inability to serve the cause of morality, the doctrine is manifestly untenable as a statement of psychological fact. Observation of the conduct of persons leaves us unable to doubt that there is a continuity binding together the several acts of each which is quite incompatible with the hypothesis that "at any moment anything may happen."'

Now, though there are many variants of this criticism, all (it seems to me) split upon the same rock. They all depend for their force upon the assumption of a dilemma which does not in fact exist. *Either* you have intelligible continuity of act with character, they urge, *or* you have what, so far as the agent is concerned, is mere 'chance.' Since the Libertarian will not accept intelligible continuity, he must accept mere chance—with all its attendant absurdities. The critic, that is (for this is the basis of the dilemma which he proposes), professes himself totally unable to attach a meaning to the supposition that an act which is not intelligibly continuous with one's character may yet be one's *own* act, determined by the self. Now the proper reply to this is just that the critic *can* attach meaning to the supposition in question: and moreover that he *does* attach meaning to it (whether he is aware of the fact or not) every time that he performs an effortful act of will. For it is impossible to perform such an act without being certain that, in the first place, it is something more than just the natural response to the circumstances of one's character (as so far formed)—since the awareness of effort is at the same time an awareness that the act is against the 'line of least resistance,' which is as much as to say that it just does *not* follow directly from his formed character—and without being equally certain that, in the second place, the act *is* one's own act, determined by one's very self.

In short, the dilemma proposed by the critic is a false dilemma. We are not compelled to think of 'chance' as the sole alternative to complete causal continuity between character and act. We *can* attach a meaning to an act which is not causally continuous with our character and is yet our own act if we look for the meaning in the right place, viz. in the actual experience of willing. I say that this is 'the right place,' not merely because we do in fact find here what we are in search of, but because it is logically the one place where it should be sought. If there *is* in the self the creative activity which is at issue between Libertarianism and Determinism, then the only way in which we *could* apprehend it would be by direct experience. It would be absurd, therefore, if the critic were to treat as ground for suspicion the assertion that the 'meaning' which escapes his dilemma is only to be grasped in direct experience. That is just precisely what is to be expected if the Libertarian doctrine is the true one.

From the same point of view we can reply to the Determinist's oft-repeated criticism that the 'free act' of the Libertarian is essentially 'unintelligible.' Of course it is unintelligible if 'intelligible' means capable of being planted in a continuous causal sequence. The act would not be 'free' if it were intelligible in this sense, and therefore to demand 'intelligibility' here is simply to presuppose that the Libertarian's case is wrong. But, equally of course, it is not unintelligible if 'intelligible' means capable of being significantly appreciated. The critic himself can enjoy significant appreciation of it if only he will emancipate himself for a moment from metaphysical prepossessions and permit an unclouded imagination to reproduce a single effortful act of will.

Section 2. Defence against Charge of Ignoring the Observable Continuity of Conduct and Character

These last few pages have been concerned rather to show that we can attach a meaning to an act that is self-determined but not issuing causally from the agent's character than to defend the *existence* of such acts. It may still be said that although direct experience gives us the notion of such acts, it is a mistaken notion; since, to mention one important reason, it conflicts with the observed facts of continuity between character and conduct. This criticism would certainly hold good, as we have already admitted, of a freedom in which 'anything may happen,' such as the freedom of mere chance or caprice that is rightly castigated. But the freedom alleged on the basis of self-activity is not a freedom in which 'anything may happen.' If we consider now what exactly is claimed for 'effort of will' we shall see, I think, that although absolutely hostile to *complete* continuity of character and conduct, it is not incompatible with the substantial *degree* of continuity which is all that the observed facts can justify us in inferring.

There are two main points to be observed in this connection. In the first place, the function claimed for effort of will is that by it we can reinforce a weaker but higher desire against a stronger but lower desire, bringing about thereby action in the line of the former. It is only in relation to an end already desired—although felt as desired with insufficient strength in relation to its value on the one hand, and to opposing desires on the other—that effort of will is held to operate. But this at once limits the field of the 'possibilities' in the way of action which belong to a freedom of the type defended. Action, although free, will be limited to those courses of action which the interests, guided by the intelligence, of the agent suggest to him as possible modes of self-satisfaction. Freedom exists only within this prescribed area. Thus it is just as inconsistent with our view of freedom as it is with the observed facts to suppose that an act can take place which is void of all continuity with the conative tendencies of the agent. The continuity admitted will, it is true, justify prediction of conduct only of a very general order. But it will justify that. Knowing within broad limits what kind of interests a person has, we are entitled to predict, within broad limits, what kind of response he will make to a practical stimulus. We may predict, for example, that the typical Philistine will not respond to a sudden access of wealth by endowing a Chair of Fine Art.

That is the first point. The second is no less important. Taking our guidance, as before, from the experience of effortful willing itself, we are aware that there is a gradation of situations from those in which only a slight and relatively easy effort of will is required to reinforce successfully the higher but weaker desire, through those in which greater and more difficult effort is required, up to those in which we feel that the effort required is so tremendous as to be well-nigh impossible. Now this gradation is determined by the ascending degrees of strength of the tendencies felt as opposing the weaker, higher desire. So that what we are recognising here, from the point of view of the freedom-claiming act itself, is that it is far more difficult for an agent to achieve the higher end, where it conflicts with tendencies that have become strongly entrenched in his nature. Thus where, for example, the powerful forces of a deeply engrained habit are opposed to the right course, we shall not expect the agent to follow that course. He *may*, we believe, but he will be a 'moral hero' if he does; and since we know that most men are not moral heroes, we realise that the probabilities are all against it. In this way approximate prediction is once more possible, even from the standpoint of freedom. The Libertarian is not compelled by his theory to ignore the enslaving chains of 'bad habits.' He will differ from the Determinist in his attitude to what look like notable discrepancies between formed character and conduct only in that while for him they are *unlikely*, for the Determinist they are *impossible*. He, like the Determinist, will be ready to explore more closely the inner recesses of the agent's personality with the expectation of finding that the discrepancy is at least less acute than appeared on the surface.

When these two considerations are duly weighed, the criticism that Libertarianism involves a rupture of continuity between character and conduct must, at least so far as it relates to our version of Libertariansim, be greatly modified. It must be so modified that it becomes no more than an allegation of

MORAL FREEDOM 165

what every unsophisticated person actually believes of himself, viz. that he is able to overcome the bias of his formed tendencies, but that this is more and more difficult for him the more powerful are the tendencies, and the more remote from their direction is the higher course in whose interest he feels it right to subordinate them. This is not a rupture of continuity which can legitimately be complained of on the score of incompatibility with the facts of observation. The facts of observation do not oblige us to assume a whit more continuity than this theory allows, although they do, I think, oblige us to assume as much. It is true that, so far as observation is concerned, we *can* adopt as an hypothesis the view that there is complete continuity, and that apparent 'breaks' would disappear for a fuller knowledge of the relevant facts. But the evidence of observation does not *compel* this hypothesis, and since the evidence of inner experience directly denies it, I see no good reason for supposing it to be true.

Section 3. Defence against Charge of Miracle-mongering

The next variety of criticism to which I wish to allude is one upon which, at the stage now reached in our argument, there is no need to dwell at length. It is a constant reproach against the Libertarian that he lives in an atmosphere of mystery, invoking incomprehensible and miraculous agencies. It may almost be said that no criticism of 'free will' is complete without its little joke against the 'mysteries' and 'miracles' in which the conception is supposed to be enveloped.

What is the assumption underlying this reproach, and needful to give the reproach the force of a criticism? It is, I suppose, that 'miracles' (meaning by that events which defy the laws of intelligible continuity) cannot happen, since the universe is intelligibly continuous throughout. That the universe is intelligibly continuous is, however, an hypothesis at best—and, if I am right, a false hypothesis. Only the critic who takes it as irrefragable dogma is entitled on his premises to consider as *a priori* absurd the conception of an agency of a 'miraculous' character. And I think I am not mistaken in crediting to many of the 'miracle' critics metaphysical views of a very much more tentative character.

Free will *is* mysterious, *is* a miracle in the sense just alluded to. No attempt should be made by the Libertarian to disguise this aspect of it. But it is perhaps worth while reminding ourselves that it is certainly not 'mysterious' in the sense of being a mere inexplicable 'bolt from the blue,' something that 'comes from nowhere.' So far is this from being so, that there is a true sense in which there is absolutely *nothing* of whose ultimate source we have such certain knowledge as we have of this creation of which we know our self to be the creator.

This is really all that it seems necessary to say on the objections to free will on the score of its mysteriousness. Truth to tell, many of these objections seem to the present writer fairly to deserve the adjective 'cheap.' The critic makes capital out of the fact that philosophy is an affair of the 'reason,' and plumes himself upon the inexorable logic which saves him from falling a victim to this 'illusion' of an occult force whose operations cannot be understood by the intellect. It does not occur to him that perhaps it would be much more mysterious if the self which knows *were* capable of being understood after the same manner as the objects which it knows. Much less does he suspect that this very 'reason' which he extols may possibly, if duly interrogated, drive us to the conclusion that reality is 'beyond reason.' These are not matters for crude and hasty dogma, but for the cautious, critical, respectful consideration which the great figures in the history of philosophy have, almost without exception, vouchsafed to them. But our 'scientific' Determinist, blinded by his idolatry of a 'reason' which he has never analysed, smiles in contempt at the very mention of 'mysteries,' and (though, it is fair to add, only half-conscious of the implications of what he is doing) calmly extrudes from the realm even of possibilities that creative

MORAL FREEDOM 167

self-activity which is an absolutely indispensable condition of the worthwhileness of human existence.

Section 4. The Privacy of Will-power. Answers to Objections

We pass on now to consider a new set of criticisms of considerably greater interest. They necessitate, however, some few words of introduction.

I have not disguised my conviction that the capacity for putting forth will-effort or will-energy is, whether ultimately defensible or not, a quite necessary condition of 'moral responsibility.' A person cannot be held morally accountable for anything save in so far as he is the real or ultimate cause of it. Now if we disallow this capacity to put forth will-effort, there seems no sense in which man can be said to be the ultimate cause of his acts. The capacity for will-effort is that which makes possible action against the line of least resistance, action in the line of a felt weaker (but believed higher) desire. If there were no such capacity for reinforcing a higher but weaker desire against a lower but stronger desire, all action would of necessity follow the bias of the agent's existing conative tendencies. We should thus be saddled with a psychological determinism, which seems to leave no room for moral responsibility. And, since the 'conative tendencies' here are just the consequences of 'nature + nurture,' and since the 'nature' in question is just as much 'given' to the agent, though in a different way, as is his 'nurture,' there can be no question of the agent ever being an ultimate cause of anything. Granted, however, the conscious capacity to put forth will-energy in the service of the weaker but higher desire, the self *can* be regarded as an ultimate cause. He is certainly never the *total* cause. But wherever there is the recognised contrast between weaker but higher desire and stronger but lower desire, it will depend upon *him here and now* whether, or how far, the moral effort is made, and what 'act' therefore takes place. In this, as I think perfectly intelligible, sense the self can, on the hypothesis of the capacity for will-effort, be viewed as an 'ultimate cause.' He will, quite justly, be held 'responsible' for this act, since it did rest with him here and now which act he performed.[1] Ultimately moral responsibility is just responsibility for the use which we make of our capacity for will-effort. We can, strictly speaking, be 'accountable' for nothing else but this, for nothing else but this is wholly within our own power.

But *is* will-energy something that is indefeasibly the self's own? Is it something for whose expenditure the self is solely and absolutely responsible? It is here that the critic will join issue with us, even the critic who may be sympathetically disposed to the general notion of 'effort of will.' He will tell us that such a theory cannot be reconciled with the known facts. For is it not a known fact, for example, that some persons are endowed by nature with less 'will-power' than others? They are born with weak wills (just as some other persons are born with strong wills) and are inherently incapable of putting up a stout resistance to 'temptation.' And if this apparent fact of diverse natural endowment is accepted, the self is *not* wholly accountable for the degree of will-energy which it exerts.

Or, again, is it not a 'known fact' (it may be asked) that the capacity for energising is decisively modifiable by external conditions also? What, for example, of the captive who is slowly starved into betrayal of a secret? Is this not a matter of failing will-power, brought about by specific physical conditions? But if this is so, the capacity for energising is not indefeasibly the self's own, and you will have to look elsewhere

---

[1] This statement is not to be understood as denying that circumstances beyond the agent's control (*e.g.* the relative power of his congenital tendencies) have much indirect influence upon the act—determining in large measure the ease or difficulty of 'rising to duty.' Considerations of this nature will rightly be taken into account in assigning praise and blame, even though the self in volition is, in the sense above indicated, the 'ultimate cause' of its act. In Chapter VII. my position in this matter will be fully expounded.

than to 'will-energy' in your search for something for which the self is solely accountable.

These criticisms are certainly very serious, if they can be sustained. And they do rest upon 'facts' frequently supposed to be beyond dispute. I think, however, that if we look closer we shall see that the supposed 'facts'—native diversity of will-power, and external modifiability of will-power—are really misinterpretations of certain observed phenomena.

Let me try to make this out first of all with regard to the supposed fact that men are endowed by nature with different degrees of will-power.

What is the evidence for this alleged diversity? Presumably it is not the (undeniable) fact that some men actually do exert less will-energy than others. That fact allows no inference to a diverse *capacity* for expenditure. Wide variation is, indeed, just what we should naturally expect to find. In the case of one's own experience, one is conscious of very different levels of achievement at different times, but one never dreams of supposing this diversity to be incompatible with an identical *capacity* throughout. The point, however, is too obvious to labour. There must be solider grounds than this for a view so commonly accepted. And I do not think we shall be far astray if we find these grounds in the phenomena of 'congenital dispositions,' the consideration of which may very easily provoke an erroneous inference as to the nature of will-power.

To see this, let us take as an example two men A and B, of whom A is afflicted with a strong inherited disposition to alcohol, while B is in this respect an average being. Very likely we find A yielding to an extravagant craving for alcohol, even although he may be acutely aware that thereby he is heading towards the destruction of all that he most deeply values. Now we are apt to say, in such cases, that A 'seems to have no will-power, where alcohol is concerned,' and to contrast him in this respect with B, who keeps under control a normal taste for this particular stimulant. But, if we look closer, we find that the facts do not warrant the inference that A has less will-power than B in respect of this object of desire, nor even the inference that A is less active than B in the actual exertion of will-energy. For we have to remember that A's alcoholic bias being much stronger, a much greater effort of will is required of A than of B to keep these tendencies within 'respectable' bounds. For this reason A will be less likely than B to achieve an externally satisfactory result, even on the hypothesis that their respective will-capacities are identical. Accordingly there is no need to interpret the appearances, which do admittedly force upon us the conclusion that A is much more likely than B to become a drunkard, as meaning that A has 'less will-power' than B, even with respect to alcoholic indulgence. The 'likelihood' in question obtains, not because A has less will-power than B, but because he has a much stronger resistance to overcome.

The case is really precisely analogous to that of strong *acquired* propensities of a bad kind. Here, too, the onlooker is apt to say (as, *e.g.*, of the confirmed drug-taker) that the agent 'has no will-power left'; the only difference in the two cases being that the defect of will in the second case is believed to be an acquired defect, not congenital, and therefore one for which the agent must accept a certain responsibility. But the mistake in interpretation is the same. The agent (as he himself well knows) retains his capacity for energising, but (as he also knows only too well) the same effort that would once have achieved total abstention now achieves only a relatively insignificant mitigation of the full demands of his craving. External results, it is important to bear in mind, are no clue at all to the effort of will expended, save where we know the relative power of the competing tendencies.

Now exactly the same principle is, I think, sufficient to dispose of the second form of the criticism, that which rests upon the appearance of 'external modifiability,' of will-capacity. It does not follow that because it is possible to starve or torture a man into submission, that starvation or torture, or any analogous external influence, have the effect of weakening the agent's will-power. What happens is not that the will-power is weakening, but that the forces to be overcome are progressively strengthened, so that an ever-greater effort is required to maintain the same external result—*e.g.* refusal to betray a secret. This, I submit, is the natural interpretation of the phenomena in question, and its accuracy can readily be confirmed by the interrogation of our experience. The case of the growing consolidation of a bad habit brings out the crucial point clearly enough. We sometimes speak as if with the process of consolidation the will was becoming progressively weaker. But it is surely evident that we do not mean by that that we are less and less able to put forth effort. On the contrary, the extreme demands which the increasingly 'difficult' situation comes to make upon our will may be the occasion of our putting forth what we feel to be a greater effort than we have ever made before. All that we should mean when we speak of the will 'becoming weaker' in these cases is that the same amount of effort or will-energy is progressively less effective in bringing about the external result that is aimed at.

I think, then, that the facts upon which these criticisms are based do not, when closely inspected, really jeopardise the doctrine that the individual self is solely responsible for the degree of will-energy expended, both in specific situations and throughout life as a whole. There are other forms which the criticisms might take. The most impressive, I think, would be that based upon the phenomena of what is called 'moral education,' which, like the phenomena previously considered, do suggest *prima facie* a dependence of will-energy upon factors not under the self's complete control. I shall touch upon this topic when we come to deal in a later chapter with the criterion of morality, but I think it will be plain that no new difficulty of principle is involved. So far as we have gone at present, I venture to assert that nothing has appeared to show that the doctrine I defend is in conflict with the findings of a sound psychology.

Section 5. *Summary of Doctrine regarding Will-energy, with some further Observations*

But before passing on to new matter it will perhaps be helpful if I bring together into a sequence of propositions the main points that have emerged, either directly or by implication, with regard to the notion of will-effort or will-energy: adding one or two further observations on points of interest in order that no dubiety may remain as to what it is that I hold to be true of the nature, range, and function of this fundamental reality.

I am prepared, then, to stand by the following propositions.

(1) Will-energy is made known to us in direct experience, and in no other way. Only by actually or imaginatively 'living through' the kind of situation in which it functions can we hope to appreciate its character.

(2) If we do 'live it through,' one thing that we find it means for us is that in that situation we could have acted otherwise. That conviction is spontaneously evoked by the experience as part of its ideal significance. We are certain that we need not have made the effort, could have made a lesser effort, or, if the situation was such as to require it, could have made a greater effort—with corresponding differences in the act in each case.

(3) The onus of proof lies upon those who deny that this experience, variously referred to as experience of 'activity,' 'effort,' or 'energy' of will, really means what it is naturally taken by the subject of it to mean. But the actual attempts to resolve the experience into a complex of elements which do not justify the unsophisticated interpretation, which show it to be in fact an avoidable misinterpretation, carry no conviction.

(4) There is no good reason for supposing that the native *capacity* for energising varies between persons.

(5) There is no good reason for supposing that the capacity for energising can be either increased or diminished by external agencies.

(6) The function of will-energy is, in any particular case, to reinforce a desire recognised as weaker but higher, against a desire recognised as stronger but lower; or, taking it in its general significance, to make it possible for the agent to rise in the direction of his ideal above the level of conduct which the actual 'set' of his desires would *per se* determine. It is inherent in the nature of a rational being (we must content ourselves here with a dogmatic statement, which will be justified in the ensuing chapters) to have present to it the concept of an obligatory ideal of conduct, which frequently contrasts more or less sharply, according to circumstances, with the conduct which it is felt would be the direct expression of the agent's existing conative disposition. Where this contrast is present, action towards the ideal is felt to be possible only through 'effort' of will, a type of action which the agent opposes abruptly to that seemingly 'effortless' action which obtains if he merely follows out the bias of his desires. The 'prospective' consciousness of required effort is, I think, a constant concomitant of the presented contrast of ideal with desire. And, on the other hand, *save* when there is this presented contrast, in some form, of ideal with desire, there is no consciousness of effort required, nor is any effort put forth. Naturally, the 'moral ideal' of the agent need not be present in its full-fledged character. It is enough, for the eliciting of the consciousness of effort required, that there should be an apprehended 'higher against lower'—action *more*, against action *less*, in the direction of the ideal—and that the existing conative tendencies should be felt as 'set' towards the lower. But save in relation to this contrast, effort of will has no *raison d'être*, and never in fact takes place.

There is one set of cases, indeed, which seems at first sight to conflict with the doctrine that effort of will can function only in repressing a recognised 'lower.' Sometimes we deliberately set ourselves to act against a strong conative disposition, not because we morally disapprove it, but because we wish to 'test' our will-power, or because (influenced by what is, I think, a mistaken psychological doctrine) we imagine that by practising 'doing what we don't like' we can improve our general will-power or will-capacity. Will-effort may undoubtedly here be produced. And it does not *seem* to be reinforcing a 'recognised higher' against a 'recognised lower.' But I think we can see, if we look closely, that it really is doing so. *Prior* to our proposing to ourselves this experiment, the conative disposition, let us say the 'tobacco habit,' is not disapproved, not recognised as a 'lower.' But *after* we have taken the decision, the situation is altered. From the new standpoint, that of the desire to strengthen our will-power by practising in a specific situation, the refraining from tobacco becomes a 'higher' by contrast with 'indulgence.' The effort that we make—if we make it, for the decision may have been made in advance of the incidence of the temptation—is thus still against something recognised as lower *in that specific situation*. The present case, therefore, does not seem to be a genuine exception to the principle maintained.

(7) Finally—this is a point we have not yet touched upon—it may be asked whether there is a limit to the degree of will-energy which it is possible for a man to put forth; whether, to put a practical case, there may not be situations in which the resistance offered to the 'ought' by the lower tendencies is so strong that there is literally not sufficient will-energy available to break it down. Now, in spite of 'reasonable expectations,' the grounds for which have been already discussed, that in these 'extreme' cases the resistance will, in fact, prove too great to be overcome, I do not think that there can ever be ground for absolute certainty. It is at least very difficult, when we consider

the experience of effort from the inside, to see how any maximum of possible achievement can be assigned. Just as, in the experience of activity or effort, we are certain that we are introducing an energy which we could have forborne to introduce, or could have introduced in smaller measure, so too, I think, we are certain that (if the situation demanded it) we *could* (whether or not we *would*) have introduced energy in greater measure than we actually do. Is it not true that however great be the effort we make at any time, we can always conceive ourselves making a greater effort still? I think that it is. And if it is, it does not appear that, from the standpoint of the experience itself, there is evidence of a definite 'limit.' Short of pathological cases, I am pretty sure that the victim of the most deeply engrained habit never really believes that even the *immediate* act of complete abstention is impossible. (I say the 'immediate' act, because *ultimate* abstention, following upon a gradual passage through intermediate stages, is, in my opinion, quite obviously possible, and is indeed the normal course of 'regeneration'). He may believe it to be almost indefinitely 'hard,' but he would, I think, utterly decline to accept the word 'impossible.' [1]

Section 6. Reaction of Present Doctrine upon Problem of Finite ' Individuality '

I want to conclude this chapter by indicating very shortly the general way in which the theory of freedom here maintained reacts upon the problem of the kind of individuality which belongs to finite selves. The problem is, of course, difficult and many-sided. No more will be attempted here than to make clear, by contrast with the doctrine of Absolute Idealism, the principle of what seems to me the more satisfactory doctrine which Supra-rationalist premises make possible.

In what sense, if any, can the finite self claim to possess genuine individuality? It is common ground that to be an

[1] On this point see Sidgwick's *Methods of Ethics* (6th ed.), p. 65.

'individual' implies being, in some sense, a self-subsistent, self-maintaining, being. Is there, or is there not, in the finite self a self-subsistence sufficiently real to entitle it to be called in any true sense an 'individual'? That, in brief, is the issue to be considered.

The answer of Absolute Idealism is unambiguous. If the universe is indeed rationally continuous, then there can be no true self-subsistence short of the Whole. Finitude and self-subsistence are, for Idealist metaphysics, mutually incompatible. Selves, accordingly, are not individuals in any full sense. The Absolute alone has genuine individuality. Selves possess individuality only (to apply the old principle) in 'degree,' according to the adequacy with which they are able, by harmonious self-expression, to manifest in themselves that character of perfect, all-comprehending unity which belongs to the one real individual, the Absolute.

Now to this doctrine there is a very natural disposition to reply that, if true, it is at least an exceedingly unpalatable truth. If this is the only kind of self-subsistence which man can claim, then it certainly seems as if something of quite paramount value has gone out of human life. Not only does the ordinary man assume as a matter of course that there is a genuine discontinuity between his personality and the surrounding universe, he is also quite convinced that without this element of discontinuity he cannot be supposed to be in any proper or valuable sense the arbiter of his own destiny. Deny this discontinuity, he feels, and the 'adventure of living' loses all its significance and savour.

The Idealist, however, is not at all prepared to agree that his doctrine is destructive of human values. He has his answer ready. In depriving the finite self of that discontinuity which is the basis of its supposed independence, imperviousness, or exclusiveness, we are not, he tells us, really removing anything which man in his best moments deems of vital importance to his individuality. On consideration, do we not see it to be true that the kind of individuality which is most profoundly admired, which we most intensely wish for ourselves, is one not characterised by 'exclusiveness' at all, but by 'organised wholeness of being'? Thus we commonly speak of a man as possessing 'grëat individuality' not when he presents the appearance of being a self-contained and 'repellent' unit, but rather where everything that he says and does is bound together by, and bears the impress of, a single dominating principle of order. 'Unity in difference,' or 'concrete universality,' is the mark of the individuality which is really felt to matter most, not that ontological exclusiveness which, in any case, a sound metaphysics shows to be a barren hope. And so, the Idealist would persuade us, the individuality that is (in its varying degrees) permitted to men to enjoy on the Absolutist metaphysic, is not only all that we *can* have, but all that we most truly *want* to have.

This line of argument has often been developed with much subtlety and eloquence, as, for example, by Bosanquet in his Gifford Lectures. Yet I venture to suggest that it is only necessary to keep clearly before our minds one simple but incontrovertible fact, for the whole imposing fabric to crumble to pieces. When people eulogise the individuality of 'organised wholeness of being' they are *not* (as is implied in the argument) decrying as relatively unimportant the individuality which consists in being a genuinely independent centre of activity. On the contrary, they take it for granted that the organised or systematic character to which they pay tribute is achieved by a self *which both was and is individual in the 'exclusive' sense*, by a self which, although finite, is endowed with an independence which makes its progress one through genuinely 'open' possibilities. The assumption that this kind of individuality persists throughout is the very condition of the recognition of any value in 'organised wholeness of being.' Banish it, as the Idealist would do, to the realm of 'mere mythology,' and the self appears to itself as no better than a spiritual automaton. No amount of 'organised wholeness' will restore by one iota the vanished sense of the worthwhileness of human striving.

For our present purpose it is not necessary to go into the question of what precisely people do mean when they speak, as admittedly they do, of organised wholeness of being as constituting the truly valuable kind of individuality. All that our argument demands is the recognition that what they do *not* mean is to affirm, by implication, that the individuality which consists in being a single independent centre of activity is worthless or insignificant. There is no thought in their minds of *contrasting* the value of 'organised wholeness' with the value of 'finite exclusiveness,' whether to the detriment of the latter or not. On the contrary, the possession of individuality of the latter sort is simply assumed as a matter of course in any ascription of value to individuality of the former sort.

The individuality which the Idealist is prepared to concede to finite persons is then, I submit, no less incapable of satisfying the value postulates of human life than the unsophisticated mind takes it to be. In ruling out, on metaphysical grounds, the possibility of real discontinuity, the Idealist thereby rules out an essential condition of the worthwhileness of finite existence. His doctrine may be true—degrees of organised wholeness *may* represent the only kind of self-subsistence to which finite beings can aspire—but we should not permit ourselves to be deluded into supposing that it is also pleasant.

But *is* his doctrine true? Must we say that although this kind of individuality is certainly not all that man wants, it is yet all that he can have? Or is it perhaps possible to assign to finite persons a self-subsistence of a more significant character? It is at this point, as it seems to me, that the doctrine of freedom which has been expounded in this and the preceding chapter shows itself indispensable as the support of a genuine individuality in finite beings. Through it we can vindicate a real self-subsistence in finite selves in despite

MORAL FREEDOM 179

of their finitude. For, if I have been right, the self is wholly and absolutely 'self-subsistent' in one definite respect, namely, in so far as concerns the expenditure of will-energy in moral situations. In this respect the control lies solely within the private and exclusive self. As has been sufficiently pointed out, I admit without question the dependence of the finite self upon circumstances and agencies beyond its control for the actual range of possible courses of action which are presented to it in practice, and again for the relative strength of the competing tendencies—a consideration of the first importance when it is the external achievement, the visible success, of the act which is under review. But these are admissions which are entirely compatible with the plain man's reading of his own powers, and are rightly believed by him not seriously to jeopardise the value of his independent individuality. If only there can be retained for man the power of self-direction which is here defended, the significance of personal strivings will be preserved, and moral judgments (a mockery for Absolute Idealism only less obviously than for crass Materialism) in principle vindicated.

Section 7. Note on Bradley's Criticism of the 'Reality' of the Finite Self

One last point. The discussion of the last two chapters has made it possible for me to set forth in a very few words my position with regard to the kind of criticism which has been levelled by Bradley against the 'reality' of the finite self (as, for example, in the well-known chapters on the self in *Appearance and Reality*).

The nerve of Bradley's argument is as follows. The test of the ultimately real is self-consistency. To nothing that fails to possess this character can we assign reality in the full metaphysical sense of the term. Now whatever by its very nature points beyond itself for the understanding of itself is assuredly not self-consistent. But this is so of the concept of finite self-hood. View the self as you may, in whatever aspect or from whatever angle, always you find in the self a necessary reference to something beyond itself which forbids us to find in it the principle of the ultimately real. You may, indeed, in your endeavour to discover the self as an unbroken unity, and thus an adequate principle, descend below the level of relational consciousness altogether to a state of mere feeling. But if you do, you are not dealing with a 'self' at all, but with an experience prior to the very emergence of the distinction of self from not-self. If, on the other hand, you accept the relational level, at which alone self-hood proper can exist, the relation to something not-itself is inexpugnable. Hence the attempt to save the ultimate reality of self-hood is in the end no more successful than the attempt to save the reality of the less dignified concepts which Bradley's dialectic has already traversed. The finite self is, in a word, like everything else save the Absolute, 'appearance' and not 'reality.'

Now with the substance of this argument I am in the fullest agreement. We cannot ascribe ultimate reality to the finite self, and Bradley has, in my view, furnished a sufficient demonstration of this. The immediate sub-relational unity of feeling is not a 'self,' and the self as it exists at the relational level is not a true unity in difference (and thus not ultimately real). But this result does not wear quite the same forbidding significance when it is considered in relation, on the one hand, to what was said (in Chapter III.) on 'final phenomenal truths,' and, on the other hand, to what has more recently been argued as to the directness of our perception of self-activity. Although it is true that we do not have in the self 'ultimate reality' in the full sense, it may also be true that we do have in the self as ultimate a reality as finite mind can hope to apprehend. As we saw earlier, there are certain matters which finite mind just has to accept as final for it, 'human ultimates,' datal or intellectually incorrigible facts, which do not, indeed, satisfy thought's demand for self-explanatory unity in difference, but which yet no conceivable advance in knowledge can either overturn or modify. Of such a character, I submit, is our apprehension of our 'self' in so far as pertains to its nature as an active centre of experience. 'Self-knowledge,' in the ordinary and fuller sense of the term, rests, of course, upon a multitude of mediate processes, and is conditioned by the progress of our cognitive contacts with our social and natural environment. And because this kind of self-knowledge is mediate, and in consequence liable to an indefinite amount of revision as the system which inspires the connections expands, the 'self' which is apprehended in this self-knowledge can never be accepted as an ultimate reality even of the phenomenal order. It is quite otherwise, however, with the self-knowledge which pertains to the self only in its formal character as an active centre of experience. This knowledge (if I have been right) is not achieved through mediate processes, but given in direct or immediate awareness. And because this kind of self-knowledge is thus immediate, and in consequence free from the conditions which impose the necessity of subsequent modification, the 'self' which is apprehended in this self-knowledge can, indeed must, be accepted as an ultimate (phenomenal) reality. Thus while we may reasonably doubt the 'reality' of the self of our self-knowledge in respect of any feature whatsoever of its apprehended concreteness, of its 'reality' simply in respect of its character as an active centre there can be no significant doubt.[1] In this character of itself the finite self can be absolutely assured of its own ultimate (phenomenal) reality. And bare and formal though this character certainly is, it is, after all, the character of central significance in self-hood, the character which we are chiefly

[1] I am not suggesting, of course, that we can apprehend bare 'activity' in and by itself. What we apprehend is always a determinate self 'active' in a determinate objective situation. But since the character of activity as apprehended remains precisely identical *whatever* be the apprehended natures of the determinate self and the determinate situation, the abstraction of the 'perception of activity' from the total experience is a valid, and not a vicious, abstraction.

concerned to justify when we contend for the reality of our finite 'self.' Even if our assured knowledge of our self's reality extends no further than this, our knowledge will yet be very far from trivial.

It is necessary to emphasise, however, that this 'ultimate reality' which we can ascribe to our self *qua* active centre belongs only to the phenomenal level. We cannot, in the end, ignore the fact that the self *qua* active centre stands in essential relationship with the self *qua* possessed of concrete characteristics, and in equally essential relationship with a determinate objective situation, and that these relationships are, for mind, merely *de facto*. There can be no question of our having arrived, in the apprehension of the self *qua* active centre, at an 'intellectually satisfying' object, and therefore a 'noumenal' reality. We have arrived only at an 'intellectually incorrigible' object—one which, because not mediately known, can suffer no modification from advancing experience. There still remain essentially askable, though by finite mind essentially unanswerable, questions as to the cosmic significance of that which we apprehend as our 'activity.' And in the absence of answers we cannot ascribe noumenal status to our object. It is, without doubt, a paradoxical situation that the finite mind should thus be able to regard as inadequate pronouncements which it yet sees to be final for itself. But it is a paradox bound up with the essential paradox of man himself, as a creature who partakes at once of finitude and infinitude. In as much as he is finitely conditioned, man is forever precluded from the vision of things *sub specie universi*: but in as much as he is conscious of his own finitude (and so far infinite), he must forever recognise the deficiencies of his limited vision, and must refuse the title of 'noumenal reality' to the objects even of his most assured insight.

To sum up. There is a significant sense in which we can legitimately hold our finite self to be an ultimate reality. It is only a 'phenomenal' ultimate. But when once we have succeeded in re-orienting our mental attitude in the way demanded by subscription to the doctrine that the ultimately real in the full sense is in principle inaccessible to human reason, and have come to recognise accordingly that we as finite beings must look for *our* ultimate realities not in *the* ultimate reality but in whatsoever by the conditions of our nature we are obliged to accept as final for us, the denial of validity to the self's indefeasible certitude of its own 'reality' will be seen to hold good, I think, only in a sense in which it is very nearly unimportant.

CHAPTER VI

THE REALITY OF MORAL OBLIGATION

Section 1. Absolute Idealism and the Status of Morality

IN the last two chapters I endeavoured to establish the validity of the belief in 'freedom,' in that common-sense interpretation of it which postulates genuinely 'open possibilities' for the human will: and thereby—since freedom thus conceived is incompatible with a Reality 'intelligible throughout'—to offer indirect confirmation of the hypothesis of the 'supra-rational' Reality. In this chapter I shall attempt to follow a like course in the case of morality. I shall argue that there is equally good reason to regard the recognition of moral obligation or 'ought-ness' as a fundamental and untranscendible characteristic of human experience: and that since belief in the moral ought has implications incompatible with belief in Reality as intelligible throughout, we have here further confirmation of the 'supra-rational' hypothesis.

The incompatibility of the 'intelligible Reality' of Absolute Idealism with the moral point of view is a matter to which I have already adverted, in considering the relation of the Idealist doctrine of freedom to the problem of moral responsibility. But Idealists as a body are so extremely averse from admitting this implication of their general position that it will perhaps be well to devote a further few pages to the effort to drive the point home.

Let us remind ourselves, then, of the very elementary, but by no means therefore negligible, difficulties which the Idealist has to face in dealing with morality.

The crucial concept of morality is the 'ought.' This I hold to be indisputable. It is not enough for moral appraisement merely to be able to say that a person would be 'better' if he acted in such and such a way. We must be able to say that he *ought* to act in this way, and is the legitimate object of our censure if he doesn't. The whole vocabulary of morals in common usage implies the centrality of the idea of 'duty' or the 'ought.' Cut away this conception, and the very bottom falls out of what ordinary men mean by morality.

But the meaning of the moral ought is destroyed on the Idealist philosophy. No one can possibly attach meaning to the idea of 'ought,' either with reference to his own acts, or to those of other persons, if he believes that finite spirits are but channels through which the Absolute Spirit pours forth its being. If I believe that I 'ought' to do so and so, I must believe that it is in my power *either* to do *or* to forbear. And if, actually, I forbear to do it, my subsequent moral censure of myself gets all its point from my conviction that I could have done what I did not do. In short, the freedom of genuinely open possibilities is presupposed in the conception of moral obligation, and any philosophy which repudiates that freedom as a fiction, as Absolute Idealism must do, cannot by any verbal or intellectual legerdemain rebut the accusation that it has thereby made morality meaningless.

It is not to be denied, of course, that the word 'ought' may still have a meaning of some kind in a Determinist philosophy. But it is not a *moral* meaning. There will still be point in saying that the background of this picture 'ought' to be darker, and so on. Wherever you have in view a standard of propriety or perfection, the word 'ought' can fittingly be used with respect to conformity. But you obviously cannot, if you are a Determinist, mean that non-conformity to the standard is blameworthy; and that implication is inherent in the 'moral' ought. The distinction is quite clear, and it finds an interesting illustration in Bentham's well-known dictum that 'the word "ought" ought to be expunged from the vocabulary of morals.'

There is no doubt, however, of the extreme reluctance of the Idealist to confess his bankruptcy as a trustee of the moral values. We have already had occasion to observe the tenacity with which Bosanquet clings to the concept of moral responsibility, even while he is compelled, almost in so many words, to repudiate it. A similar alternation of thought may be detected in his treatment of that other ethical crux of Idealism, the nature of moral evil or the 'bad self.' What Bosanquet ought to say, as a consistent Monistic Idealist, is that the bad will is one in type with the good will, differing only in degree. And this is the view which he does perhaps most uniformly urge. But what he wants to say, as a man to whom it is as repellent as to anyone else to suppose vice to be other than the thing it is, is that good and evil are as vitally opposed in principle as white and black. And this, when the pall of metaphysic does not hang too heavily upon him, he permits himself to say too. It will be instructive, I think, to consider this conflict in Bosanquet's thought in some detail, for it illustrates excellently the kind of difficulty with which the Idealist is faced in his effort to be true at once to his metaphysical principles, and to the moral experience which he shares in common with his fellows.

The relevant passages occur for the most part in the chapter on 'Good and Evil' in *The Value and Destiny of the Individual*. In the course of that chapter Bosanquet gives us an analysis of the bad will which seems definitely to imply its ultimate antagonism of principle to the good will—an account, indeed, with which I, for my part, find myself in almost verbal agreement. But before many pages have passed the need emerges of exhibiting the place of moral evil in the Idealist Absolute, and Bosanquet, completely in the thrall of his false metaphysic, jettisons the antagonism to which the moral consciousness (and his own earlier argument) testifies, and makes moral evil identical in structure with moral good.

To take the earlier position first. The essential point which it is sought to bring out is that while there is a contradictory element present in all willing (since all willing, good and bad, implies the effort to realise 'self' through the inclusion of an obstructive 'not-self'), the bad will has as its distinctive feature the attempt to realise self not merely against a contradiction but 'in and as a contradiction.' Each self naturally builds up, in Bosanquet's view, out of the material furnished by its diverse interests, its own ideal of the best life, a 'relative world of perfection,'[1] comprising the system of activities regarded as best calculated to promote harmonious experience. Against this ideal there stand in sharp contrast for the self such divergent activities as are recognised to be (however attractive *per se*) inimical to harmony, to the satisfaction of self *as a whole*. When the self identifies itself in will with the former type of end, its will is, so far, 'good'; when with the latter type, 'bad.' The essence of the good will is thus the attempt to realise oneself (against a contradictory element) in the direction of recognised harmony of being. The essence of the bad will is the attempt to realise oneself (against a contradictory element) in the direction of recognised discord. The latter is, as Bosanquet in forthright terms here expresses it, 'interested to realise itself in and as a contradiction.'[2] Or, again (and the opposition of principle between good and bad could hardly be more starkly defined), 'the point of the content [of the bad will] is not in any whole which it subserves, but in hostility to the identification of the self with such a whole.'[3]

This doctrine seems to me to be fundamentally sound; although naturally a much ampler development would be demanded in any systematic exposition of it. But the present

---
[1] *Value and Destiny of the Individual*, p. 206.
[2] *Ibid.*, p. 207.
[3] *Ibid.*, p. 209.

point is that we do surely get in it perfectly clearly the admission of a radical antagonism between good and bad willing. The good will is the willing of an end recognised as conducive to harmonious being, and the bad will is the willing of an end recognised as opposed to this harmony. The good will is a manifestation of the 'nisus towards totality.' The whole point of the bad will is that it is *not*.

Thus, if this were the whole story, we might well wonder what such a doctrine is doing in the pages of an Absolute Idealist. How is it possible to maintain *both* that Reality is a single systematic whole animated by the 'spirit of non-contradiction' (to use one of Bosanquet's own expressions), *and* that certain manifestations of that Whole have as their special characteristic the direct opposition to the 'spirit of non-contradiction'? It certainly seems as if one of these doctrines must go. Either the doctrine of the Rational Absolute, or the doctrine above offered of the bad will, is a false doctrine. And Bosanquet does in fact, as I have already indicated, supply us almost immediately with a virtual recantation of the latter.

At this next stage the distinction between good and evil is expressly declared to be parallel to the distinction between truth and error. And we know what Bosanquet makes of the latter distinction. In the present chapter he sums it up thus: 'Error differs from truth simply in systematic distinction and completeness. Its character of falsity is a matter of degree, normally reducible to exaggerated emphasis on some one element in a whole.'[1] The difference is simply one of degree. And so it is, we now find, with the difference of good from evil. Even earlier in the chapter, indeed, we had been told that good and evil were 'of the same stuff.'[2] But this identity might merely have referred, and from the context seemed merely to refer, to the unfashioned 'raw material' of

---

[1] *Value and Destiny of the Individual*, p. 214. [2] *Ibid.*, p. 205.

REALITY OF MORAL OBLIGATION 189

willing. Good and bad willing do draw from a common storehouse. Now, however, it becomes evident that the identity is affirmed not merely of the raw material, but of the finished product also, the spiritual act of willing. The defect of the bad will turns out to be, not that it repudiates the end of self-completion, but that, seizing on a false clue, it aims at self-completion where self-completion is not to be found. It differs from the good will merely in the less adequate character of the content in which self-completion is sought. Far from there being any mortal antagonism between them, there is, we are informed, 'room in good for the character of all evil, redistributed and resystematised.'[1] Or, again, 'there is nothing in evil which cannot be absorbed in good and contributory to it.'[2]

What, then, we may ask, becomes of the thesis expounded but a few pages back, that the bad self 'is interested to realise itself in and as a contradiction?' Bosanquet seems dimly to realise that what he is now saying clashes with that thesis, and in a highly significant passage he suggests that we may perhaps have to return to the Socratic doctrine that 'no one sins voluntarily.' We may have to agree, he tells us, that 'in the moment of evil volition the inherent contradiction is blunted, and the system willed and recognised as good . . . is modified by self-deception so as apparently to accept for the moment the evil attitude.'[3] In other words, we 'may have to agree' that the earlier doctrine of the essence of the bad will was just a mistake.

This later position represents, I think, Bosanquet's real or dominant attitude. There is a passage in the earlier volume of his Gifford Lectures which prepares us for it, and is worth quoting. We find him there eulogising the ethical theory of T. H. Green on the ground that 'it is undoubtedly not easy in this theory to distinguish otherwise than in degree between

---

[1] *Value and Destiny of the Individual*, p. 216.
[2] *Ibid.*, p. 217.   [3] *Ibid.*, p. 216.

moral good and evil. And I believe this to be an indication that its main outline, its metaphysical fabric, is sound.'[1]

But whether or not this is Bosanquet's more considered position, the thing of chief importance is to see that it is the only position logically consistent with the metaphysics of Absolute Idealism. For Idealism the bad will must, like the good will, be 'in the end' a manifestation of Perfection, of 'the principle of individuality and value': and the only way to save this 'in the end' from being a mere phrase, expressive of a blind faith, is to try to show (as Bosanquet here recognises) that the bad will is just as truly, though not as apparently, an instance of the 'nisus towards totality' as the good will. The return to the Socratic moral psychology is for Idealism not so much a matter of 'may' as of 'must.' 'There is nothing in evil,' says Bosanquet, 'which cannot be absorbed in good.' Yes, the obvious answer surely runs, *except the evil will itself*. It is perfectly true that each and all of the component impulses which are the material of the bad will could be conceived, if considered in abstraction from the act itself, as 'absorbed in good.' But the bad will as such, the component elements in the concrete effective unity of the spiritual act, can *not*; unless, accepting the Socratic psychology, we believe that the bad will is really one with the good will in 'direction' as well as in abstract components.

I submit, then, that for Absolute Idealism there can be no significant distinction between moral good and moral evil. And this is the virtual destruction of the category of moral value. I am not saying, so far, that Idealism is in error in thus discrediting the moral point of view. But I do insist that it must discredit it if it is not to play false to its own fundamental principles.

Now on the Supra-rationalist hypothesis there will at least

---

[1] *Principle of Individuality and Value*, p. 242. Observe that in a footnote to his argument Bosanquet roundly identifies himself with the Socratic psychology.

not be this metaphysical necessity of exorcising moral value. But a difficulty of another kind has come into view. If the Socratic theory of willing to which the Idealist makes tentative return is a valid theory on its own account, as it may very well be for all that we have as yet said to the contrary, then our own more 'plastic' metaphysical principles will avail us nothing so far as the defence of morals is concerned. On this moral psychology—or so I at least should agree—morality is but a name. It seems obligatory upon us therefore to pause for a little and make some inquiry into the credentials of this theory which denies the possibility of man 'knowing the better and choosing the worse.'

Section 2. The Socratic Theory of the Will

How, in the first place, does this theory get itself suggested? It is certainly not the natural report of introspective observation. Moreover, the moral judgments in literature and practical life are, in general, based on the assumption of the contrary, as are, of course, society's penal institutions also.[1] It arises, I think, from the adoption of a 'self-realisation' theory of ethics, for which 'better' means 'better for self.' This type of ethical theory is itself dependent upon the psychological doctrine that every deliberate act of choice aims at something conceived to be a 'good' for the agent. For if all willing is thus directed to *a* personal good, it does not seem possible to define the moral ideal, the object of the best will, save in some such terms as *true* personal good. Now when this, or some similar ethical position is arrived at, the phrasing 'knowing the

[1] There are indications that the penal institutions of some future societies may not be based on this assumption. But if they are not, then they will not really be 'penal' institutions. To talk of 'punishing' where you do not admit 'blameworthiness' is just nonsense. Prisons will be quite literally 'Houses of Correction,' and nothing more, under the new assumption. The drift of contemporary opinion in this direction, under the influence of the 'New Psychology,' is, I think, deeply to be deplored. If this book did something to counteract it, I could accept with tranquillity the rejection of almost everything else for which I have argued.

better and choosing the worse' must be interpreted as 'knowing what is better for oneself, a truer personal good, and choosing what is worse for oneself, a less true personal good.' But when the phrase takes this form, there do arise understandable doubts as to whether it can represent any actual psychical reality. Why should a rational being deliberately choose what he knows to be less good for himself? The apparently paradoxical character of such an act suggests the advisability of returning to make a closer examination of the phenomena of choice with a view to discovering whether what appear, *prima facie*, to be 'acts of incontinence' may not be capable of a different construction—one more in accord with what we should expect of a rational being.

Since I for my part accept the substance of the 'self-realisation' psychology, the problem is one which it is not possible here to ignore. Looking at the facts with the initial bias which such a psychology induces, there is no doubt, I think, that there is a strong *prima facie* case for the doctrine of Socrates.

Now what the doctrine has to do to establish itself is, of course, to explain intelligibly how it is that people often believe that they know and approve the better and choose the worse, if in fact they are incapable of such a choice. There is no doubt that the ordinary man imagines, after many of his acts, that a, the course which he rejected, was clearly conceived by him at the moment of choice to be 'better' than b, the course which he adopted. And only on this account does he experience 'remorse.' The Socratic doctrine has to make it plain that he is, in so believing, the victim of self-deception.

One explanation of this self-deception would run as follows. Let us suppose a, the rejected course, to be a component of the agent's standing ideal of the better. It is part of his general habit of mind to think of it as better than b. But that general habit of mind is not formed in response to *all* varieties of concrete practical situations. Actually, in *this* concrete practical situation, the attractiveness of *b* is rendered so peculiarly powerful that at the moment of the choice it supplants *a* as the 'better.' But *after* the act, the agent automatically relapses into his 'general habit of mind' with regard to the relations of *a* and *b*. Considering them, as he does *now*, in abstraction from the vividness of the concrete situation, he is sure that he thinks *a* better than *b*, and supposes that he always thinks *a* better than *b*. And this induces in him the belief that he has acted contrary to what he believed to be best, and brings about in him the emotion of remorse. But the truth is that if he could imaginatively reconstruct the competing alternatives in the concrete setting of the practical situation, he would realise that *b*, with all its attendant details—perhaps, if it is a round of golf, the fineness of the morning, a new brassie to handsel, the availability of a congenial partner, and so on—might well have appeared a greater good to him than *a*. His self-deception arises, in short, from too abstract a consideration of alternatives whose competition was in a highly concrete complex.

In some situations a slight variation of this account would be demanded. There are some occasions—for example when a man gives way to a 'dope' which he knows is rapidly undermining his whole mental, physical, and moral being—with respect to which the agent cannot possibly bring himself to suppose, when he thinks of the act in retrospect, that he could ever have believed *b*, indulgence in the drug, to be better than *a*, abstention from it, *if the alternatives were ever before his mind at all.* The explanation of incontinence in such cases must be sought in 'gusts of passion.' The thought of the drug raises a craving so overwhelming that all else is swept from the mind, and '*a*' simply does not present itself. At the actual moment of choice, then, *a* did not appear as the 'better,' because it did not appear at all.

Making allowance for the simplifications of brevity, these seem to me to be the lines along which the 'illusion' of having acted incontinently may best be explained away. And they have some plausibility, more especially if considered in connection with the general difficulty one feels in understanding how a rational being can deliberately reject what he regards as best for him. I should even be prepared to say that the explanation actually does cover certain cases, that people do on occasion deceive themselves in the manner suggested. But I do not think that it can be stretched to cover all cases. There are some situations in which there really seems no room for the possibility of illusion. And if any cases of indubitable 'incontinence' can be established, and the universality of the psychological principle opposed to it thus impugned, legitimate doubt may be reflected back upon a good many of the cases which the explanation could be abstractly conceived to cover, but did not necessarily cover.

In the first place, it is fairly evident that it is with respect to 'impulsive' conduct, and generally to transient practical decisions rather than to relatively permanent policies, that the follower of Socrates can maintain his case with best hope of success. Yet even in this field there is a good deal to be said on the other side. For it is important to observe that the kind of 'explaining away' which we have illustrated is effective only in regard to acts in which there is not good evidence that the emotion of remorse was present at the actual time of choice. If remorse is present at the time of choice, then it is clear enough that the belief in the 'betterness' of a (keeping to our former symbols) was neither temporarily upset by the attractions of b as appreciated in the concrete situation, nor extruded from the mind by the violence of passion. In either contingency the remorseful colouring of the act would be unintelligible. But surely it is extremely difficult to persuade oneself that instances of this sort do not occur? Is it not plain matter of fact that the enjoyment of 'illicit pleasures' is often poisoned by the sense of wrong-doing that accompanies their indulgence? Such is the common belief, and, for my own part, introspection leaves me in little doubt that the common belief is true.

But when we leave the sphere of momentary choices and pass on to cases where choices remain effective over an appreciable period, the assertion of the possibility of incontinence hardly appears to require such qualified language. It is just barely conceivable that memory deceives us in every single case in which we think that we experienced the emotion of remorse in a momentary choice. It does not seem conceivable at all in respect of cases of continuously effective choice. If a drunkard informs us that he was conscious of remorse while yielding to a sudden temptation to drink a glass of whisky, we can appreciate the possibility that he has 'mis-dated' the emotion, and that it was not really contemporaneous with the choice. But if he informs us—and instances of the kind are far from uncommon—that he was frequently weighed down with remorse during a long evening in the bar-parlour, through the recurring remembrance that it would be far better for him really to be spending the evening soberly at home, there is no room for a lapse of memory *here*. He *did* feel remorse as he sat there. And his feeling of remorse must have rested upon the awareness that it would be better for him not to be sitting there. Why then, if it is a psychological necessity that we always choose what seems best to us at the moment of choice, why then did he make no move to depart, but, even while the remorse was upon him, choose to continue where he was?

I do not know what answer that is even plausible can be given in cases of this kind. After all, there is a limit to the range of 'self-deception' as an explanatory principle. We are all aware that there are many genuine cases of self-deception, *e.g.* in the 'rationalisation' process whereby a person unconsciously sets himself to find good 'moral' reasons for pursuing a course which is in fact dictated by some unworthy passion, and comes eventually to believe that it is for these reasons that he does pursue it. Self-deception like that is readily intelligible, for it is aimed at preserving the agent's good opinion of himself. But the odd thing about the 'self-deception' to which the critic of incontinence appeals is that it leads the agent to adopt a poorer opinion of himself than he need. This is by no means a fatal objection to the hypothesis, but it should lead the experienced student of human nature to apply the hypothesis with a good deal of caution.

I think, then, that the actual facts of psychological observation are rather strongly in favour of the reality of the bad will, in the sense of the will which 'knows the better and chooses the worse.' If one rejects the interpretation suggested by the facts on the *a priori* grounds of a metaphysical theory, one would have to be extremely confident of the truth of one's metaphysics—as Bosanquet no doubt was. The natural reaction of the psychological investigation would be to throw back doubt upon a metaphysic which demands the Socratic interpretation. We venture to claim it as at least an advantage in the supra-rational metaphysic as against the metaphysic of Absolute Idealism, that there is no need for us to adopt an interpretation of the 'bad will' which the psychological facts seem ill-fitted to sustain.

Section 3. Statement of the Problem, and of the Method to be Adopted

We come now to the main problem of the chapter. I have tried to show, with special reference to the metaphysic of Absolute Idealism, the difficulty—nay, the impossibility—of any reconciliation of the moral point of view with a rationalistic interpretation of the nature of reality. It follows that if we can exhibit the moral point of view, the recognition of 'oughtness,' as an integral, untranscendible, aspect of human experience, we shall be able to claim that human experience in one of its ultimate aspects confirms the validity of our supra-rational hypothesis. If moral obligation *is*, then the 'intelligible Reality' *is not*. I shall try to demonstrate, then, that moral obligation indubitably *is*. The 'approach' here is important, and it will be advisable to consider the problem first in its general bearings.

The plain man never doubts the reality of moral obligation any more than he doubts the reality of personal freedom. And here too his belief rests upon a supposed 'direct' experience. He does not profess to be able to 'explain' this experience to anyone who does not possess it. For it is essentially *sui generis*, is just itself. He can do no more, by way of communicating its meaning, than distinguish it off from certain other experiences which bear a superficial resemblance to it, and might be confused with it. But he is sure that from time to time he does have this experience, this consciousness that he 'ought' to act in such and such a way. If he becomes a little less of the 'plain' man, he will admit the possibility of being mistaken as to *what* it is he ought to do. For he can soon be brought to see that into the determination of the 'what' there enter many factors besides direct experience. But this, he will be justified in telling us, does not render it doubtful that he ought to do *something*. For so long as he is being persuaded that he ought not to do X (which he had previously approved) only on the ground that he 'ought' to do Y, the argument is being carried on within the circle of the 'ought.' And the recognition that there is an 'ought' is just the recognition of the reality of moral obligation and value.

Now (again as in the case of 'freedom') the onus of proof certainly lies upon those who choose to reject the all but universal testimony of human experience. And so far as I can see, there is really but one way in which the critic can hope to persuade those who suppose themselves to have direct experience of the 'ought' that moral obligation is not a reality. He must induce them to see that the experience in question is resoluble without remainder into non-moral ingredients. If a man can be brought to believe that what he has taken to be direct experience of a unique meaning—of the 'ought'—is in fact a disguised fear, or a disguised wish, or some other complex of non-moral elements, then, and then alone, he may be ready to agree that moral obligation, with all that it implies, is a mere chimera, the product of a mental muddle. Doubtless this is not the only way in which it has been sought in practice to discredit morality. But it is the only way which can pretend to logicality of method. The popular plan of seeking to establish a positive relationship between particular 'moral sentiments' and the particular 'desires' of the community in which they occur, carries with it an a-moral inference only by confusion. The dependence upon desires may very well be established. But to show that particular moral sentiments *depend* on a particular context of desires is not to show that they *are* merely such. The recognition of the 'ought,' which is what makes moral sentiments *moral* sentiments, has got to be explained away, or the moral sceptic has made out no case. He has got to try to show, by analysis of the so-called 'moral' experience, that it is only through an understandable illusion that the agent has supposed there to be anything present other than 'non-moral' components.

It follows that it should in principle constitute an adequate defence of the reality of moral obligation, if one can show that the sceptic's attempts to dissolve so-called 'moral' experience into something non-moral are in fact incompetent to explain the experience which they set out to explain. And this does not seem to be at all a difficult task. It has often been undertaken effectively enough as a mere preliminary incident in the exposition of an ethical system. For the would-be champion of moral experience does not have to face sceptical analyses of anything like so formidable or authoritative a nature as does the would-be champion of 'effort of will.' It has proved in practice a simple enough business to overthrow the sceptical analysis of moral experience by making it clear that if that experience were really as it appears in the analysis, the nature of the emotional and ideal responses called forth by the experience, as attested in common speech, becomes quite unintelligible.

Nevertheless, in spite of the fact that the great bulk of philosophers are agreed that moral experience cannot be 'explained away,' there does not seem to be anything approaching universal application of this belief to metaphysical practice. If the reality of moral obligation is accepted, then surely a place should be left for morality in any metaphysical theory of reality that is adopted? Yet many thinkers who would repudiate the suggestion that moral experience can be 'explained away' seem quite ready to adopt, for example, a deterministic view of reality. And the two positions are mutually incompatible.

Why is there this reluctance to accord to moral experience its full metaphysical significance? There can be little doubt, I think, that the leading influence is the immense authority which belongs, for most thinkers, to the belief which runs directly counter to the implications of moral experience, the belief in the intelligibility of reality. The belief may be taken to be guaranteed by the cumulative success of scientific inquiry, or it may be supposed to be an actual postulate implied in all thinking. In either case the security of its lodgment in human experience is regarded as well-nigh indisputable. Now when against this deep-seated belief are set the implications of an experience which, after all, is of but sporadic occurrence in human life, an experience which, although acknowledged to occur as a matter of fact, is not visibly embedded in the very structure of human nature (as a necessary postulate of thought is embedded), it is hardly surprising that if, in the interests of consistency, *one* side must give way, the 'moral' is felt to be the side which must be sacrificed. (It is only justice to add, however, that the presence of moral experience, however sporadic, is constantly felt to be embarrassing. Hence the divers attempts to concoct an interpretation of morality for which the freedom of 'open possibilities' is not required—a forlorn hope indeed, but natural enough if both morality and an 'intelligible reality' are felt to have inescapable claims.)

These considerations suggest a line of treatment for our problem which, if successful, should be a good deal more effective in establishing the reality of the 'ought' than any re-hash of the arguments against the sceptical analysis of moral experience. Is it not possible, we must ask, that moral experience too may be 'visibly embedded in the very structure of human nature'? If this can be shown, if moral experience can be exhibited as a permanent and indefeasible element in the kind of experience which man has, then it becomes manifestly impossible to ignore or gloss over the implications of moral experience in the construction of metaphysical theory. Its claim to recognition will be on the same footing as the claim of 'thinking' experience. And if these two claims in the end prove incompatible (which we have, in earlier chapters, seen reasons for doubting) there will be no option but frankly to admit ourselves saddled with a metaphysical dualism.

My argument 'in defence of the ought' will, therefore, pursue the following course. I shall try to show that the psychological situation in which moral experience occurs (or in which 'oughtness' is apprehended) is one of definitely assignable conditions, which conditions are permanently rooted in the nature of man: that, accordingly, so long as human nature is what it is, recognition of 'oughtness' must remain an inseparable element of it. I shall not, I may add, be propounding any very novel doctrine. In large part I shall follow the account given by T. H. Green of the setting of the moral principle in the economy of human nature.[1] But if this view (at present, one fears, almost without disciples) can be established, the significance of it within our present context of thought will be, I think, very great indeed.

---

[1] It will be observed that I regard it as possible to disentangle the essential truth of Green's moral theory from its unhappy relations with the 'eternal self-consciousness.'

Section 4. Exposition and Defence of the Idealist Doctrine of Desire

It is not possible, nor perhaps desirable, to expound in full detail here the psychology of conation which underlies Green's account of the moral principle. But one prominent doctrine in that psychology it is absolutely necessary that I should state and defend at length: because, in the first place, its acceptance is of basic importance to the position which I am to try to make good here; and because, in the second place, it has called forth far more hostile criticism than any other of Green's psychological tenets—being, indeed, very largely responsible for the disrepute in which at the present day his psychology is commonly held. The offending doctrine (which is common to almost all Idealists) is that which makes the object of desire always a 'conceived personal good of the agent.'

How, first of all, is this formula arrived at? There is nothing very mysterious about the procedure, despite the critics' professions of inability to see any grounds for the result. The general method is one of 'self-reflection,'[1] by the very nature of the case. For it is a phenomenon of the inner life, desire as a psychical experience, that we are interested to understand. But, more in particular, the procedure adopted and recommended by the Idealist consists in the endeavour to make clear to oneself the basis of the distinction which we feel to exist between the experience we call 'impulse' or 'appetite' and the experience we call 'desire.' In each of these experiences we have inclination directed to an object. But, it is pointed out, we certainly do distinguish between them. The Idealist's contention is (and I believe him to be right), that if

---

[1] This general method is inevitable, but Green is always careful to insist that we must pursue it with great circumspection, guarding ourselves against arbitrary interpretations by 'constant reference to the expression of that [inner] experience which is embodied, so to speak, in the habitual phraseology of men, in literature, and in the institutions of family and political life.' (*Prolegomena to Ethics*, p. 105.)

we carry out our introspective analysis with due care we shall see that what distinguishes impulse from desire is just that in impulse there is lacking any recognition of the object as a 'good,' as *something which the self wants*. The object in 'impulse' is, as it were, *merely* object. Or, as we might put it (using the expression which Butler has constantly, but mistakenly, been applauded for applying to desire), impulse 'terminates upon its object'—whereas in all desire there is present the *reference* of the object to the needs of the *subject self*.

The point comes out perhaps even more clearly in relation to action. We all distinguish off 'instinctive' or 'impulsive' action from action preceded by desire for the object. And only the latter do we regard as strictly 'motivated' action. Now if we try to make clear to ourselves what it is that marks off instinctive or impulsive action from motivated action we find, Green points out, that we can only say that the former is an act '*not* determined by a conception, on the part of the agent, of any good to be gained or evil to be avoided by the action.'[1] The implication as to the nature of motivated action, where the end is the end of a desire, is evident.

'Yes,' it may be retorted, 'no doubt the "motive" of action is always a "conceived good." But you have not shown that it is a conceived *personal* good.' To this, however, Green's reply in the passage immediately following that just quoted seems to be perfectly adequate. 'It is superfluous to add,' he explains, 'good *to himself*; for anything conceived as good in such a way that the agent acts for the sake of it, must be conceived as *his own* good, though he may conceive it as his own good only on account of his interest in others, and in spite of any amount of suffering on his own part incidental to its attainment.'[2] Is this claim of Green's really disputable? I cannot think that it is, unless a meaning be read into it more extreme than its author intends—upon which more later. Nor does there seem to be any greater difficulty in making the point

---

[1] *Prolegomena to Ethics*, p. 104. [2] *Ibid*.

in specific reference to desire rather than to motive. To conceive an object as something which *I* want (which is characteristic of desire as distinct from impulse) seems precisely identical with conceiving the object as a good 'for me,' as a 'personal good.'

It is the element of 'self-reference' inherent in desire which the Idealist psychology is especially concerned to bring out. Desire, it may be said, is what impulse becomes when it enters into the experience of a self-conscious subject. Self-consciousness, in relation to the flow of the impulses, is not a mere otiose contemplation which leaves the impulses as they were.[1] A self which is conscious of its impulses as impulses of *it* will naturally consider their objects in the light of their capacity to satisfy not the mere particular impulse, but the *self*, their common subject. And unless and until this action of self-consciousness, this self-reference, takes place, we do not have the phenomenon which we call 'desire.' And, it may be added, we do not have the kind of conative experience which is typical of rational beings, and which is the necessary basis for any conduct which we can regard as morally imputable.

This must suffice by way of exposition. A fuller understanding of the theory's precise import will be reached by the discussion, to which we now turn, of the objections commonly alleged against it.

Almost all of these objections centre upon the supposed 'egoism' of our theory. Now, as I shall show, the theory does not even raise the question of 'egoism or altruism.' But before developing this point I wish to remind the reader that the view of desire which is commonly set against our so-called 'psychological egoism' is one whose weakness has already been exposed in the course of the foregoing analysis.

---

[1] It is not denied that under certain conditions such a state, or a close approximation to it, may occur. But where it does, the impulse has *not* 'entered into the experience of a self-conscious subject.' It is, and is recognised by the subject to be, external to his experience as a subject, almost a 'foreign body.' Such cases are, of course, exceptional.

I refer to the view, especially associated with the name of Bishop Butler, that desire 'terminates on its object.' It may be granted readily that there is an element of real value in Butler's thought here, for the point which the phrase carried for him lay in its implicit repudiation of the fallacy of 'psychological hedonism.' The object of desire is certainly not necessarily, nor even generally, the pleasure expected to accrue from the attainment of some object: and it was important to place it beyond all reasonable doubt that there is no such 'ulterior' end in normal desire. But neither is the object in desire just 'object.' If I have been right, to take desire in this wise is to abandon all possibility of making a distinction between desire and impulse. It is impulse which 'terminates on its object.' In desire the 'object' is raised to a new level by being regarded in the light of its capacity to satisfy the *self*, charged by the reflective consideration that 'this is something which *I* want.'[1]

It is the presence of this element of 'self-reference' in desire which explains the fact that the desires of a rational being show always a more or less well-marked unity. A man's desires bear the impress (as mere appetites do not) of their common relationship to a single self. This is accepted matter

[1] I am far from wishing to decry the great services of Bishop Butler to moral philosophy, but it does seem to me definitely unfortunate that so few ethical writers, in pausing to bestow a well-earned compliment upon Butler's exposure of the fallacies of Psychological Hedonism, have not paused a little longer to point out the defect in Butler's own theory of desire. This defect has been pointed out on more than one occasion by Idealist writers—notably by E. Caird (*Critical Philosophy of Kant*, vol. ii. p. 213, note)—and it has been plainly enough indicated that a main point in the Idealist theory is to restore to desire that characteristic in virtue of which alone desire can be distinguished from animal appetite. It is a little disturbing, therefore, to find philosophers of eminence like Dr Broad speaking of the theories of Bradley and Green as though they belonged to a pre-Butlerian stage of thought, and had long been refuted in principle by Butler's arguments against Psychological Hedonism. It would be a great deal nearer the truth to say that these are the only genuine *post*-Butlerian theories, in that they have not only appreciated the element of value in Butler's view, but have also understood, and indicated clearly, the respect in which that view falls short of being an adequate theory of desire.

REALITY OF MORAL OBLIGATION

of fact, and we can see why it must be so. To consider the object (as happens in desire) in the light of its capacity to satisfy the self, is to consider it in the light of its compatibility with the other objects which the self is conscious of wanting. And the perception of compatibility will naturally heighten, while the perception of incompatibility will naturally weaken, the self's desire for the object. This is by no means to say that each particular desire will be automatically adjusted, through its reference to the good of the self, the common subject of many desires, to that precise degree of strength in which it will best harmonise with the self's other desires. To say this would be to lose sight of the fact that desire has its roots in instinctive impulse, and that the dominating determinant of the strength of desire is (prior to deliberate volitional effort towards adjustment) the intensity of the impulse. It is obvious that where the underlying impulse is strong, as it may be, *e.g.* in extreme hunger, it is not always enough to secure harmonious adjustment that the consideration of the object 'eating food' in the light of its capacity to satisfy the self should show (as it may under certain conditions) that 'eating food' is contrary to the self's interests. All that is claimed is that it does naturally promote *some* adjustment in the way of harmony; and that it is this 'self-referent' aspect of desire, accordingly, which explains why it is that the desires of each individual do as a matter of fact exhibit a certain characteristic unity. That consideration of the object of the impulse in the light of the self's good, in a situation where the conflict of the two is manifest, should fail to produce in the desire any modification of the initial strength of the impulse, seems unthinkable, save in pathological cases: save in cases, that is, where the self is not regarded as behaving like a 'rational being' at all.

But we need not dwell upon the difficulty of accounting for the facts which must beset any attempt to evolve a positive theory of desire without recognition of the element of self-reference. For such attempts originate, almost always, as deliberate reactions against the supposed egoism of the self-referent theory; and if we can show that this egoism is a myth, by far the most serious objection felt against the theory disappears. In what follows I shall consider the problem chiefly in regard to 'motive,' since it is in regard to the special case of motive that the problem appears in its most crucial form. It is urged that if the motive of action is always a 'personal good' of the agent, then all action is *ipso facto* egoistic.

Let us try to get clear upon the meaning of 'egoistic' in reference to a concrete case of behaviour. Suppose a man gives a munificent donation to a hospital. It is commonly recognised that although such an act is outwardly altruistic, it *may* be inwardly, or really, egoistic. It all depends, we say, on his 'motive.' The ultimate end he had in view may have been to bring health and happiness to less fortunate fellow-creatures. If so, if the act is dominated by his interest in the well-being of others, we have genuine altruism. On the other hand, the ultimate end the donor had in view may have been the social or other advantages which might be expected to accrue to him from the act. The act may be dominated by interest in his own private person, by desire for a satisfactory state of himself which he expects by this means to achieve. If so, everyone would agree in calling his act 'egoistic.' The question of whether the act is egoistic or altruistic is, roughly, just the question of whether the controlling interest is in a state of one's self or in a state of other persons.

So far all is simple. But now consider the following point. On *either* of the alternative motivations above illustrated, the 'altruistic' no less than the egoistic, is not the ultimate end aimed at conceived by the agent as a 'personal good,' in that meaning of the expression which our theory alone claims to be true of the object of desire? If the act was not dictated by mere impulse, if it was a *deliberate* act at all, then the end in question was conceived by the agent as something which *he* wanted, *i.e.* a good for him, *i.e.* a 'personal good,' even—

although such terminology approaches the danger zone—as a 'mode of self-satisfaction.' There is not an atom more of difficulty in regarding the 'altruistic' act as directed to a 'personal good' in this sense than there is in the case of the 'egoistic' act. If the agent has not so far disengaged himself from the life of mere impulse as to place before himself the well-being of the prospective beneficiaries as an end which he wants, and therefore as something which he regards as a 'good' for himself, the act was not a willed or responsible act at all.

If this is so, as it surely is, there is no inherent egoism, any more than there is inherent altruism, attaching to the willing of an end as a 'personal good.' As we hinted earlier, the question of egoism and altruism simply does not arise here. What matters for the decision of the latter question is the *nature* of the end in which the agent seeks his personal good. That end may be a prospective state of the private self. But it may equally well be the happiness of other persons. 'Conceived personal good' is just the common characteristic of motivated action, and is entirely neutral as regards egoism and altruism.

I make no apology for lingering over this distinction,[1] for its appreciation is indispensable to any understanding of Idealist moral psychology. The failure to grasp it, combined, it must be added, with the Idealist's omission to emphasise it, lies at the root of an enormous mass of unproductive controversy. Failing to grasp the distinction, the critic very naturally denounces the Idealist doctrine as egoistic, and, because egoistic, in palpable contradiction with the actual facts of the moral life. And he is right, I think, in so far as he insists that selfish motives, in the proper sense of selfish, are far from universal. It is nonsense to explain away the act of the martyr (to take an extreme instance) who immolates himself for some great cause, as really motivated by desire for some future state of bliss which the present act is expected to ensure

---

[1] *I.e.* the distinction between 'personal good' and a 'satisfying state of the private self.'

There are any number of recorded martyrdoms in which no future life is believed in at all. The martyr is not (or certainly not as a rule) thinking of a future state of his private self. He is thinking of the well-being of his 'cause'—perhaps his country's safety. *But* his country's safety does present itself to him as something which *he* wants, as a 'good' for him. Otherwise his act could not be a deliberate act at all. And that is all that the Idealist contends for when he insists that even the martyr's act is directed to a conceived 'personal good.'

It is, again, nothing but this general failure to recognise that 'object conceived as a personal good' is *not* equivalent to 'object conceived as a means to a future state of private satisfaction' that has led so many critics to aver that the Idealist theory of desire is open to the charge of involving a 'hysteron proteron' of the same kind as that of which Psychological Hedonism is generally supposed to be guilty.[1] Since according to these critics 'conceiving an object as a personal good' means 'conceiving it as a means to a future state of private satisfaction,' they have no hesitation in saying that on the Idealist theory I can be moved to perform a deliberate act for the welfare of others only by the anticipation of a satisfying state of myself expected to accrue from having acted 'benevolently.' It is then very easy for them to point out that the existence of a *direct* desire for the welfare of others is the precondition of there being any felt satisfaction in having promoted that welfare: and that we can thus come to desire the private satisfaction of benevolent activity only on condition of a prior desire that was not for private satisfaction. But

---

[1] Even against Psychological Hedonism the charge of involving a hysteron proteron is sometimes made in a manner which cannot be sustained. It is not true that every desire for pleasure presupposes an independent desire for the object whose attainment conditions the pleasure. A great many 'pleasures' are discovered 'accidentally.' Bo-Bo's discovery of the pleasure of eating roast pork was not the outcome of a desire to eat roast pork. In this and all similar cases of accidentally discovered pleasure it would be absurd to hold that the subsequent desire for the pleasure is conditioned by a prior independent desire for the object.

this criticism just does not touch the Idealist theory of desire (and will). All that the Idealist holds is that if my benevolent act is not to belong to the category of mere 'impulse,' I must have exercised such reflection upon the object as enables me to hold it before me as something which I want, *i.e.* as 'a good for me.'

In the same way, Dr Rashdall's failure to appreciate the all-important distinction to which I have been calling attention is the only conclusion which really follows from the 'dilemma' with which he confronts, and by means of which he proposes to confute, the Idealist doctrine of desire. That doctrine, he tells us, must mean either of two things. Either it means that the object is always a prospective state of private satisfaction; or it means just that a man's desires are his own desires. The former assertion, he points out, is false to the facts; and the latter assertion is an insignificant tautology which carries us nowhere.[1]

But the Idealist doctrine means neither of these things. The former meaning has been sufficiently considered, and I wish to add only one observation here. The Idealist has spoken much, and it may be at times with insufficient caution, of all desire being for 'self-satisfaction,' and of the object of desire being conceived as a 'mode of self-satisfaction.' It is at least understandable that, where due warning is not given, this manner of speech should be taken as meaning that no object can be desired save in so far as it is conceived to be a means to self-satisfaction. But on reflection it is surely evident that to conceive an object as a *means* to self-satisfaction is by no means the same thing as to conceive an object as a *mode* of self-satisfaction. The latter is a legitimate enough

---

[1] Rashdall's *The Theory of Good and Evil*, Book i., chap. ii., section 6. '... I can only understand the idea of "aiming at self-satisfaction" to mean that my motive is a certain future state of my own consciousness. And later: ' Of course there is a sense in which every action is interested. ... It simply amounts to saying that a desire which is to move me must be *my* desire.'

expression for the Idealist doctrine that the object in desire is always conceived by the agent as something which he wants, a 'good for him.' The former expression, on the other hand, undoubtedly suggests that the agent is always dominated by interest in the future state of his private self, *i.e.* that all desire is ultimately egoistic. This is not the meaning of the Idealist doctrine, and where (if at all) the Idealist slips into a form of words which suggests it, he must certainly accept some responsibility for the misconstruction.[1]

What of the other horn of the dilemma? If not asserting universal selfishness, is Idealism asserting the insignificant tautology that my desires are my own desires? Far from it. In maintaining that the object of desire is a 'conceived personal good' the Idealist is contending for the recognition of an important aspect of desire which is not suggested by saying simply that 'my desires are my own desires,' or anything of the sort. He is drawing attention to the fact that it is characteristic of desire, as distinct from mere impulse or instinctive appetite, that in it the self so disengages itself from the flow of its impulses as to present the object to itself as a good for the self. He is drawing attention, in other words, to the self-referent aspect of desire which is made possible by the fact of self-

---

[1] Perhaps Bradley is, of all Idealist philosophers, the most addicted to the use of questionable language with regard to the nature of desire. His delight in paradox not infrequently impels him to choose precisely that form of words for the expression of his views which will most deeply shock the sensibilities of his opponents. Thus a great deal has been made of the dictum in *Ethical Studies* that ' all we can desire is, in a word, self ' (p. 66). And I am ready to admit that such an expression, if taken by itself, is liable to mislead. But I must protest against those who have fastened upon it with avidity as an uncompromising confession of psychological egoism, that any philosophical statement must be read in the light of its context. If we study the context here, what do we find ? We find that Bradley not only expressly distinguishes his view from the view that we always desire a future state of our ' self ' as this or that individual man (footnote, p. 67), but, moreover, actually goes on to explain (appendix to same chapter) what else he *does* mean by saying that in desire our object is always ' self.' The critic who wants to make Bradley out an egoist will (to adopt one of Bradley's own phrases) ' do well still to ignore ' these and a host of other passages.

consciousness, and without which there would be no such thing as morally responsible conduct. This is, at the lowest estimate, a valuable service to psychology: but it may very well prove to be of first-rate importance for moral theory also.

Section 5. The Contrast of the 'End of the Self-as-such' with the 'End of Desire'

The remainder of the argument will fall into two parts. On the basis of the psychology just expounded I shall try to show, in the first stage, how there must arise and persist for every self from its very nature, a contrast between two general 'ends,' one of which may be called the 'end of the self-as-such,' and the other (somewhat more loosely) the 'end of desire.' This, the simpler task, will not demand lengthy treatment. In the second stage I shall try to show that the 'end of the self-as-such' presents itself as 'obligatory' as against the 'end of desire'—that it wears the garb of the moral imperative. If this can be made good, then no more is required for the proof of the thesis which the chapter set out to maintain. It will have been shown that the recognition of an 'ought' is bound up with a form of experience which is fundamental and irremovable in human nature; wherefore the 'ought' must itself be accepted as fundamental and irremovable. The implications of such acceptance for metaphysics have been sufficiently dwelt upon.

Let us make a start, then, with the emergence of the contrast between the 'end of the self-as-such' and the 'end of desire.'

We have already seen how a being not merely immersed in the flow of its impulses, but capable of distinguishing itself from them, *i.e.* a self-conscious subject, will consider the objects of the impulses in the light of their capacity to satisfy the *self*. This self-reference is what transforms rude animal impulse into the desire characteristic of rational beings. The 'mere object' of impulse becomes in desire 'object conceived as a good for the self.'

We have seen also how the 'self-referent' factor in desire has the effect of promoting a certain natural harmony in the several desires of the individual rational being (a feature which is absent from the mere impulsive material). The viewing (as in desire) of the object towards which an impulse is felt in the light of its capacity to satisfy the self raises the question of the object's compatibility or incompatibility with the other interests which the self is conscious of having, and this reflective consideration exercises a qualifying influence upon the original impulse, heightening or diminishing its force, according as its object is found to be in alignment with, or in opposition to, the interests of the self as a whole.

But we have also noticed in passing, and must now observe more closely, that this self-referent factor, although it operates naturally in the direction of harmony, does not of itself suffice to effect harmony. To consider the object of impulse in the light of its capacity to satisfy a self which is conscious of many other interests also claiming satisfaction involves the formulation of some conception as to the precise amount of indulgence (if any) which may be permitted consistently with the good of the self as a whole. It tells us what we should here desire, if our desire is to be in accord with what will best satisfy the self as the common subject of many desires. But this 'considering' does not have the effect of producing in the desire, 'automatically' as it were, the precise adjustment whose fitness is conceptually clear. The conceived fullest or truest good of the self is often in opposition to the direction not merely of impulse, but of desire also. Desire is always for *a* conceived good of the self, as we have seen. *The* conceived good of the self may be something very different.

It will be helpful, perhaps, to see how these distinctions function in a concrete case. Let us suppose the case of a scientific explorer travelling alone through some desert waste. His store of water has by some mischance failed him, and, while still a day's journey from known supplies, he finds

REALITY OF MORAL OBLIGATION

himself afflicted with a thirst that is almost unendurable. Suddenly he comes upon a wholly unexpected pool, and great is his elation until, on drawing closer to it, he finds unmistakable signs of pollution. He has not present, we shall suppose, the means of ascertaining the exact nature, and consequent danger, of the impurity, but he knows enough to be sure that there is at least grave risk in partaking.

Now let us consider the conative situation that may fairly be expected to arise here, from the point of view of the distinction of 'ends.' The dictate of impulse, *per se*, is to slake his thirst to the full. That is the first 'end.' But as a self-conscious subject he presents to himself the end of drinking the water in the light of its capacity to satisfy the self. And that self has many interests whose fulfilment, it is at once clear to him, will be seriously endangered if he allows even any indulgence to the impulse; and very much more seriously if he allows to the impulse completely full rein. For even slight indulgence, he sees, may mean death, either directly, or through such incapacitation as will unduly delay his reaching the near-by depôt. Thus when he reviews the situation in the light of these manifold interests which drinking will endanger —his interest in bringing a difficult project, now all but achieved, to a satisfactory termination; his interest in collating and studying and circulating the valuable scientific data that he has amassed; the interests that affect him as husband, parent, and friend; his interest in new expeditions which he had promised himself for the future; his interest in mere living itself, or, what is perhaps the same thing, his aversion from the thought of physical death (to mention but a few of the more typical interests)—it is certain that he will regard it as really best for him that he should resist wholly the cravings of his parched throat and push on as rapidly as may be to the source of fresh supplies. Here then we have a second 'end,' the end representing the conceived good of the self-as-such, or of the self as the unity of its manifold interests. But there is a third end also. When the act of self-reference has taken place, and a conception thereby formed of what course of action is in accord with the good of the self as a whole, our traveller does not, unfortunately, find the 'set' of desire inclining straight to this good. Without a doubt the antagonism of impulse will have undergone modification through the self-reference which constitutes it as a 'desire.' It is improbable that he will 'desire' to drink unrestrainedly. Such an end is too crassly self-destructive to be even present to his mind once the act of self-reference has taken place. But almost certainly the modification will still leave a desire to drink—to drink perhaps just enough to relieve the first urgency of his distress. This is the third end, the 'end of desire,' and its presence as a factor opposed to the end of the self-as-such is manifested in the inner conflict which ensues. The traveller, if his thirst be as intense as we have hypothesized, will assuredly be conscious of having to exert will-power in order to achieve the 'end of the self-as-such.' He may, indeed, speak as if it were mere 'impulse,' his 'animal nature' which offers combat—'flesh warring against spirit.' And this is in a sense true, since it is the power of the original 'animal impulse' continuing on, though in modified form, in desire, that is the ultimate source of the opposition. But strictly considered, that which offers the opposition must be named 'desire,' not 'impulse.' Impulse has ceased to exist as such with the incidence of the act of self-reference.

The above illustration is typical. And indeed the presence in human experience of this contrast between 'end of self' and 'end of desire' is in one sense plain matter of fact. But I think we can see now how its emergence and persistence are conditioned by the very constitution of human nature. It is, at bottom, the old story of the union of animality and rationality in the one being. Were man purely animal, there would be no conception of a 'good of the self as a whole,' of an 'end of the self-as-such.' Were he purely rational, there would be nothing which could effectively oppose itself to the conceived 'good of the self as a whole.' But in the mingling of the two natures lie the conditions of that conflict which is at once the source of human greatness and human degradation. In virtue of his rational or 'self-conscious' being, man formulates to himself an idea of self-satisfaction which is the satisfaction of his self as the recognised common subject of manifold interests or desires: an ideal end which, by contrast with the ends of desire, is the objective counterpart of the *unity* of the desiring self. In virtue of his 'animal' being, through which he owns a variety of instinctive impulses which are not by nature in any kind of 'pre-established harmony,' he feels himself from time to time powerfully desiring ends which, though recognised as satisfactions of partial aspects of his self, are recognised also as inimical to the satisfaction of the self as a whole. The conflict will manifest itself in an infinitude of forms, determined by diversity of circumstance, of nature, and—perhaps not least—by diversity of success in past volitional control. In some persons, where natural conditions are fortunate, and volitional control has been notably effective, it may well be that the 'end of desire' which opposes itself to the 'end of the self' is actually of a more refined character than that which for the average person constitutes the 'end of the self.' But in some form, and at some level, the conflict pervades all human life. That it should be fully and permanently resolved seems possible only under conditions of a change so cataclysmic that human nature would cease to preserve its identity.

Before passing on to consider the problem of the *authority* of the end of the self-as-such, as against the end of desire, there is a possible difficulty attaching to certain implications of our present argument which it may be well to clear up. On my view, the emergence of the contrast of the two ends is coeval with the emergence of morality, and is almost as old as human nature itself. But for some theories of the constitution of primitive group life it may seem that this thesis implies on the part of primitive man a more distinct consciousness of his private individuality than actually obtains. Primitive man, it is urged, is more properly conceived as a function of the tribal life than as an 'individual' self. He does not set before himself private policies or projects. The tribal purposes determine his purposes, and tribal success or failure are felt as *his* success or failure.

But unless the theory is held in an extreme form in which it seems obviously false, there is no real difficulty here for the thesis we are maintaining. That extreme form would consist in a literal acceptance of the phrase 'a function of the tribal life' as applying to primitive man. But it is doubtful if this meaning has ever been seriously intended. The swing of the pendulum in sociological thinking from atomic individualism to organic societism has been violent enough. It has resulted, in my opinion, in an exaggerated emphasis upon the communal factor in primitive groups. But the interpretation of primitive man as just 'a function of the tribal life' involves, if pressed, too gross absurdities to find serious championship. It would involve, for example, that primitive man not only never sins deliberately against the group's interest for a private end, but that he is not even conscious of the possibility of so sinning. And the annals of savage life, even in the most closely knit communities, hardly bear out so wild an hypothesis.

What is certainly true is that primitive man is ordinarily endowed with a far more intense consciousness of his one-ness with the group than civilised man is. Both natural conditions and deliberate artifice contribute, as sociologists have explained, to bring this about. There is no need to try to minimise this unity, for it does not at all demand the hypothesis of members who have no consciousness of separate individuality, in the sense implied by our thesis. All that is required for the emergence of the contrast of 'end of self-as-such' with the 'end of desire' is the capacity to consider 'practical' objects in relation to the satisfaction of the self. And this capacity cannot be denied to primitive man, unless we are going to say that his conduct is not merely in large part (which is true), but *all*, 'impulsive.' The truth is that the closer community-life of primitive peoples has no effect on the principle of the contrast, but has a very great effect upon the actual terms of the contrast. It will ensure that the 'end of the self-as-such' will have the most intimate relation to tribal welfare, and it will, moreover, give to the end of tribal welfare so powerful an attractive force that it will in very many practical situations be also the 'end of desire.' Hence the relative paucity of anti-social behaviour in primitive communities. The closer the approximation in practice of the end of desire to the end of self-as-such, the less is the need for exerting will-energy, and the more common, accordingly, is conduct which conforms to the standard.

Section 6. The Moral Authority of the 'End of the Self-as-such'
(a) *Removal of Obstacles to its Appreciation*

Granted that the contrast of 'end of self-as-such' and 'end of desire' is thus characteristic of the conative experience of self-conscious or rational beings, our final task is to show that the former end presents itself to the self, as against the latter end, with all the authority of the moral imperative. Formally to 'prove' this is, of course, out of the question. In the last resort appeal must be made (as always in the case of 'ultimate' ends) to intuition. And perhaps even the word 'show' is too strong in this context. Nevertheless I think that a great deal can be done 'from without' to induce agreement, more especially by the removal of certain common prepossessions which are apt improperly (if unconsciously) to prejudice the issue. By this means, as well as by drawing attention to considerations which point to the *a priori* probability that the 'end of the self-as-such' should carry with it a unique claim upon the agent, it seems possible at least to dispose the reader favourably for that intuitive recognition of 'obligation' which, as I believe, must accompany any imaginative realisation of the contrast in question, if only it be unfettered by preliminary bias. I shall consider first some prejudicial prepossessions.

Among these hostile influences one of the most prevalent, I think, springs from what may be called the 'religious texture' of our common moral notions. To a great many people the idea of moral authority is so inextricably interwoven with their beliefs concerning the Deity that they find it hard to conceive of an 'ought' as having any meaning at all in a context which is (as they would describe it) purely 'secular.' And this attitude is, I think, natural enough. Once anything that can fairly be called a 'religion' has emerged, it is well-nigh impossible that one's moral ideas should not be linked up with, even in a manner absorbed by, one's religious ideas. The cosmic supremacy of the Deity can hardly be interpreted in a way which leaves to the moral imperative an independent authority, more especially since the Deity is as a rule conceived as embodying in Himself the perfected consummation of those values to which the moral imperative summons us.

But natural as it is thus to clothe the moral imperative with a religious significance, it seems sufficiently clear that it does not *require* for its recognition, or imply in its meaning, anything that would ordinarily be called religious belief. For a simple, but I think effective, answer it is only necessary to contemplate one of the outstanding characteristics of the spiritual life of our time. No one can deny the existence of a very considerable body of persons in our contemporary civilisation who, though candidly professing themselves devoid of any kind or sort of religious belief, declare both in their conduct and by verbal testimony their respect for the 'voice of Duty.' There seem no adequate grounds for gainsaying this, and much similar, evidence for the independence of moral experience.

I am saying no more, be it noted, than that the moral imperative may be recognised independently of religious ideas. I am far from suggesting that a religious significance may not legitimately be infused into morality. And in a wider sense of the word 'religion' than is customarily employed, in which its essence would consist in the conviction that the Perfect alone is ultimately real, it is possible, I think, to make out a pretty strong case for the view that morality is itself implicitly religion; that the recognition of the essential religious postulate is implicitly present in the moral self's consciousness of *obligation* to aim at 'harmonious' being. But these are high matters upon which we cannot enter here. Suffice it to point out that the independence of religion which I claim for moral experience, and which, so far as religion in its usual interpretation is concerned, seems sufficiently obvious, is not conceived as ruling out *a priori* all doctrines of the ultimate fusion of morality and religion.

In the second place, it may be felt to be an objection that the 'conceived good of the self as a whole,' since it confessedly gets all its content from the self's desires, will in many natures manifest itself in ends of a somewhat low and materialistic character—such ends, it may be suggested, as cannot without offence be supposed to be deliverances of our 'moral consciousness.' But the fact (for it is, of course, a fact) that often no very exalted content will pertain to the 'conceived good of the self as a whole,' ought surely to be regarded as a merit rather than a demerit of the present theory. We are searching for a 'moral principle.' But a genuine moral principle must be adequate to the facts of moral experience. And among the facts of moral experience must be counted those felt obligations on the part of undeveloped races towards ends which we should regard as 'low and materialistic.' The 'felt obligations' of uncivilised man belong just as truly to the data of ethics as the felt 'obligations' of you and me. We shall not really have laid hold of the principle (or the principles, admitting for the moment the possibility of ethical pluralism) of our moral nature, if that principle (or those principles) be not such as to make intelligible the moralities of all men, civilised and uncivilised alike.

And there is certainly nothing *essentially* materialistic about the ideal of the conceived good of the self as a whole. Doubtless in the earlier stages of man's development the end representing the unity of the self's interests—the good of the self as a whole—would be concerned largely with the satisfaction of physical wants. Yet even here, and without having recourse to venturesome speculations as to the spiritual aspirations of savages, we can see that the end will not be wholly physical. The social interest is alive from the beginning, and must bring it about that the 'conceived good of the self as a whole' is felt to involve the satisfaction of the physical wants of the family, or the clan, as well as of one's self. The 'end of the self-as-such' therefore will include, even at the lower levels, the satisfaction of social as well as physical wants. But furthermore, however materialistically oriented at primitive levels, the principle in question is plainly capable of expanding, without loss of continuity, into something which bears little trace of its crude beginnings. As the human self advances in the fullness of time to a more developed consciousness of its own nature and possibilities, new and powerful interests emerge—interests in knowledge, in beauty, and, perhaps dwarfing all others, the religious interest in the union of the soul with God. When interests such as these develop, and manifest themselves, as they must, in the conceived good of the self as a whole, that end or ideal will have little in its nature to provoke the imputation of materialism.

But by far the most potent of the prejudices against which our doctrine has to make itself good is that which arises from the failure to understand that it is not just a more or less refined form of egoism. I have already said a good deal on this matter. In principle the whole case of the objector was met when it was pointed out that what determines conduct as 'egoistic' is not that the agent seeks 'personal good,' but that he seeks personal good exclusively or predominantly in states of private satisfaction. But the importance of a right decision in this matter is so great that some further observations seem called for.

In the first place, I should like to make clear my position concerning the relation to morality of egoistic ends properly so-called. I am in full agreement with the critic of egoism in holding that no egoistic principle can exhaustively express the moral principle. But some critics go a great deal further than that. They maintain that the moral principle cannot express itself in an egoistic end at all; that morality, strictly speaking, only begins when universal ends, transcending the individual, claim allegiance. Following Croce, they would describe all egoistic action, in whatever circumstances, as directed to merely 'economic' good.

It does not seem to me that this distinction can be sustained. We may note first what seems plain matter of fact, that obligation of *some* kind may in suitable circumstances be felt towards an egoistic end. To take an obvious instance, there is the man who has a strong desire for a glass of wine, but is confronted by the remembrance that for him indulgence in wine means a headache and general malaise the following day. Even if his consideration of consequences keeps entirely within the universe of his private feelings, will he not feel that he 'ought' here to refrain from drinking? Will he not feel that, of the two courses, that which he clearly sees to be the more conducive to a satisfactory state of his private self 'ought' to be pursued as against that which, in spite of the ardour of his desire, he knows to be less conducive? It is pointless to reply that this is just a matter of 'prudence,' not of obligation. It *is* a matter of prudence, but it is also *more*. The agent does deem it more 'prudent' to refrain, but he also—and this is the significant thing—is conscious that he 'ought' to follow the more prudent course. He is conscious of *an obligation to be prudent*.

'But not a *moral* obligation,' it is said. Why not? I have been totally unable to discover any serious reasons offered for distinguishing off the kind of obligation experienced here from moral obligation. What essential difference is there? The agent will use precisely the same language in regard to it, and to its implications, as he would if the obligatory end were a social one. He will say that he knows he ought not to yield to the desire, and, if he does yield, he will consider himself a just object of censure. In fact, the only reason for denying to this obligation the title of 'moral' seems to be the quite arbitrary one that the objector has already defined morality to himself in terms which exclude egoistic ends. But definitions, if they are not to be purely formal, must wait upon experience, not dictate to it.

It remains to point out that on the view of the moral principle which I am trying here to maintain, the experience of obligation in the above illustration is fully understandable. I have been anxious to insist that there is no obstacle to the entry of 'altruistic' interests into the 'conceived good of the self as a whole'; but nothing has been said to suggest that 'egoistic' interests, even of a purely hedonic nature, are debarred from it. In point of fact, private pleasure is obviously *one* of the things which man wants, one of the 'personal goods,' therefore, which have to be considered in determining the 'good of the self as a whole' (though in some cases, as we know, it comes to be regarded as of so little value by the side of certain other 'personal goods' that it is definitely among the least influential factors in that determination). Taking pleasure in this way as 'one' personal good, there is no difficulty in seeing that for a self who is conscious of himself as a perduring identical subject it must appear to be in accord with the good of the self as a whole that he should forgo any immediate pleasure which involves future pains far outweighing it. Even where no considerations of consequences save those affecting private pleasure and pain are before the mind—as a rule the situation is immensely more complicated—there is, therefore, for my view nothing surprising in the presence of a felt obligation. In the illustration taken, the agent will conceive it to be more in accord with the good of his self as a whole to refuse indulgence to the desire for wine, and will in consequence be conscious of an obligation to abstain.

There is this much truth, then, in Butler's famous doctrine of the 'manifest obligation' of 'Reasonable Self-love.' Man does recognise an obligation to follow that course which reason tells him is the more conducive to his 'happiness' on the whole —*provided that* the practical situation is not complicated by other considerations than those of his private feelings. What Butler fails to see is this *limitation* of the obligation, which arises from the fact that the obligation is in reality only a specific case of the general obligation to pursue the 'conceived *good* of the self as a whole.' Into this latter end all kinds of interests besides that of private happiness normally enter. And it is this end alone which is a 'manifest obligation' in any absolute sense. Butler's advocacy of the claims of Reasonable Self-love rests probably on a dim apprehension of the truth that 'personal good' can alone be deliberately sought. But his confusion of 'personal good' with 'private pleasure' makes it necessary for him, in order to be true to moral experience, to erect a second moral principle which will do justice to our sense of 'altruistic' obligations. Hence his dualism of Conscience and Reasonable Self-love, and the ethical chaos to which a duplication of 'ultimate' moral principles inevitably leads.

The 'conceived good of the self as a whole' may, then, find expression in certain circumstances in an 'egoistic' end: a fact which does not, however, disqualify it in any way as the principle of morality. On the other hand (to return to our old theme) it is not true that it can find expression only in egoistic ends. For consider. The various 'personal goods' which are the material out of which is constructed the conceived good of the self *as a whole*—the 'end of the self as such'—need not be solely, nor even dominantly, egoistic. That we saw in our discussion of the nature of desire. Why then should the 'construct,' the conceived good of the self as a whole, be solely, or even dominantly, egoistic? It seems just worth while pointing out that it not only need not, but in fact normally will not. The policy of life expressive of the good of the self as a whole (which, though not for most selves recognisable in this guise, is yet evolved naturally by a self conscious of its own perduring identity) will normally be charged with many altruistic elements. The interest in the welfare of others is not an exotic plant that blooms only in a rarefied atmosphere. It is of the very stuff of human nature. The problems which centre upon the origin and nature of the social instinct are too formidable even to allude to in a passing reference, but, whatever their solution may be, it is incontrovertible that man has normally an interest in, or desire for, the well-being of at least *some* other persons. Moreover, although this interest is confined in the early stages of civilisation to the family or the clan, a survey of the facts suggests strongly that there is such 'a natural principle of attraction in man towards man,' that the inclusion of all humanity within the ambit of the social interest may not extravagantly be called its natural termination. As Green has said, what needs to be explained is not the width and depth of modern expressions of the social interest, but rather the limitations to which it has been subject in previous history. Contact of man with man does spontaneously generate a sympathetic interest. We find this to be matter of fact, true to a surprising degree even where the character of the person 'contacted' is in many respects displeasing to us. Through contact we come to appreciate other men, who may previously have been 'foreigners' to us in every significant sense, as *men* like ourselves; and once this realisation of a common humanity is aroused, interest in their welfare seems to follow instinctively.

However this may be, there are certainly few persons in whom the social interest is not alive, even if its range be often distressingly restricted. And the present point is that this interest must function in precisely the same way as other interests—interests in sport, or culture, or wealth, or 'sex'— in determining the conceived good of the self as a whole. Furthermore, this interest will be enormously enhanced in effectiveness where, through the teachings of philosophy or religion, or by some other 'humane' influence, the agent has been brought to realise the unique ontological significance of 'self-hood.' When this happens, there is generated a respect for personality as such which is utterly antipathetic to a selfishly oriented 'good of the self as a whole.'

The vital thing to keep in mind in this whole matter is that the self's interest in private satisfactions is normally only *one* interest among many. Private happiness is *one* of the manifold ends of our manifold desires, and it has absolutely nothing peculiar about it as an end which gives to it any special centrality in the determination of 'the end of the self as such.' It is perhaps not possible to deny that it *may* become the object of so overwhelming an interest that all other ends are conceived to be of insignificant value beside it. We should then have the 'good of the self as a whole' conceived in purely egoistic terms. But such ego-centricity, if it ever is, is definitely an abnormality. Strong social interests are part of the natural equipment of human nature, and determine the content of the 'conceived good of the self as a whole' in a way which sharply contrasts it with the end of sheer egoism.

A further line of argument may be utilised against those who deprecate our doctrine as 'egoistic.' It may be pointed out that all moral education rests on the tacit presupposition that the moral principle is 'egoistic' in exactly our sense. From Socrates onward, the characteristic method of the moral teacher and the moral reformer has been to show the pupil, by inducing a more vivid and accurate insight into the nature of his self and his world, that *this*, and not *that*, is what he *really* wants. The appeal throughout is to interests which are latent, or whose applicability to the ruling 'circumstances' has not been realised, in the confident belief that they will, once stimulated, express themselves effectively in the pupil's conception of the good of his self as a whole. How, for example, does one seek to give a child (or an adult, for that matter) a 'conscience' on the matter of kind treatment of dumb animals? Are not our chief efforts directed to stimulating a lively realisation of the actual sufferings of these creatures under ill-usage, in order that the natural sympathy with fellow-sentients, unawakened here so far because of sheer lack of imagination, may be at last aroused? Or how, again, does the intelligent administrator in 'outposts of Empire,' or the missionary, in so far as his strictly ethical mission is concerned, seek to reform the moral ideals of savages? Is it not just by leading them to see, by enlargement of their vision of the factors involved, that what they *really* want will be better achieved in the new way than in the old? Only through this appeal to real, as against apparent, '*personal* good' can moral persuasion, so far as I can see, have any effect at all.

No, it may be said, the appeal is to 'good,' of course, but not to 'personal good.' The appeal is to those objective, independent goods which are obligatory in their own right, and are recognised to be so wherever the 'moral faculty' is permitted to function purely. These self-evident eternal obligations, binding everywhere and always, are the sole principles of morals, and only through appeal to them can anything which deserves the title of 'moral' education be effective.

'Intuitionalism' in ethics is, in some form or another, sponsored by so many eminent thinkers at the present time that no one dare treat it with less than respect. Yet I am convinced that it is in principle an untenable type of theory: untenable, moreover, for reasons which have long been a commonplace of ethical literature. If I may be pardoned a partial digression, I should like to state shortly what seem to me to be the outstanding objections to Intuitionalist ethics, paying regard, at the same time, to certain recent attempts to counter these objections.

Section 7. Digression upon the Crucial Difficulties of Intuitionalist Ethics

The most obvious objection to Intuitionalist ethics is as follows. It is of the essence of this type of theory to lay down a number of moral rules, each of which is supposed to be absolutely or unconditionally binding in its own right. But practical situations arise in which these rules seem to dictate mutually exclusive courses of action. Thus there may be a rule prescribing truth-telling, and another prescribing the prevention of needless suffering, and I may find that in my particular situation I can obey the first rule only by disobeying the second. What then am I to do? Intuitionalism can give no answer, for each rule is for it, *ex hypothesi*, *absolutely* binding. We are left with a conflict of professed ultimates. We are told that we ought to do *a, and* ought to do *b*; which means in this situation that we both ought, and ought not, to do *a*.

The point is a simple one, but it seems so directly fatal to Intuitionalism as commonly held that it may repay us to dwell upon it a little longer. Intuitionalist ethics, I am affirming, lands us in crass self-contradiction. For consider. According to the theory, we are given, let us say, *five* absolutely binding 'ends,' A, B, C, D, E. Now if A is absolutely binding, that means that all other ends must defer to A. But then 'all other ends' must include the ends B, C, D, E. Yet each of these latter is, *ex hypothesi*, absolutely binding, and each is such, therefore, that all other ends, including A, ought to defer to it. We are being told, therefore, both that B (likewise C, D, E) ought to defer to A, and that A ought to defer to B (likewise to C, D, E).[1]

A very interesting attempt to circumvent the difficulties inherent in the presence of a manifold of ultimate obligations has recently been made by Mr W. D. Ross in his book *The Right and the Good*. We must distinguish, he tells us, between *prima facie* duty and absolute or actual duty. The term '*prima facie* duty' is 'a brief way of referring to the characteristic (quite distinct from that of being a duty proper) which an act has, in virtue of being of a certain kind (*e.g.* the keeping of a promise), of being an act which would be a duty proper if it were not at the same time of another kind which is morally significant. Whether an act is a duty proper or actual duty depends on *all* the morally significant kinds it is an instance of' (pp. 19–20). It is only to the category of '*prima facie* duty' that, for Mr Ross, the intuited 'general rules' or 'principles' of morality belong. We intuit promise-keeping, for example, not as something which we unconditionally ought to do, but as something which we ought to do wherever the case is not complicated by the relevance to the particular act of *other* moral principles.

It is pretty evident that this view successfully avoids the self-contradiction inherent in the ordinary Intuitionalist theory. That contradiction had its source in the alleged absoluteness of the obligation of each moral principle. But with the 'condition' introduced by the present view the possibility of contradiction between the principles disappears. On the other hand, as I shall try to show, the temporary advantage gained is of little avail. If the older theory could not tell us what we ought to do where two ultimate obligations come into conflict, the present theory is in no better case where two *prima facie* obligations come into conflict.

[1] In expressing the argument in this way I have especially in mind a passage in which Caird criticises the Kantian resolution of morality into so many absolutely binding moral rules (*Critical Philosophy of Kant*, vol. ii. p. 175).

By way of bringing out the difficulty for Mr Ross's theory, we may note briefly the manner in which the monistic moralist views the conflict between traditionally accepted 'moral rules.' For him, too, these moral rules possess a certain authority. But it is not an authority which belongs to them *in their own right*. It is an authority derivative from the authority of a single supreme moral principle. The accepted moral rules of any community represent the ways of behaving, in certain typical and important practical relationships, which respect for the one supreme moral principle has seemed to prescribe. Since they are the product of the accumulated moral wisdom of generations, they are obviously not to be lightly discarded. On the other hand, if we lose sight of the spirit behind the letter of the law, we become impotent, in the first place, to discern when, owing to special individual circumstances, or perhaps to a change in the general conditions of life, the letter no longer manifests the spirit: and we become impotent, in the second place, to resolve any conflict which may arise between the claims of different rules. But since in truth the only authority which these rules possess belongs to them in respect of their capacity to express the one ultimate moral law or ideal, the principle for the solution of any conflict between the courses which they dictate is always available. We have simply to ask ourselves, which of the proposed (mutually exclusive) courses of action is the one best calculated to realise the ultimate ideal? We shall feel no compunction in disobeying the 'rule' which this inquiry decides us to reject, for we recognise that the authority of that rule was conditional, and that the condition upon which it rested is not here fulfilled.[1]

Now Mr Ross's moral rules have, in a sense, only 'condi-

[1] I need scarcely say that I am not for a moment intending to suggest here that there are not very serious difficulties in the way of exhibiting the different moral rules as derivations of a single principle. My purpose here is only to draw attention to what appears to be a technical superiority of monistic to pluralistic ethics.

tional' authority likewise. They are merely '*prima facie*' obligations. But the difficulty is to see what it is for Mr Ross that has absolute or unconditional authority. For monistic ethics there is a single supreme standard by appeal to which we can in principle adjust and compose the conflicting claims of different 'conditional' duties. What is there to fulfil this indispensable function in Mr Ross's theory?

Mr Ross is, of course, perfectly well aware of the necessity of offering some answer on this matter. On p. 23 the difficulty is explicitly raised. It may be objected, he says, 'that our theory that there are these various and often conflicting types of *prima facie* duty leaves us with no principle upon which to discern what is our actual duty in particular circumstances.' What, then, is his answer?

We may begin by considering briefly the answer which follows immediately upon the statement of the difficulty, although we do not here, I think, have Mr Ross's whole mind on the matter.

Mr Ross points out first of all that what he calls 'the rival theory'—Mr Moore's 'ideal utilitarianism'—is not in a position to urge the present objection. For it is in a like case. 'When we have to choose between the production of two heterogeneous goods, say knowledge and pleasure, the "ideal utilitarian" theory can only fall back on an opinion, for which no logical basis can be offered, that one of the goods is the greater.'

This, I think, is true. But we must not forget that the appointment of ideal utilitarianism as 'the rival theory' rests upon the discretion of Mr Ross—not upon any agreed characteristic of the nature of ethical science. Most people would be prepared to allow that there are other 'rival theories,' and at least some of these do not, with ideal utilitarianism, accept a plurality of ultimate goods, and therefore are not saddled with this disability of having no single standard to which to refer in cases of conflict. Not, of course, that it is always, or even often, easy to apply in practice the standard of a monistic ethics with confidence in the accuracy of one's results. As Mr Ross says, when 'we consider the infinite variety of the effects of our actions in the way of pleasure,' it is evident that even hedonism offers no 'readily applicable standard of right conduct.' But it is one thing to have no 'readily applicable' standard, another thing to have no 'standard' at all, but rather many 'standards,' each equally authoritative. The former is a disability pertaining perhaps to all ethical systems; but all ethical systems do not share with ideal utilitarianism and (it may be) Mr Ross's theory the latter disability.

Even as an *argumentum ad hominem*, then, this point has only a limited effectiveness. But Mr Ross, in any event, professes himself unwilling to be content with an *argumentum ad hominem*. (After all, a theory is not really made more tenable by the fact that its defects are shared by opposing theories.) 'I would contend,' he goes on to say, 'that in principle there is no reason to anticipate that every act that is our duty is so for one and the same reason.' If, after reflection, *prima facie* duties, like keeping a promise and redressing an injury, do not appear reducible to one another, we are not entitled on any *a priori* ground, he urges, to assume that such a reduction is possible.

The exact significance of this contention does not seem to me to be altogether clear. Mr Ross is replying to the objection that on his theory we are left with no principle by which to discover our actual duty in cases where *prima facie* duties prescribe mutually exclusive courses. Is he admitting that he has no such principle, and alleging that there is no *a priori* ground for supposing that there should be one? Or is he saying only that he has not, and that there is no *a priori* reason why he should have, a principle *of the kind sponsored by monistic moral theories*—leaving open the question of whether there is or is not *some* kind of principle to which appeal may be made on his theory?

I think we may take it that the second is Mr Ross's real meaning. The passage under consideration, with its context, certainly suggests the former, more sceptical meaning, but it is not, I think, definitely incompatible with the latter meaning. And although at this juncture the subject is abruptly discontinued, later parts of the chapter seem to make it clear that for Mr Ross there is a principle of sorts to which we can refer for the determination of our 'actual' duty. As is surely, indeed, very necessary—even *a priori* necessary, if ethics is to be possible at all. There cannot be a 'science of right and wrong' if there just is not any intelligible principle upon which we can ever decide what is our actual duty.

What, then, is the principle of 'actual' or 'absolute duty' to which we may refer for the settlement of conflicts between *prima facie* duties? Mr Ross's answer is, as I understand it, that we have to consider which of our possible acts will produce the greatest balance of *prima facie* rightness over *prima facie* wrongness. We 'must reflect to the best of our ability on the *prima facie* rightness or wrongness of various possible acts in virtue of the characteristics we perceive them to have' (p. 32), for 'right acts can be distinguished from wrong acts only as being those which, of all those possible to the agent in the circumstances, have the greatest balance of *prima facie* rightness, in those respects in which they are *prima facie* right, over their *prima facie* wrongness, in those respects in which they are *prima facie* wrong' (p. 41).

Mr Ross is very ready to agree that the use of this principle can never allow us to attain *certainty* as to what in particular is our duty. And he mentions two main causes of uncertainty. In the first place, each act obviously originates countless effects, many of which are unforeseeable, and of these unforeseeable effects some at least have moral significance (*i.e.* make a contribution to the balance of *prima facie* rightness and wrongness). We cannot, then, attain certainty that we are ever choosing the act which really promotes the greatest balance of *prima facie* rightness over *prima facie* wrongness. The most that we can do is to reflect as carefully and as comprehensively as we can upon the consequences of our possible acts, in the confidence that we are 'more likely' to do our duty thus than by acting without thought. In the second place—to give Mr Ross's own words—'for the estimation of the comparative stringency of these *prima facie* obligations no general rules can, so far as I can see, be laid down. We can only say that a great deal of stringency belongs to the duties of "perfect obligation"—the duties of keeping our promises, of repairing wrongs we have done, and of returning the equivalent of services we have received. For the rest, ἐν τῇ αἰσθήσει ἡ κρίσις' (pp. 41, 42).

Now the first of these 'reasons for uncertainty' raises no special difficulty. A similarly conditioned uncertainty of particular moral judgments is admitted by most ethical theories, and the validity of the ethical theory is not impugned thereby. An ethical theory must supply us with a principle for moral guidance, but there is no *a priori* necessity that the principle should be such that the conditions of its practical application are simple. But the second reason for uncertainty indicated by Mr Ross appears to me to belong to a different category altogether. The first reason for uncertainty was just that we never have complete information as to the facts. But the second reason—our lack of 'general rules' for 'estimating the comparative stringency of these *prima facie* obligations'— means that *we don't know how to appraise the information that we have*: that even if our information as to the fact was perfect—even if the 'countless effects' were fully known in respect of their contributions to the different *prima facie* rightnesses and wrongnesses—we *still* should not be able to tell what our 'actual' duty is. For, being ignorant of the 'comparative stringency' of the different *prima facie* obligations, we have not the knowledge by which we can even begin to calculate which act promotes the greatest balance of *prima facie* rightness over *prima facie* wrongness. And if this is so, we have here a defect which, unlike the former, does impugn the validity of the ethical theory.

And surely it *is* so. 'Calculation' implies the reducibility to a common measure of the things to be calculated. But it is just this reducibility to a common measure which seems here to be clearly impossible. Our 'common measure' should, I suppose, be units of *prima facie* rightness on the positive side, and units of *prima facie* wrongness on the negative side. But on the theory we do not, and apparently can not, know the relative number of units which belong to each *prima facie* obligation. According to Mr Ross, we know (doubtless by intuition) that certain characteristics of acts (*e.g.* the characteristic of promise-keeping) possess *more* units of *prima facie* rightness than certain other characteristics (*e.g.* the characteristic of relieving distress). Such, at any rate, seems to be implied in the known 'greater stringency' of the 'duties of perfect obligation.' But we do not know *how many* more units the one possesses than the other. And such knowledge is indispensable to moral calculation. It may not seem to be required if we have a simple case where we have to choose between keeping a promise on the one hand and relieving distress on the other, no further moral factors being relevant (though no case is really quite so simple, and certain difficulties which we shall notice later are ignored in the very postulation of such a case). It might seem that here our knowledge that promise-keeping has more *prima facie* rightness than relieving distress is all that we need, since our ignorance of *how much* more rightness belongs to the former will not introduce any difficulty into the determination of which act is our 'actual' duty. But whatever we may say of these 'simple' cases, our ignorance matters vitally in those more complicated cases in which we have to choose, let us say, between keeping a promise, on the one hand, and, on the other hand, relieving distress *plus* manifesting gratitude to benefactors. In cases like this, it is absolutely impossible to discover what is our 'actual' duty, what act will produce the greatest balance of *prima facie* rightness over *prima facie* wrongness, unless we can assess the values of the different obligations relatively to one another in terms of the number of units of *prima facie* rightness which each possesses. It is not that the calculation is, otherwise, a *difficult* one. The point is that it is in principle *impossible*. We are asked to do a sum which we do not, and can not, know how to do.

It is all-important to appreciate in its proper character the 'uncertainty' which belongs to our particular moral judgments in terms of this aspect of the theory under review. It is quite other than the uncertainty which is due to our inadequate information as the effects of our action—an uncertainty which we can progressively diminish (thereby advancing towards 'more probable' opinions) by widening the scope of our reflections. The present 'uncertainty' is one which no amount of reflection will even begin to diminish. In respect of this cause of uncertainty, we have no means of advancing towards 'more probable' opinions.[1] The *impasse* which confronts the moral self is absolute. Even were the self's information as to 'effects' ideally complete, it would not know what to do with its information in order to determine what act is its duty. And if the admission of this is not tantamount to ethical scepticism, the difference is not easy to detect.

Thus the principle offered us for the solution of conflicts

[1] Mr Ross is, very naturally, loath to admit this consequence. He wants to be able to say that the more we reflect upon our duty, the better will be our chance of coming to a correct decision (see, *e.g.*, the suggestion of a parallel between the attempt to do our duty and the attempt to do what is to our personal advantage, on pp. 31, 32). But, on his premises, no amount of reflection is going to lessen by one jot our uncertainty as to *how* we should calculate. We may certainly vastly augment our knowledge of the 'facts of the case,' but that will not help us if we don't know how we are to deal with the facts when we've got them.

between *prima facie* obligations turns out, after all, to be of no avail: not, indeed, to be an intelligible 'principle' at all. And it is worth pointing out, I think, that even if Mr Ross had *not* recognised differences in the 'comparative stringency' of *prima facie* obligations, we should still be without a real principle for the calculation of the balance of *prima facie* rightness over *prima facie* wrongness. For suppose it were to be maintained that each obligation has the same degree of stringency, possesses an identical amount of *prima facie* rightness. We are faced at once with the new difficulty that at least some of the obligatory acts admit of a *more* or *less* intensive performance. There is, let us agree, a *prima facie* duty to improve the conditions of our fellows. But, obviously, the amount of 'improvement' which we bring about may vary indefinitely. Just how much 'beneficence' should there be to constitute that act of beneficence which is equal in *prima facie* rightness to, say, the act of promise-keeping? Or again, just how much 'unmerited distress' must be relieved for the act to equal in *prima facie* rightness the act of requiting a benefit received? Or again, may the highly intensive performance of one *prima facie* duty equal in *prima facie* rightness the less intensive performance of two other *prima facie* duties? The questions of this sort are legion, and there is no answer to them, so far as I can see, on the premises of the intuitionalist theory. Yet the answers must be capable of being known if any computation of the greatest balance of *prima facie* rightness over *prima facie* wrongness is to be possible even in principle.

It may be objected that I have said nothing of the 'ἐν τῇ αἰσθήσει ἡ κρίσις.' I have said nothing of it, because I do not really think that Mr Ross wishes to take refuge in some mystical intuition which solves the problem, before which reason is helpless, of the comparative values of the *prima facie* duties. Even with αἴσθησις, Mr Ross admits that our judgment of our particular duty is 'highly fallible.' For my own part, I doubt whether we should find ourselves having moral 'perceptions' of *any* kind, let alone correct moral perceptions, in situations in which we are conscious of conflict between *prima facie* obligations, and conscious also of lacking any principle for the adjustment of the competing claims. A state of sheer moral deadlock seems to me the natural consequence of such conditions. But in the absence of any full account of the nature and functions of αἴσθησις, it is perhaps not desirable to pursue the matter. I am content to submit that *unless* αἴσθησις is meant to be some non-rational faculty of moral intuition, Mr Ross's theory lands us in ethical scepticism. If it *is* meant to be such a non-rational faculty, the case for its existence can hardly be said to be established in his pages.

The first main objection to Intuitionism is, then, that it is incapable of affording us a principle for the determination of our actual duty in cases where its self-evident obligations prescribe contrary courses—even if these self-evident obligations be conceived as not 'absolute' but merely *prima facie*. The second main objection is this: Intuitionism offers us a definitive set of obligations which, it affirms, may be intuitively discerned to be self-evident. How are we to reconcile this intuitive self-evidence with the prodigious diversity of historical moral codes? If these obligations are really 'self-evident,' why do so many persons, and so many races, fail to recognise their authority—nay more, frequently accept the authority of obligations which seem directly contradictory of those claimed to be self-evident? Can the findings of comparative ethics really be squared with the hypothesis of a definitive 'set' of self-evident obligations?

I am well aware that many Intuitionalists (and even some critics of Intuitionalism) do not admit that there is here any difficulty at all. They believe themselves to be in possession of a simple but perfectly satisfactory answer. I agree that the answer is simple. But I am convinced that any close scrutiny of its nature will reveal it to be anything but satisfactory.

What then is the Intuitionalist's answer? It is, in effect, as follows: It is pointed out that to be 'self-evident' does not mean to be evident 'at once, or to all.' It may well be necessary that certain conditions be fulfilled, a certain stage of development achieved, before the mind is competent to discern the truths in question. Thus, the truth of mathematical axioms is not luminous to the young child or the savage. But no one supposes that this failure to be evident to undeveloped minds makes these truths one whit the less genuinely 'self-evident.' When 'self-evidence' is claimed for a moral truth, we mean (to quote Mr Ross) 'not . . . that it is evident from the beginning of our lives, or as soon as we attend to the proposition for the first time, but . . . that when we have reached *sufficient mental maturity* and have given sufficient attention to the proposition it is evident without any need of proof, or of evidence beyond itself. It is self-evident just as a mathematical axiom, or the validity of a form of inference, is evident.'[1] When this is understood, no difficulty remains in the divergence of historic moral traditions from the definitive set of self-evident moral obligations. We can always suppose that the conditions necessary to the apprehension of these obligations were not fulfilled.

I think it is fairly plain that the ability or otherwise of this explanation to meet the facts turns upon the phrase 'sufficient mental maturity.' If the *kind* of mental maturity which may legitimately be regarded as a condition of the apprehension of self-evident truths is such as may plausibly be supposed to be lacking in those who fail to appreciate the alleged self-evident obligations—whatever they may happen to be—of the Intuitionalist, then there is force in the Intuitionalist's argument. But if, as I suspect, that hypothesis cannot be sustained, the Intuitionalist's argument breaks down. Let us consider, then, what kind of 'mental maturity' may justly be demanded as a condition of the apprehension of self-evident truths.

[1] *The Right and the Good*, p. 29. Italics mine.

We may eliminate one kind of mental maturity at once. It is not necessary to have the mental maturity which consists in the ability to maintain before the mind a complex system of conceptual relationships. That ability, in greater or less degree, is indispensable for the apprehension of inferential truths—e.g. for the apprehension of the truth of the conclusion in a geometrical demonstration. But it is of the essence of 'self-evident' truths, admittedly, that the proposition in question can be seen to be true 'within the four corners of its own being.' Its 'evidence' lies wholly within itself. The mind, therefore, does not need to be capable of sustaining anything in the nature of a train of reasoning in order to be capable of apprehending a self-evident truth. Hence, although primitive peoples are, no doubt, 'mentally immature' in this regard, this kind of immaturity should not preclude them from the capacity to apprehend self-evident moral truths.

And we can eliminate another kind of mental maturity likewise. The mental maturity which consists in the possession of an ample store of knowledge of facts—the 'well-stocked mind'—can have nothing to do with the present case. To most people, it is true, this kind of maturity seems extremely important for moral knowledge. But that is just because to most people the rightness of acts is at least largely determined by the *consequences* they produce—information as to probable consequences being thus indispensable to the ascertainment of particular rightnesses. But for the apprehension of the Intuitionalist's 'self-evident' obligations information as to the consequences of the acts to which they relate is plainly irrelevant The evidence of the 'self-evident' obligation lies (to repeat) wholly within itself.

What, then, *is* the kind of mental maturity that can be legitimately supposed to be a condition of competence to apprehend self-evident truths? So far as I can see, it is of this nature. The mind must have such maturity as enables it to understand the meaning of the different terms in the proposition, and it must have such maturity as enables it to make the effort of abstract thought required to 'hold together' the different 'terms' in their propositional relationship. Granted these conditions, it seems to me that a truth that is really self-evident must be evident to any mind that attends to it.

Is this not, after all, what we all assume with regard to the self-evidence of mathematical axioms? Take the proposition 'if equals be taken from equals, the remainders are equals.' Given a mind which understands the meaning of the different terms, and which is capable of holding the terms together in their propositional relationship (and thus of understanding the meaning of the whole proposition), and that mind, we all assume, cannot, if it attends to the proposition, withhold its assent from it. For what is there which could obstruct its apprehension, granted these conditions, and granted that the proposition is really self-evident? Nothing, it would seem, but the possession of a different kind of mind, a mind that works according to quite different principles. And no one is likely to wish to take refuge in the sceptical hypothesis that there are 'minds' intrinsically different in the principle of their operation.

But if it be admitted that it is only the kind of mental maturity which we have just described which is rightly esteemed a pre-condition of competence to apprehend self-evident truths, is it really plausible to explain the apparent incapacity of so many persons to apprehend the alleged self-evident truths of the ethical Intuitionalist as being due to their 'mental immaturity?' It is very difficult, indeed, to believe this. Undoubtedly, primitive peoples are seriously defective both as regards insight into 'consequences' and as regards capacity to perform any intricate piece of abstract reasoning. But these defects, we have seen, are irrelevant to the present issue. What matters is that they should be able to understand the meaning of terms like promising, lying, gratitude, benefactor, etc., and also, of course, what is meant by the term 'ought' itself: and again, that they should be sufficiently developed in their thinking powers to be able to take in the meaning of a total proposition like 'gratitude ought to be shown to benefactors.' Surely it is paradoxical to maintain that these very elementary conditions are not in very large measure satisfied among all save the most barbaric races? Yet many of the communities which sharply dissent from the Intuitionalist's set of obligations are far removed from the status of the 'barbarian.'

It is just conceivable, however, that the Intuitionalist might be prepared to admit that most of those who acquiesce in other codes do have the *capacity* to apprehend the alleged self-evident obligations. He might try to explain their failure to apprehend them on the ground that they have not had occasion to give proper attention to the general propositions in which they are expressed. And it is true enough, of course, that not many of the persons in question have set themselves, or been set, to 'consider' these propositions. On the other hand, if they have not had the opportunity to appreciate the 'general proposition,' they have had ample occasion to appreciate its particularised expression in reference to individual acts in their experience. And this particularised expression is supposed by the Intuitionalist to be equally a self-evident proposition. Indeed, if we are to believe Mr Ross,[1] it is from the apprehension of the self-evident rightness (for Mr Ross, *prima facie* rightness) of an individual act of a particular type that we ultimately come to apprehend the self-evident 'general principle' relating to that type. Yet the actual facts of the case are that these persons who have failed to apprehend the alleged self-evident principles have been every bit as unsatisfactory in failing to apprehend the alleged self-evident particularised expression. The failure does not seem to be accounted for, therefore, by mere lack of opportunity.

I think, then, that if the Intuitionalist's set of obligations

[1] *The Right and the Good*, p. 33.

really were self-evident, it is reasonable to suppose that they would manifest themselves in the lives and minds of primitive peoples in a very much more decisive and consistent way than is actually the case. And this view of the matter is confirmed in a very significant manner when we consider the operation on the primitive mind of certain truths that really *are* self-evident, viz. the axioms of mathematics. These axioms are not apprehended as general principles by primitive peoples. But at least many of them *are* apprehended in their particularised expressions. Primitive man does not state to himself the general proposition 'a straight line is the shortest distance between two points.' But in individual situations he will show that he recognises it to be true by formulating his action as though it were true. Thus there is all the difference in the world between his response to particularised expressions of mathematical axioms, and his response to particularised expressions of the 'self-evident' obligations of the Intuitionalist. If the latter really are self-evident, I can see no good reason why there should be this difference.

And there is a further important point which must not be neglected in connection with the attitude of the Intuitionalist to 'comparative ethics.' The Intuitionalist has not merely to face the fact that primitive peoples, and many peoples not so primitive, *fail* to apprehend the Intuitionalist's obligations. He has also to face the fact that they *do* recognise *other* obligations, obligations sometimes even contradictory of those posited by the Intuitionalist. How is the Intuitionalist going to explain these moral recognitions in terms of his own theory? They are, in some sense, manifestations of man's moral consciousness. They bear every mark of being continuous in kind with the deliverances of the most 'civilised' moral consciousness. But it is extremely difficult to account for them on the assumption of a moral consciousness which is the seat of the apprehension of a special set of definitive obligations. To say that they are due to 'inadequate development' of the moral consciousness is to explain only in words. For what are we to understand by the 'development' of a moral consciousness of the sort posited by the Intuitionalist? And even if the possibility of 'development' were granted, what kind of 'development' could it be in which some of the earlier phases are in actual *contradiction* with the final phase?

As far as I can see, the Intuitionalist is debarred by the nature of his theory from offering any positive account of the multitudinous diversities of historic moral codes. Yet we must be in earnest with these facts, for they belong to the very data of ethics. If we are in earnest with them, if we do really seek to account for these diversities, there seems to be little doubt that headway cannot be made save in terms of an ethical theory which recognises the closest of connections between the 'moral consciousness' and 'desires.' Any serious scrutiny of these diversities almost compels the conclusion that the cardinal factor in determining the specific character of each code is the special nature of the dominating interests or desires of the community in question. Assuredly *mere* interests, *mere* desires are not enough. There would be no 'moral' recognitions if there were nothing but the particular 'interests.' But that there is a connection, intimate and positive, between the concrete moral consciousness of any community and its dominant interests, seems to be the plain lesson of comparative ethics. With this clue before one, one may thread one's way not unsuccessfully through the labyrinth of the world's moralities. The variations of codes cease to be mere *de facto* variations, become intelligible variations. Without this clue all is confusion.

Nor (finally) does it really seem unfair to remind the reader of the signal failure of Intuitionalists to make their 'self-evident' principles evident even to those who, unlike savages, cannot fairly be suspected of 'mental immaturity': even to those, indeed, who are predisposed to sympathy by general agreement with the Intuitionalist mode of approach to ethics. In this respect our most important contemporary Intuitionalists are in no better case than their predecessors. Is it too venturesome to suggest that the reason for this may be just that of every one of the 'self-evident' obligations in the Intuitionalist's lists the question may still intelligibly be asked '*why* is this obligatory?' Of *one* end only (as I hold) can this question not be asked intelligibly, because the obligatoriness of this end is in truth intuitively discerned. This is the end which I have called the 'end of the self-as-such,' or 'good of the self as a whole.'

Section 8. *The Moral Authority of the 'End of the Self-as-such': (b) its Intuitive Appeal*

I have admitted frankly that formal demonstration of our one ultimate obligation is not possible. The final appeal is, and must be, to intuition. The main work of its recommendation consists in the removal of obstacles which obstruct the attainment of that intuition. Trusting that at least something to this end has been achieved by what has been said, I must now invite the reader to give his attention (bearing the foregoing considerations in mind) directly to the crucial experience itself.

Let him imagine himself in a practical situation in which two conflicting ends, x and y, present themselves as rival motives. For convenience, the ends are restricted to two; and, also for convenience, we may choose the simple case of an alternative between doing and forbearing—say indulgence in some drug (x) and abstention from it (y). When he reflects upon these ends (as is natural to a self-conscious being) in relation to the divers goods which he, the common subject of manifold interests, is conscious of wanting, it becomes evident to him at once that to follow x is to bring into hazard much that he holds dear: so much so that, though he 'burns with desire' for it, he cannot regard it as truly representing, in this situation, *the* good of the self. It is *a* good, for he is conscious of a desire for it, conscious that it is a satisfaction of his self in one aspect of his being; but it is not *the* good, for it appears to him as less conducive than y to the satisfaction of the self in its unity or as a whole. y, therefore, presents itself as 'the end of the self-as-such,' as against x, the end of mere desire. In contrast with one another, y is 'self-fulfilling,' and x 'self-destroying.' And what I maintain is that you and I and every other self, when confronted with this plain issue between an end that is self-fulfilling and an end that is self-destroying, do feel, and cannot help feeling, that one 'ought' to resist the latter end and follow the former.

The obligation is just, at bottom, the obligation to respect one's self. It is the obligation to pursue those ends which are truly the ends of the self, in opposition to ends which, while 'desired' by the self, are recognised as not correspondent with the self's fundamental nature, *i.e.* with its unitary being. Self-consciousness *is* the awareness on the part of the self of its own unity. The self-conscious self must therefore regard its unitary nature as its 'real' nature, and must regard ends which are not correspondent with that unitary nature (*i.e.* the ends which are inimical to the good of the self as a whole) as not correspondent with that which is truly its 'self.' The root of morality might thus be said to be the self's obligation to respect, and in respecting to be, its true self. Further than this, in the way of explanation, I do not think it possible to go. If it still be asked why we should be under any obligation to respect what we feel to be our 'real' nature, I think it must be said that there is no answer. We have got down here to a simple bedrock fact of finite rational beings. It is not reasoning now that will help us in assuring ourselves of the obligation's reality, but only actual immersion in the living stream of experience itself. It is at this point that appeal must perforce be made to the reader's own intuition.

Or again, the obligation might be called the obligation to be rational. For this end which we 'ought' to follow is in a special sense the 'end of reason.' It is man's rationality or reflective capacity which forces him to disengage himself from immediate ends and to view them in the light of their contribution to the good of the self as a whole. 'The good of the self as a whole' is thus peculiarly the end sponsored by rational nature. And to describe our obligation in these terms, as 'the obligation to be rational,' is to give it what will perhaps be its most generally acceptable formula. The sense of the inherent propriety of 'acting rationally' finds such wide acknowledgment among men that this formula may make appeal to some who are unmoved by the ascription of moral authority to 'self-respect.' But it *is* only a new formula. We are no nearer than before to an ultimate explanation or justification of the obligation. Immediate experience is, as before, the final court of appeal, the only solvent of ultimate doubts. In the last resort, the proper answer to those who will not acknowledge that there is an obligation to act rationally is just, 'go and see'—or better, 'go and feel.'

Section 9. *Concluding Remarks on the Implications of the Position Reached*

The thesis of the chapter must now be left to take its fortune. I shall close by reminding the reader, in a very few words, of certain further results which must be accepted if the present conclusions be subscribed to.

An important result is that what has been called 'the ethical argument for freedom' now acquires apodeictic force. This argument states that if you believe in the 'ought,' you must believe likewise in freedom, since the 'ought' is meaningless without the postulate of freedom. Valid so far as it goes, the argument yet fails in its ultimate intention unless the necessity of believing in the 'ought' is sufficiently demonstrated. The present chapter, in so far as it is valid, supplies that condition. I have tried to show that recognition of the 'ought' is rooted in the very nature of self-conscious experience, that, accordingly, the moral life with all that it implies is for man an inexpugnable reality, which constructive philosophy can ignore only by doing violence to the very datal facts of the world which it sets out to explain.

Again, the recognition of the 'ought,' because it is the recognition of freedom, is also the recognition that Reality is not rationally or intelligibly continuous. It has commonly been felt, and I have tried in an earlier section to show that this feeling is *bene fundatum*, that only by subterfuge can a case be made out for the significance of morality on a metaphysic like that of Absolute Idealism. But there is a certain reluctance to allow that freedom, and therefore morality, is inconsistent not only with the Idealist theory of the universe, but with *any* theory of it which maintains its thoroughgoing 'intelligibility.' Yet that the universe is 'intelligible throughout' means, if it means anything, that the intellect could, under ideal conditions of information, pass inferentially from point to point within the Whole; and meaning this, it means determinism, and the denial of morality. I am not convinced that this implication of thoroughgoing intelligibility is always squarely faced. There seem to be some thinkers at least who are prepared to defend freedom, and a good many more who are resolute in their claims for morality, who nevertheless look askance at the doctrine that Reality is not 'intelligible.' But unless morality be construed after the non-moral manner of the Spinozistic 'ethics,' and freedom be accorded a similarly Pickwickian meaning, the contradictoriness of this attitude is patent. For myself, believing that both freedom and morality are real in their common-sense meanings, I must draw the inference that Reality is not rationally continuous, and regard the doctrine of the Supra-rational Absolute, arrived at on epistemological grounds, as receiving substantial confirmation from the consideration of practical experience.

CHAPTER VII

THE PRINCIPLE OF MORAL VALUATION

Section 1. Moral Valuation and 'the Moral End'

IF this were a treatise on moral philosophy, there is a multitude of subsidiary matters which would now require to be dealt with, consequent upon the discussions of the last chapter.[1]

[1] One of the more important of such tasks would be that of showing how the 'conceived good of the self as a whole' develops a content both deeper and wider in response to the advancing refinement and elaboration of the self's interests which cultural enlightenment brings in its train. A detailed account of this progress would, I think, furnish an unanswerable refutation of those who persist in regarding the 'conceived good of the self as a whole' as a 'mean and grovelling' makeshift for a moral principle. But the principle of the refutation has already been indicated (see especially Section 6 of the previous chapter) and the benefits of an ampler treatment are not, in my judgment, commensurate with the space which would require to be devoted to it.

It would be interesting to consider also the deeper implications of that 'unitary self-consciousness' which, we have seen, lies at the root of the self's recognition of a morally obligatory course of conduct. I am entirely opposed to views of the Greenian type which strive to see in the finite self-consciousness a temporal and partial manifestation of an 'eternal self-consciousness.' Indeed the reader who has laboured on thus far will not need to be informed that anything in the nature of a 'metaphysical' explanation of finite self-consciousness is for me in principle impossible. On the other hand, it might be worth while to show how, just as in the sphere of knowledge complete theoretical satisfaction is not possible short of immersion in the Whole, so, too, complete practical satisfaction—the 'end' which would answer with perfect and final adequacy to the demands of a self-conscious self—is incapable of finding expression in any *finite* system of life. The implication which would suggest itself would be that the moral impulse (which seems, in my interpretation of it, to be at first glance so 'unspiritual') is in reality a manifestation of man's kinship, *in some sense*, with the Infinite.

These (and much else that is here neglected) are important matters, but their bearing on our central thesis is not, I think, sufficiently direct to make the consideration of them an obligation.

The plan of the book imposes other demands, however. It is necessary to limit attention to those more fundamental questions in the ethical field whose settlement importantly affects, or is importantly affected by, the general philosophical doctrine which I am concerned to establish. The significance of the problem of Chapter VI. in this respect has been sufficiently made out. But there is another central ethical issue which, as I hope to show, has an almost equal significance. This is the problem of the true principle of moral evaluation. The only solution of that problem, I shall argue, which does justice to actual moral experience, is one which presupposes the truth of some of the main positions which I have been advocating. For this reason (as well as for others which will engage us later) it is a solution which there is, of course, almost universal reluctance to adopt. But if we follow 'the wind of the argument, whithersoever it leads,' refusing to allow the cross-currents of metaphysical predilections to divert us from our course, we can reach, in my opinion, no other possible termination.

Now at first sight it may appear as if this our present problem were the same as the problem of determining the nature of 'the moral end': that the 'moral end' is, almost by definition, that in terms of which moral valuation should proceed. If the moral end means that which man 'ought' to do or be—and why otherwise call it the 'moral' end?—it may seem to be self-evident that we should judge conduct to be morally good or bad according as it attains to or falls short of the moral end.

But although there is a sense (dependent, as a matter of fact, upon a rather special interpretation of the term 'moral end') in which this is true enough, a mere glance at the several moral ends proposed by the great ethical systems of the world should be enough to raise grave doubts as to whether the identification of 'moral end' with 'principle of moral evaluation' can be so simply effected. For one feature common to almost all of these ends is that they are in their nature such that the mass of men, with their environmental, cultural, and other limitations, are quite incapable of attaining them. Such an end cannot be an end which all men 'ought' to attain (if 'ought' implies 'can'), and cannot therefore be set up as a universal standard of moral praise and blame.

Nevertheless, unless language is being abused, the expression 'moral end' must be intended to signify something that in some way has obligatory force. There must surely be some sense in which this significance can be understood to attach to the 'moral ends' even of highly sophisticated ethical theories. Can we not find a justification for the ascription, by these theories, of the adjective 'moral' to the ends which they offer us?—for this is what it comes to.

I think that if the attempt were made its best hope of success would be along some such lines as these. We do not intend by the term 'moral end,' it might be said, that it is the end which all men ought to *attain*. We understand well enough that it is impossible for the multitude, and perhaps, in its completeness, for any man, to attain. What we mean is rather that it is the end which all men ought to *strive to* attain. And since all men can 'strive to attain' the end proposed by our theory, the objection to calling it a 'moral' end vanishes. Persons can in an intelligible sense be morally esteemed or censured according as they do or do not 'strive to attain' our end.

This is better, if only because of its recognition that moral valuation implies an 'ought' which is meaningless without a 'can.' But it will not suffice. It is still impossible to hold that these suggested ends are 'moral' ends, even in the sense that all men ought to 'strive to attain' them. For, when we think the matter out, it becomes clear that there is only one end which we can say in strictness all men ought to strive to attain, and that is the end, be it what it may, which each individual agent presents to himself as morally best. Of no concrete end whatever set up 'from the outside' can this be justly said. For no matter what it be, it will be true that a great many people (and it must be borne in mind that the savage as well as the sage must be considered in the determination of a universal moral criterion) not only do not, but *could* not, present such an end to themselves as morally right. It will be, for many, beyond their mental horizon, or outside their mental perspective. And you cannot call such persons 'bad' because they do not strive to attain an ideal which they do not and cannot apprehend as such. You may say they are stupid, if you like, but if the end in question could not be their moral end, it is nonsense to suggest that they 'ought' to be aiming at it. On the contrary, often it will be true that they definitely ought *not* to aim at it, for it may enjoin something which is in direct conflict with their own moral end. It is the extremity of theory to hold that a man 'ought' to do what he believes to be wrong.

These considerations are all very simple. So simple, that one would be ashamed to dwell upon them were it not that very few ethical writers seem prepared to take them in real earnest. If they are taken in earnest, it seems an unavoidable inference that we are only entitled to evaluate conduct in terms of 'the moral end,' if by 'the moral end' we mean, not some ideal laid down *ab extra* by 'enlightened' thinking, but just the ideal of the morally best which presents itself to the agent whose conduct is under review. Some qualifications will, of course, require to be introduced to take account of the obvious fact that the agent's present ideal may, owing to his own past faults, be less enlightened than it could have been. But, apart from refinements, the gist of the matter is as I have expressed it. I can see no way of evading the result unless we insist, against all the implications of language, that moral valuation has nothing to do with an 'ought' or an 'ought not,' and has no implications of 'praise' and 'blame.'

There is, indeed, an easy solvent often proposed, resting on a distinction between 'subjective rightness' and 'objective rightness.' It is 'subjectively right,' we are told, for each man to follow his own ideal, the dictates of his own 'conscience': but this conduct will only be 'objectively right' in so far as the individual ideal coincides with the ideal endorsed by enlightened ethical thinking. In terms of this distinction, it is claimed, we can see that the ethical systems which offer us 'moral ends' are offering us ends which are 'morally right,' but in the sense of possessing 'objective moral rightness,' not 'subjective moral rightness.'

But there is no way of escape in this direction. The short but sufficient answer to all theories of the kind is a question. 'Which, subjective or objective rightness, is the criterion which we are to use in appraising the *moral* worth of persons?' When once we face this question fairly, we find that no advance has been made by the distinction. For unless we are prepared to banish the 'ought' from the meaning of morality, we are forced to reply that it is in terms of the 'subjectively right,' and of that alone, that moral appraisement must function.

As to this whole conception of 'objective rightness,' I must confess that it seems to me one of the most confused, and confusing, in the sphere of morals. One would suppose that (if it is to deserve its title) it must give us that which *all* men ought to do. But it cannot support this meaning. For it seems undeniable that what *each* man ought to do is to pursue his own ideal (which may, of course, undergo refinement, elaboration, or even reform, in the course of experience). If we ask, then, *who* it is that ought to follow the so-called 'objectively right,' the only answer seems to be, that rather small body of persons to whom, in virtue of its happening to be their individual ideal, it is at the same time 'subjectively right.'

And I do not think the use of the term can be defended by analogy with subjectivity and objectivity in the sphere of 'truth.' It is the case that in this sphere we assign the title 'objective' to the truth as it appears to fully enlightened thinking. But there is a justification for this which does not obtain in the case of morals. What is 'true' to enlightened thinking is 'true,' we are all ready to agree, for every person, whether 'every person' apprehends it or not. That is the warrant, and it is a sufficient one, for our calling it 'objective' truth. But what is 'right' to enlightened thinking we may not similarly suppose to be 'right,' *i.e.* morally obligatory, for every person, irrespective of every person's apprehension. The 'apprehension' in this case seems quite vital. It seems to me, therefore, that the propriety of assigning the title 'objective' to 'intellectually enlightened' moral content is not to be made out by analogy with the sphere of truth.

Is there any way out of all these difficulties? I can see none, except the frank avowal by theories of the 'moral end' that they are using this term only as signifying 'the most satisfying state of mankind,' or something of the sort, without any direct implication of 'oughtness.' And if this line is taken, then I reply that you have not got in your 'end' a principle by which you can evaluate man's moral worth, whatever else you may have got. And that is all that I here contend for.

These brief remarks may have conveyed some indication, if only by exclusion, of the kind of theory of the principle of moral valuation which I am now to expound in detail. Perhaps I may venture to hope that the difficulties which have appeared in the conventional type of theory will have influenced the reader to regard with tolerance an attempt which will differ at least in offering no obvious violence to actual moral experience. However that may be, I propose now, making a fresh start (though not scrupling to emphasise further some points that have already been broached) to raise the direct question 'what is the true principle of moral valuation?'

Section 2. *Approach to, and Exposition of, the Positive Theory to be Defended*

It is desirable to glance first of all at the subject-matter of moral valuation. Here, fortunately, we discover a pretty general agreement. Moral valuation is concerned with 'conduct,' and with 'character' as the symbol of conduct. And 'conduct' may be taken to mean, in its primary significance, the deliberately purposed acts of beings for whom the distinction of a 'good' that ought to be followed, and a 'bad' that ought to be eschewed, has both a general meaning and a concrete content. It is true, of course, that we often pass moral judgments upon, and give the name 'conduct' to, behaviour that is not *directly* animated by deliberate purpose. But wherever this happens (as it may, *e.g.* in judging 'habitual' action now become 'unconscious') the reference to deliberately purposed acts is implicitly present, and is the real foundation of our judgment. We praise or censure acts not deliberately purposed now only because they are the reflections of acts that were deliberately purposed in the past. The moral judgment in these cases is in fact essentially a retrospective judgment, 'you are blameworthy in acting so now, because you ought to have acted otherwise in the past.' And the judgment has present force against the agent just because we regard him, and he regards himself, as somehow the self-same person as he who performed the past bad acts. It is the past bad acts, deliberately purposed, that are the ultimate object of censure. Hence here, as elsewhere, moral valuation refers essentially to deliberately purposed action.[1] If we abstract from this aspect of behaviour, nothing remains upon which a reflective person who is free from prepossessions would think of passing moral judgment.

[1] I may, perhaps, be excused from considering independently moral judgments upon the emotions, for it is apparent that, *mutatis mutandis*, the same principle of explanation will serve. We do not praise or blame 'natural' emotions, but only those which are what they are in the individual through his own 'responsible' behaviour in the past.

PRINCIPLE OF MORAL VALUATION

Now in deliberately purposed, *i.e.* 'volitional,' acts there are two aspects, one constant and one occasional, each of which has a *prima facie* relevance for moral valuation. Every volitional act has in the first place, and in the very nature of the case, a conceived 'end' at which the agent aims. And the nature or content of this end is, of course, for very many persons the thing of chief significance in morally evaluating the act. In the second place, the volitional act may, or may not, be charged, as we have seen in an earlier chapter, with 'will-energy.' The actuality of will-energy, whose function consists in reinforcing the felt 'weaker but higher' end against the felt 'stronger but lower' end—or, as we have now come to regard it, reinforcing the 'end of the self-as-such' where this is in contrast with the 'end of desire'—is not only popularly assumed, but, as I have tried to show in Chapter V., is philosophically defensible. And it too must be granted at least *prima facie* significance in the moral valuation of conduct.

At the risk of vain repetition, I wish at this juncture to remind the reader of two points in connection with the concept of will-energy which it is essential to bear in mind if what follows is to be adequately understood.

First, will-energy is not to be identified with what, for want of a better expression, is called volitional activity. The formal act of identifying one's self with a conceived end does not of itself involve 'energising.' We are all very well aware of this wherever we deliberately choose what we regard as the 'easy' course as against the difficult 'energy-demanding' course which we believe to be right. Here obviously is volitional activity without will-energy. We are aware of energising only in these volitional acts in which we rise superior to the set of our desires in the direction of our ideal, transcending, as we may put it, the *status quo* of our existing conative tendencies.

And secondly, will-energy is not to be confused with either physical or mental energy. We may be conscious of intense physical or mental energy in situations which from the point of view of the *will* we know to be effortless, mere yieldings to 'the line of least resistance.' Conversely, we may be conscious of intense will-energy in situations in which body and mind are well-nigh passive—indeed, the very end which it is the function of will-energy to reinforce may sometimes be (as in the case cited on page 134) the suspension of all bodily and mental energies.

To proceed. We have distinguished as the two factors in volition that have *prima facie* relevance in moral valuation, the omnipresent factor of the end, or concrete content, willed, and the occasional factor of will-energy. On the basis of these two factors we can make a broad classification of the possible competing views as to the true criterion of moral valuation. These views will be three in number. We may hold (*a*) that it is solely the nature of the concrete content willed that matters, conduct being good or bad according as that content does or does not express what is taken to be the ultimate moral principle (or principles); or (*b*) that consideration must be given to both factors, concrete content willed and degree of will-energy (if any) expended, if full justice is to be done to the actual moral judgments of mankind; or (*c*) that will-energy is the sole thing that matters; that the only situation which has any direct [1] moral significance is that in which there is a felt contrast of end of self-as-such and end of desire, with consequent demand for the expenditure of will-energy; and that moral value is proportionate to the degree of will-energy put forth.

The above classification is, I think, exhaustive of the possible principles of moral valuation, in the broad sense in which we are at present viewing them. It does not, to be sure, cover theories which measure the moral value of conduct in terms of its external consequences, *e.g.* pleasure-productiveness. For

[1] The significance of this qualification will become evident as we proceed.

such a theory, it will be a matter of indifference what kind of end is actually willed, or again whether any effort was required to rise to the act. What matters will be simply, what kind of effects does the act in fact produce? But the failure to take account of such theories is not really a defect in the classification put forward. For theories like Benthamism in its strict form—or so at least I should be prepared to argue—are styled 'ethical' theories only, as it were, by courtesy. It is not so much that Benthamism has arrived at the wrong destination, as that it has never really started. For it has failed to recognise the primary characteristic of its ostensible subject-matter, failed to recognise that morality, and therefore ethical theory, has to do essentially with *personal* worth, as manifested in conduct. Benthamism has really a far closer affinity with Economics than with Ethics. Economics is concerned to discover what are the kinds of action that produce wealth. Benthamism is concerned to discover what are the kinds of action that produce pleasure. Neither is in principle at all interested in the doer of the action save in his capacity as producer. But, as Aristotle long ago pointed out, morality cannot be regarded as an art whose value lies solely in its external effects. The inner nature of the act matters profoundly in our estimation of its moral worth. Benthamism in abstracting from this aspect—doubtless because its deterministic psychology left, for honest thinking, no room for genuine differences in personal worth—*ipso facto* abandons all claim to be considered as an *ethical* theory.

Let us take it, then, that (*a*), (*b*), and (*c*) cover all possible principles of moral valuation. I want to show now, in as pointed a way as I can, the rock upon which, as I see it, all theories of type (*a*) and type (*b*) inevitably split. There will here be no intricate chain of reasoning. The essence of the matter is essentially simple. But I take the liberty of expressing the hope that the reader will not be deceived by its simplicity into regarding it as unworthy of attention. For simple as it is, it has got to be remembered that there are strong reasons why considerations which, by disposing of (*a*) and (*b*), leave no option but (*c*), have tended to be slurred over in most ethical thinking. The objections on general philosophic principles to theories of type (*c*), *i.e.* theories which take 'will-energy' as the thing of primary importance in moral valuation, are very commonly assumed to be quite insuperable. Type (*c*), therefore, tends to be ruled out *ab initio* from the ranks of respectable ethical hypotheses: and the considerations which suggest it, accordingly, to be depreciated. Now these general philosophic prepossessions our earlier chapters have shown, or tried to show, to be grounded in error. It seems fair to claim, therefore, that the argument which I am about to put forward demands to be considered in relation to a good deal of preceding doctrine if its proper force is to be appreciated.

The crucial objection to all theories of types (*a*) and (*b*) is, then, as follows: In moral judgment we claim to be appraising the worth of persons, expressed in conduct. Now if the nature of the concrete content willed be that in terms of which we judge, or in so far as it is, we are judging in terms of something which is in large measure outside the agent's control. This is an assertion, I should think, that is quite beyond the range of controversy. No matter what view we happen to favour as to the relation of man to his environment, no matter how strongly we may insist that nothing can affect the conscious self save it be first internalised by the self, it still stares us in the face as indisputable fact that what anyone is able to will, the range of his possible choices, is conditioned by many factors with whose existence he has nothing to do. It may be (and this is, of course, what I myself contend) that the conditioning is only of a general character, determining a *field* of possible content, but not any particular content. But that it is real at least in this measure it seems wilful blindness to deny. The uneducated slum-dweller cannot, just cannot, will the enlightened content of the man of culture. And the inevitable, if unwelcome, inference from this is that 'content' cannot constitute a valid principle for the appraisement of personal worth. For to judge a man on the basis of the content of his will is to judge him on the basis of something largely not his own, and this is the very parody of justice. The aspect of 'content' has, as we shall see later, a certain derivative value as a criterion, but simply as such, as mere content, it is utterly irrelevant to moral valuation.

The kernel of the matter is that to judge in terms of the nature of the content willed is not, strictly speaking, to judge the *man*. We cannot in this way appraise 'personal' worth, and in consequence cannot in this way evaluate conduct from the moral point of view. And if it be rejoined that there is no other 'man' to judge, that the 'man' is not something other than his 'content,' the answer to be made is twofold. In the first place, the objector may be reminded of all that has been said in Chapters IV. and V. on personal activity, with special reference to the Section on the individuality of finite selves. And, in the second place, it must be pointed out once more that *if* man is to be regarded as no more than some complex of content, a mere current in the great ocean of Being, then perhaps some kind of valuation may be possible, but not *moral* valuation. We cannot say then that a man 'ought' to have been better than he is. He is what he is, and there's an end on't. To say that he 'ought' to be better implies that he is somehow a real initiator. Deny that man is at least this, and you thereby deny the validity of each and every principle of moral valuation.

I take my stand on this. If we are going to evaluate conduct morally, *i.e.* in terms of personal worth, we must confine ourselves to that aspect of it which is strictly the agent's *own*. And if we do confine ourselves to that which is strictly the agent's own, we must look elsewhere than to concrete content.

But is there anything at all of which we can say that it is strictly the agent's own? The question brings us in one leap to theory (*c*). There is one thing, and one thing only, which man can with any show of plausibility claim to be indefeasibly his own. And that is 'will-energy.'[1] No ordinary reflective person would hesitate to agree that his 'content' is in large measure externally conditioned, that the range of ends which are suggested to him in practical experience is dependent on factors at least partially outside his control. But I believe it to be equally certain that no one who experiences, or who imaginatively reconstructs his experience of, will-energy, can do other than believe that its exercise depends solely upon his self, that it is the creation of his own private, world-excluding core of being. It is just because men know in their hearts that energising, will-effort, is the one thing which is indefeasibly their own, the one thing for which they are solely responsible, that in their deepest moments of self-appraisement they scorn the formal codes of moral valuation, and recognise in themselves nothing that is truly deserving of credit or censure save their employment of this unique power.

Do men really, in their deepest moments, believe this? Do they really believe that effort of will, or will-energy, is the one thing of moral value? I am sure that they do, most commonly with regard to themselves, but also, when their spiritual vision is unobscured, with regard to others. It will be a large part of my subsequent business to show that wherever moral judgment ostensibly adopts a different principle there are factors in the situation which are obstructive to clear vision. Meantime, before concluding this Section, I shall for the sake of clarity express in propositional form the essence of the theory which I wish to maintain.

(1) The ultimate subject-matter of moral valuation is volitional action.

(2) All volitional action possesses a concrete content, or end, and may possess, in different degrees, will-energy.

(3) The only kind of practical situation in which volitional

[1] For discussion of the 'privacy' of will-energy see Chapter V., Section 4.

action is directly significant for moral valuation is that in which there is a felt contrast of the self's ideal end with the end of desire, and in which, accordingly, there is a felt demand for the exercise of effort of will or will-energy.

(4) In such situations moral value is proportionate to the will-energy put forth.

(5) Although the content of will is not, *merely as such*, relevant for moral valuation, it does have a certain indirect relevance. For within limits (we shall see how later) the kind of content willed offers a clue to the degree of will-energy, if any, put forth by the agent. Where, as in the case of our judgments upon others, there is no direct access to the volitional process, we are bound to judge, if we judge at all, through the medium of content. This is legitimate enough if we are careful to remember that we are evaluating the content not in and for itself, but only in so far as it reflects the will-energy put forth in the act.

Section 3. *Discussion of the Difficulties in Practical Application of the Principle*

We must now try to justify this doctrine by reference to some of the more important difficulties that are likely to be felt in its regard.

The first difficulty is one suggested by proposition (5) above, and has to do with the possibility, on our theory, of passing moral judgment upon the conduct of others. It is quite evident that only in the case of ourselves have we direct access to what is, on the theory, the ethically relevant aspect of willed action. It is not so evident that an indirect access is available in the case of our judgment upon others. To some it will appear that the principle of moral valuation which we have advanced destroys all possibility of legitimately passing moral judgment upon the conduct of anyone but ourselves.

I shall try to show that this is not really so. But it is worth asking, '*if* it is, what then?' It does not, surely, impeach the validity of a principle that its application to practice should happen to be obstructed by ignorance of matters of fact? The principle, if valid, must indeed be 'universally applicable' in the sense of 'holding good everywhere and always,' but not necessarily in the sense that we can always in practice apply it. That opens up another and quite different set of considerations.

And, after all, is not a theory for which the principle of moral valuation is one difficult to apply in practice, just recognising explicitly a fact of which most of us show ourselves fully aware in our calmer judgments? In the heat engendered by the clash of warring interests one is apt, it is true, to forget how hazardous a matter is the passing of judgment upon others. But the recognition of its essential precariousness does return in the detachment of sober reflection. And it will hardly be disputed that the latter 'atmosphere' is the more favourable of the two for the pure functioning of the moral consciousness, more likely to produce an attitude representative of authentic moral experience.

But, as already hinted, our theory does not, after all, leave us entirely devoid of means for ascertaining the moral worth of others. Their 'concrete content' does afford us a clue: not sufficient, indeed, for the determination of the finer distinctions, but amply sufficient, as a rule, to distinguish the saint from the scoundrel, and in general to form rough but reasonably probable opinions upon the broader differences in moral status.

Let us see briefly how this works. We know that every person has, in the nature of the case, a moral ideal—the conceived 'end of the self-as-such.' And we know that this ideal meets in practice with frequent oppositions from the desires, oppositions which can be overcome only by the exertion of will-energy. Roughly speaking, therefore, we may suppose that a life which exhibits marked conformity of conduct with the agent's own ideal is a life in which much will-energy has been exerted, and *vice versa*. Thus (although there are a host of other facts about the agent of which it would be helpful to be informed in the interests of accuracy), the primary condition of judgment upon others is that we should be able to know how far a man's conduct accords with his ideal.

Now to know this it is obviously necessary for us to know pretty definitely the constitution of the individual's ideal. Otherwise we cannot possibly gauge the extent of his devotion to it. But this condition is surely satisfied with fair adequacy in at least the bulk of cases. What I have earlier admitted as to the bearing of external factors upon the determination of an individual's content, I must now emphasise. Environmental and educational influences are all-important in determining what kind of ideal a man will have. And the nature of these influences, in respect of most of the persons upon whom we are accustomed to pass judgment, we do in large part know. Thus if we find a person who has, we know, been subjected to the orthodox moral education of school, parents, and society, and who is sunk in a life of sordid debauchery, it will involve no great theoretical presumption on the part of a 'moral judge' to infer that the agent's practice falls pretty far short of his ideal. We can tell, at least with approximate accuracy, the kind of ideal which a person so circumstanced must possess, or must at one time have possessed (for ideals have a tendency to deteriorate concurrently with the failure to live up to them): and his conduct flagrantly violates what must be the most elementary constituents of that ideal. If by any chance the society's ideal has genuinely failed to make appeal to him even with respect to these elementary constituents of true well-being, if he has honestly repudiated as false the precepts of his instructors, it can only be, one is entitled to suppose, on account of some definite abnormality in his make-up. And in this event it is highly probable that we shall already have had indications of something unusual in his disposition, in which case our moral judgment will naturally make the appropriate allowances.

That, however, brings us up against a second important condition which should be satisfied if one is to be confident of even the limited accuracy which I am claiming for moral judgment upon others. We ought to be cognisant of any serious disproportion or abnormality in the natural disposition of the agent. If we do not know this, we shall misinterpret the degree of will-energy which his conduct really involves. It would, of course, be absurd to pretend that on this head our information is at all adequate. But it does seem true that at least fairly often we are able to detect the abnormality in these cases where the impulse in question is of such excessive intensity that it introduces eccentric elements into the agent's ideal of true well-being; or, in the event of its leaving his ideal sound, exerts such overwhelming motive force against the ideal, that the agent must make a quite uncommon effort of will in order to carry his ideal into practice. Plenty of instances of these predispositions have come within the experience of all of us, and one's regular habit of 'making allowances' is, of course, precisely what the present theory of the principle of moral valuation would dictate. It is indubitable, I think, that such 'allowances' are made in the practice of moral valuation, at least by those on whose moral judgments we are accustomed to set any store. People do normally recognise [1] that there is greater moral worth in the control of desire in

---

[1] Some of the exceptions are, I confess, disconcerting. For example, in the spate of articles and reviews that followed upon the recent publication of certain letters of Dostoieffski, and some parts of Madame Tolstoi's Diary, it was astonishing how few of the writers, in appraising the characters of the two most remarkable men in Russian literature, either manifested the diffidence in moral judgment appropriate in dealing with persons of exceptionally complex mental processes, or (which more concerns our present point) appeared to feel that there was anything grotesque in criticising by normal standards the 'aberrations' of men whose vitality was obviously, by contrast with the normal man, titanic. Surely the slightest reflection is enough to convince one of the ineptitude of a moral imagination which permits an attitude of this sort.

obedience to the ideal on the part of 'passionate natures,' than in a similar control on the part of the douce, 'tideless-blooded' folk of Burns's satire; and, conversely, less moral culpability in 'lapses' on the part of the former. And if so, it suggests rather strongly that practice is not so far removed as may at first sight appear from our seemingly paradoxical doctrine that will-energy is the sole thing of moral value.

But the present point is just that there *are* facilities available for ascertaining, though only in a rough general way, the will-energy expended by others besides ourselves. And perhaps enough has been said on a matter which is, after all, not of the first philosophic importance. Anything like precise valuation is, I agree, utterly impossible, if only because we cannot know either the exact nature of the passionate equipment with which the individual starts his course, or how far subtle external influences may have been at work throughout his experience, nursing, perhaps, an originally normal impulse into tyrannical vigour. Ignorant of these things, and of much more besides, we can never pretend to ascertain with any rigorous accuracy how much 'moral effort' there has been in the life of anyone but ourselves.

Before passing on, we may notice very briefly one implication of what has been said about the influence of external factors in determining the content of the individual's ideal. It is this, that our highly 'subjective' theory of moral valuation is not nearly such 'dangerous doctrine' as it looks. This theory, holding will-energy to be the sole moral value, and recognising that will-energy is manifested in devotion to one's ideal, accepts 'devotion to one's ideal' as the practicable measure of goodness. And in so doing it may seem to lend countenance to all kinds of divergences from the currently accepted moral principles. But this is true only in a very limited sense. Our moral judge's readiness to condone individual eccentricities will be profoundly modified by his awareness of all the educational influences of the social medium which operate upon the individual in the plastic years of childhood and youth, influences directed to awakening and strengthening his interests in the things which, to the mind of the particular society, are most worth seeking, and to teaching him how he must order his ways if these interests are to find adequate fulfilment. When we take account of the pervasive force of these factors in determining the material, and even the organisation, of the individual's ideal of 'the good of the self as a whole,' it becomes a reasonable assumption that any well-marked and genuine unorthodoxy in ideals will be exceedingly rare. In the absence of definite reasons for expecting aberrations, the 'moral judge' will be justified in assuming that the individual's ideal is substantially identical with that of current morality. Radical departures from current morality he will be scarcely more ready to extenuate than will the more 'objective' moralist. Some kinds of departures he will be virtually certain are departures from the agent's own ideal also—*e.g.* persistent indulgence in idleness or sensuality: for only a pervert or a cretin, he will know, can suppose that such conduct is conducive to the 'good of his self as a whole.' Moral valuation which proceeds on our present principle, then, will not be such an 'anarchic' matter after all. The 'social' standard, though it will not be its sacred touchstone, will be at least its respected guide.

Moreover, our moral judge will always bear in mind that even where a person does really possess an ideal which is 'unenlightened,' the lack of enlightenment may be due to the agent's own fault. It may be due to his failure to take the trouble which he knew he ought to take over assimilating the practical instruction received in his youth. Or he may have failed to take the trouble (which again he knew he ought to take) to give any serious thought to the merits of his accepted code, in spite of recurring indications of probable shortcomings in that code. Or, again, it is quite conceivable that the agent may once have possessed a high ideal, but that it has suffered deterioration on account of the agent's prolonged failure to live up to it. For there is the notorious tendency, already alluded to, to lower one's ideals to one's conduct, when one fails to raise one's conduct to one's ideals; to cheat oneself with sophisms into believing that obligations which one consistently violates do not exist, rather than have to face the humiliating contrast between what one knows one ought to be and what one knows one is. In all of these cases lack of present enlightenment is due to defective willing, insufficient moral effort, in the agent's past life, and the agent is blameworthy in consequence. Thus intelligent moral judgment proceeding on our principles will consider not merely how far the agent is 'acting up to his lights,' but also (and especially where the 'lights' are 'lower' than one would be led to expect by the agent's general circumstances) how far any deficiencies in these lights are the outcome of past failures in moral willing.

Section 4. Reply to Criticism based upon the Moral Consciousness's apparent Acceptance of the Relevance of Content. (Part I)

We pass now to a criticism which is of much more fundamental import, one which it is vital that we should dispose of satisfactorily if our theory is to gain credence. It may be put briefly in the following terms. 'You do not dispute,' it may be said, 'that the ultimate court of appeal in deciding what is and what is not relevant for moral valuation is the "moral consciousness." And you do not, we suppose, mean merely your own moral consciousness, but the moral consciousness of mankind generally. But if one does refer for guidance to the common moral consciousness, does one really find that its deliverances, in this or in any other age, support your assertion that "content" is ethically irrelevant? If that were so, it would be the practice to assign a like value (other things being equal) to the man who dedicates his life to an enlightened ideal and to the mere "fanatic," the deluded victim of some childish dream. But the facts are surely otherwise. It is characteristic of the moral consciousness, in so far as this finds expression in common moral judgments, to place the latter personage in a definitely lower moral category. The falseness of an ideal is clearly taken to vitiate in large measure the moral worth of the most conscientious pursuit. And if this be so, what becomes of your doctrine that devotion to one's ideal, or, more precisely, the will-energy which manifests that devotion, is the only thing that counts for moral valuation?'

It is scarcely necessary for me to express my sense of the importance of confirmation of any moral theory by the common moral judgments of mankind. If the moral consciousness has any principle—which is just to say, if there is a moral consciousness at all—that principle must manifest itself (though it may be disguisedly) in *all* deliverances that really issue from the moral consciousness. Nevertheless, when I ask myself how I should react to the hypothetical presentation of a clear proof that the 'moral judgments,' so called, of every other person took account of 'content' in evaluating conduct, I find that I should be powerless to abandon my present principle. This not from immodesty, but from the simple incapacity to understand, by reference to my own moral experience, what can be meant by holding that a person 'ought' to do what he 'cannot' do, and is morally estimable (or culpable) for aspects of conduct over which he has no control—tenets which are implied in the view which assigns moral value to content as such. I should be compelled instead to hold that if this is really for others the testimony of what they mean by 'moral experience,' then the term 'moral experience' has for them a different reference. They and I are using the same name for quite distinct types of experience. This would be, indeed, a highly undesirable position to have to take up. Out of respect for the common use of language, I should be compelled to say that my doctrine, in not referring to what is ordinarily meant by 'moral' experience, was not an 'ethical' doctrine at all. But undesirable or not, it would seem preferable to flouting the unmistakable testimony of one's own fundamental experience.

But fortunately there is no need to adopt this drastic attitude. The common moral consciousness of mankind is only 'at the first look' hostile to the principle of valuation here maintained. It does often *seem* to assign important status to content in the determination of moral worth. But, I am prepared to argue, it is only 'seeming.' Where such judgments are passed, it is not the 'moral consciousness' that is responsible. The authentic utterance of the moral consciousness has been obstructed, either by the intrusion of selfish interests, or by the commission of a certain assignable confusion of thought. Upon each of these disturbing influences it is necessary to speak at some length. I shall deal first with the former.

That the intrusion of selfish interests biases the moral judgment in the way I suggest is best observed in a very common phenomenon of both private and public life. I refer to the revision—often of the nature of a reversal—which so frequently takes place in the estimate of the moral worth of the man whose ideals are (in the valuator's view) unenlightened, *after* that unenlightenment has for some reason ceased to affect the valuator's personal concerns. The significant thing about such revision is this. The original valuation, carried out while the unenlightened agent is injurious to the valuator, appears to regard the nature of the content as of prime importance. Its lack of enlightenment is treated as a grave delinquency, and the agent tends to be condemned as little better than a rogue. The subsequent valuation, on the other hand, carried out when the agent has ceased, through death or otherwise, to be a danger to the valuator, shows an exceedingly well-marked tendency to treat the unenlightenment of the content as of no account whatever. The tendency is now to consider as the thing that really matters, how far the man did sincerely follow the light that was in him. Instances of the sort abound (they are almost a commonplace in the political arena). I shall refer to one or two by way of illustration in a moment. And it will scarcely be denied that it is in the second of the two psychical situations involved, where there is nothing to disturb judicial impartiality, that the purer, more authentic expression of the moral consciousness is likely to be found.

As it is obviously most suitable that instances should be selected in which the actual facts are widely known and beyond dispute, we may turn to public life for our illustrations. And we might look far without coming upon an example more impressive and suggestive than the fluctuation in the British people's moral estimate of the great Indian patriot and mystic, Gandhi.

Most readers will be able to recall at least the general tone of public opinion during the period when Gandhi's activities first became a serious menace to the welfare of the British people. And if they do recall it, they will agree, I think, that in most quarters Gandhi was subjected to almost unqualified vilification. So far as that *vox populi* the Press was concerned, almost no language was deemed too strong for the denunciation of this 'criminal lunatic'—to use one of the more charitable epithets in currency. The 'content' of the ideal (for that Gandhi was honestly following his ideal was seldom seriously questioned) was obviously treated at the period as of prime importance in moral appraisement. The fact that Gandhi's ideal was stupidly misguided (as was sincerely enough believed by most people) not merely detracted from his moral worth, but seemed sufficient, in the prevailing state of opinion, to brand him as a miscreant.

But what a transformation in the years which followed Gandhi's withdrawal (temporary, as it now appears) from the crusade which spelt so much inconvenience to British interests! Before many years had passed, that profound sense which abides in the common heart of man, though so often obscured by the clouds of passion, that profound sense of the imperishable worth of a life that spends itself in the quest of the ideal, manifested itself in numberless ways. A great Gandhi literature rapidly arose, almost wholly flattering. Studies of 'Gandhi the Man' appeared and multiplied, each vying with the other in doing honour to the Mahatma's nobility of spirit. Gandhi the Arch-villain was now Gandhi the Saint. Even the 'man in the street,' insensitive as he is to the less obvious, less external evidences of spiritual worth, shared in the general reassessment of the man who but a few years back had been the subject of his most extravagant flights of vituperative eloquence. And what, one asks, is to be inferred from this but that when the fetters of prejudice are loosened, and the moral consciousness is permitted to function in its purity, misguidedness of content is deemed as of no moment whatever? The travail of the spirit in striving after its ideal is, for the unperverted moral consciousness, the sole thing that matters.[1]

Let us take one other illustration, scarcely less striking—the contrast in the attitudes of the British public towards the individual German soldier during and after the War respectively. During the War it was more than enough for most people that the German was fighting for a bad cause. The fact that he honestly believed the 'bad cause' to be the best of all causes was tacitly accepted as irrelevant to moral valuation: if, indeed, it did not give a keener edge to the common reprobation, on account of the greater 'power for evil' which the 'idealisation' of the cause would create. Anyone who at this period ventured to suggest that, after all, the German soldier was only doing what he thought to be his duty, ran a serious risk of being suspected of 'pro-German' sympathies. But peace had not long been declared, the German soldiery had not long ceased to endanger British interests, before a markedly different public attitude set in. Free now to make a dispassionate estimate,

[1] It will be noticed that the point of the present illustration receives confirmation from the swing back of the pendulum of public opinion which has now taken place, following upon Gandhi's renewed interest in 'twisting the lion's tail.'

our people speedily began to realise that spiritual values were not confined to the side of the Allied forces, that indeed the individual German who sacrificed himself on the altar of *his* ideal was no less worthy of honour than his British counterpart. The ideal *was* misguided: so it was still, at least commonly, believed. But any reproach that arose from that fact was now directed against the 'Prussian system,' not against the ordinary individual citizen who, inoculated with the 'Prussian virus' almost from birth, could do no other than believe in the supreme value of this 'misguided' ideal. In a word, 'content' was now accepted as immaterial for moral valuation, and anyone who still employed it as his standard was regarded—very rightly—as a Philistine and a Jingo.

Of course there were honourable exceptions, both in the case of Gandhi and in the case of the German troops, to the common execration called forth by their 'misguided' activities. And it seems to me, when we look at it closely, a somewhat significant fact that perhaps the most notorious exception in the latter case was the combatant soldier. As a rule our soldiers went overseas burning with moral indignation against the 'Hun.' But, save with the coarser spirits, this attitude of personal hatred and condemnation was seldom able to survive —even though conviction remained that the opponent's 'cause' or 'content' was misguided. Examples of signal devotion to their cause within the enemy ranks called forth honour and respect almost precisely as did similar examples within our own ranks. 'Devotion to ideal' was everything, the concrete content of the ideal counted for nothing. I say the fact is significant because, although there were minor contributing influences, by far the profoundest reason for this attitude was just, I believe, that the conditions prevailing in the line were uniquely favourable to the unperverted functioning of the moral consciousness. Doubtless, indeed, these men had more to lose than anyone else from the 'misguided content' of the enemy's ideal. But the bias which this might otherwise engender would be far more than compensated by another circumstance. When men are living from day to day on the very brink of Eternity, not only are they forced back upon ultimate spiritual issues, but, further, their thoughts are little likely to be coloured by the comfortable self-deceptions and hypocrisies of ordinary 'civilised' life. It is Truth, and Truth only, that can avail them now. Against the background of Eternity the paltry passions of a day dwindle into insignificance, and become impotent to warp the vision and distort the judgment. Men look upon the stark elemental realities of human existence with eyes unscaled. And it is, I think, just because the circumstances of the man in the line were in this way favourable to an intenser and more penetrating spiritual insight, to a more than usually pure functioning of the moral consciousness, that 'concrete content' was, in his judgment, of no account as against 'devotion.'

The two illustrations I have offered are, as it were, historic. But everyone can furnish a host of other instances from the stock of his own experience, all pointing to the same conclusion. In our most sober and dispassionate judgments, where it is reasonable to assume that the moral consciousness functions in its purest integrity, it is, I submit, the inner heart of conduct, the spiritual striving, that is our sole concern.

And I would remind the reader of a consideration to which passing allusion has already been made. Upon what principle does a man pass moral judgment upon *himself*, upon the one person whose conduct is known to him in any accurate and complete manner? Does he ever censure himself for what he may now see to have been 'misguided' ideals animating past conduct? Only, surely, where he is clear that these ideals would have been more intelligent if he had not been insufficiently earnest in his moral thinking. Is it really doubtful that the one thing, in the last resort, that he feels to be shameful in him and deserving of moral censure, is failure to act up to his ideal, in at least a reasonable approximation? And, correspondingly, that the one thing which he values in himself, which exalts him in his self-respect, is the effort, the energising, whereby he has overcome the 'path of least resistance' beloved of the natural man in him, and drawn nearer to the man he feels he *ought* to be? And if this be the criterion we use for ourselves, as it surely is in all self-searching that is honest and serious of purpose, why should we suppose a different criterion to be applicable to others?

Section 5. Digression on the Supposed Distinction of Merit from Goodness

We must now face an objection, the discussion of which will lead us eventually to a recognition of the second major influence which causes the moral judgments of mankind to seem often to be concerned with 'content.' The objection is as follows: 'Are you not,' it is asked, 'omitting to notice the familiar and very necessary distinction between "Merit" and Goodness.[1] We are quite prepared to admit that in

[1] The distinction of Goodness from Merit may be given a different signification—Goodness as implying 'effortless' conformity to the standard which in meritorious conduct is conformed to only with 'struggle.' The manner in which I should deal with the distinction in these terms will perhaps be apparent from what has preceded, but a condensed statement may be helpful. I should maintain that what is here called 'Goodness' either has no moral value, or if it has moral value, that value is 'retrospective,' being derived wholly from the 'effort' of past 'meritorious' acts of will. Let us consider. An act (first) which issues *merely* from a 'natural disposition' may elicit approval, but does it ever elicit that 'respect' which is inherent in 'moral' approval? Surely the question answers itself, and in an emphatic negative. Often, however, a good act issues from a natural disposition which has been stabilised through much willing in the past which *was* effortful. Then the case is different. We do then morally commend the agent, but only in virtue of his identity with the person who by 'effort' made this 'effortless' action possible. The moral commendation is essentially retrospective. The agent's present effortless action is commended *as an evidence of* past effort. 'Good' action from 'acquired' habit, where the acquisition involves effort, falls under the same category. And I am confident that our moral approval of the 'saint' finds a similar explanation. Moral approval here, in so far as it is really 'moral,' is elicited by our consciousness of the long and arduous self-denying discipline, involving hard and sustained 'effort of will,' which must have gone to make him the man he is now.

judging the "meritoriousness" of conduct it is the will-energy involved, the aspect of spiritual striving, which it is proper to consider. But it does not by any means follow that the "goodness" of the conduct is measurable by the same principle. Goodness, we should insist—and we should claim here to have behind us the suffrage of common sense—is a wider term than Merit, and does accept the relevance of "content." Two acts of hypothetically identical will-energy may be of like "merit," but if one is directed to the ideal of an ignoramus, and the other to the ideal of a man of wide culture, it is paradoxical to say that they are equal in "goodness." The latter person is, by general consent, "the better man."'

There is a good deal of plausibility in this contention. The distinction which it notices is commonly recognised, and it will be needful to consider its nature and significance at some length if its innocuousness for our theory is to be completely established. But meantime there is no difficulty in exposing its fundamental defect in so far as it purports to offer a relevant comment upon strictly *moral* theory. It is necessary only to ask (as we did in the case of the similar distinction of 'subjective' from 'objective' rightness) *which* of the two criteria, that of 'Merit' or that of 'Goodness,' is the proper one to apply in the appraisement of strictly *moral* goodness? If the critic says that it is that of 'Goodness,' then he has to face all the difficulties that assail the introduction of content into matters of the 'ought.' And if he admits that it is the criterion of 'Merit' that is to be used, then he is really accepting all that I contend for, viz. that 'will-energy' alone counts in the appraisment of *moral* value. Merit and Moral Goodness are now implied to be identical, and the distinction between Merit and so-called 'Goodness' must be admitted to be a distinction which does not fall within the sphere of morality proper at all.

This reply does, I think, dispose of the objection in principle. The so-called distinction of Merit and Goodness turns out to be really a distinction between Moral Goodness as such, and an intelligent or cultured form of Moral Goodness. Yet it would not be altogether satisfactory to arrest our argument here. The objection obstinately recurs, claiming impressive support from the mass of general opinion, that the 'cultured' moral person is 'the better man,' even if he be not a 'morally better' man. It is highly desirable to understand the significance of this implicit acceptance of a 'value' which is not 'moral value,' and which stands, *prima facie*, in possible competition with 'moral value.' Actually it arises, in my view, as one indirect consequence of the original too common error of regarding certain contents as possessed of moral value in their own right. I have already dealt with one of the factors which incline us to make this mistake—the intrusion of private interests. But this factor will not account for anything like all of the cases in which value is ascribed to content as such. There is another factor much more general in its scope, a factor not of the nature of personal bias but rather of loose thinking. If we consider it now, we shall be led, I think, to see the ground of the common acceptance of an objective value which is yet not a moral value.

Section 6. Reply to Criticism based upon the Moral Consciousness's apparent Acceptance of the Relevance of Content. (Part II)

We may remind ourselves once more that every rational being has in the nature of the case a 'moral ideal,' something which he is conscious that he 'ought' to do or be. And this ideal is no mere vague nebulosity. Through the influence of social education working upon the material of his native impulses, it takes concrete shape in every man as a more or less coherent system of definite activities.

The individual's consciousness that he ought to follow his ideal is thus always in practice a consciousness that he ought to act in certain definite ways. Accordingly the moral value which he feels attaches to following his ideal, he naturally ascribes to these particular ways of acting, which are what his ideal means concretely for him. He will think and speak of such acts as 'moral values,' which indeed they are so far as his own behaviour is concerned, since to perform them *is* to follow his ideal.

But the trouble is that it will be perilously easy for him to lose sight of the fact that to act thus has 'moral value' *only because and in so far as these acts are the expression of his ideal.* The more he thinks and speaks of them as morally good, and comes to make his moral judgments automatically by reference to them, and, especially, the more he finds other persons referring to them in these same terms, the more liable he will be to slip into the error of looking upon these acts, these 'contents,' as moral values not merely in relation to an agent whose ideal they represent, but in their own right.

A certain level of moral reflection is necessary, indeed, in order to avoid this mistake, which rests at bottom on a failure to recognise the distinction between the ideal *qua* ideal, and the acts which are its temporary, *de facto* embodiment. But there does always lie latent in the mind the awareness that what gives the acts their moral value is their nature as expressions of the ideal; an awareness only awaiting, for the possibility of becoming explicit, the recognition of the distinction alluded to. The conditions required to incite this recognition are just the general conditions, needless to detail here, which arouse doubt as to the validity of one's inherited moral code. When I come to 'doubt,' when I come to ask of my hitherto accepted moral 'content,' 'Is this what I really think I ought to do?'—*i.e.* 'Is this the proper concrete embodiment of my ideal?'—I am obviously recognising the distinction between ideal as such and its *de facto* embodiment. And it is only a short step from this to the explicit consciousness that it is only *as* expressing my ideal that my concrete acts have moral value. For when I ask of my hitherto accepted content, 'Is this what I really think I ought to do?,' I am aware that I ought not to do it if it is *not* what I really think I ought to do, *i.e.* that my acts have no moral value if they do not express my own ideal: and conversely I am aware that I ought to do whatsoever my reflections now lead me to think I ought to do, *i.e.* that my acts have moral value if they are expressive of my own ideal.

The level of moral reflection involved is certainly fairly elementary, but it is probably not even within the capacity of the more primitive peoples. For there is very little in the experience of a member of a primitive community likely to stimulate doubt as to the validity of his code, and to arouse in consequence this recognition of a distinction between ideal as such and *de facto* embodiment. Close relations of a friendly order with other persons who subscribe to other codes is the most common stimulus of moral reflection, but primitive man is unlikely to be touched thereby. It is quite as we should expect, therefore, that among ruder peoples moral judgment is passed consistently in terms of a rigid standard of 'content.' It would not even occur to the savage to ask whether his fellow-tribesman who violates a taboo is perhaps doing what *he* thinks right.

But even in more developed communities it is surprising how many fail to reach the elementary level of moral reflection required. The capacity of the average man to retain immunity against the manifold influences which must breed doubt of the validity of one's own code in the most mildly reflective intelligence, is truly astonishing. The more sensitive, of course, are affected. And they, recognising that the ideal may, indeed must, vary in its embodiment, do often take the further step of recognising that the supreme moral law is not, 'Do this, or that, particular thing,' but 'Do the particular thing which you think right, which manifests your ideal.' They have come to see, that is, that devotion to one's ideal is the one thing of sure moral value. But they are the exceptions.

Most people, even yet, tend to regard as 'good in their own right' the modes of conduct which happen to constitute *their* concrete ideal (and which are thus morally good so far as *they* are the agents concerned); more especially so with regard to those central modes of conduct which are relatively common constituents of the society's ideal, and which are in consequence constantly spoken of and written of in terms of direct admonition and command.

It is through a quite understandable misinterpretation, then, of the essential nature of that which one's moral consciousness really approves and disapproves, that moral value tends to be ascribed to certain concrete ends in their own right—to paying one's debts, honouring one's parents, helping the needy, and so on. And on the whole this illusion that certain concrete ends are as such good and bad may be said to work moderately well in the actual practice of common moral judgment. It seldom leads to gross injustices in moral valuation, by reason of the substantial identity of the moral ideals of the several members of a single community. To censure the promoter of bogus companies, to commend the honest and the diligent—judgments of this kind must be acknowledged to be tolerably safe. On the other hand, when it comes to less central 'duties,' upon which, once reflection is stirred, difference of opinion is natural, our 'standard' judgments will often go wildly astray. And if we are stupid enough to apply our rigid standard to the conduct of alien races it is certain that our judgments will often grotesquely misrepresent the real moral value in the case. But even if the 'concrete' standard did work satisfactorily always, led to no injustices of valuation, it would be no more valid in theory than if it never worked satisfactorily at all.

Section 7. *The Fiction of 'Non-moral' Objective Values*

Now the notion of another objective value which is not moral value—to take up again the problem which we found it necessary to shelve temporarily—arises, I think, as an indirect consequence of this common but false assumption that the concrete ends in which our ideal is embodied possess moral value 'in their own right.' It arises in this way. Among the ends which constitute the ideal of educated persons in a civilised community, knowledge, æsthetic feeling, and culture generally can hardly fail to find a prominent place. The interest in these ends is widespread and powerful, and will naturally secure expression in the 'conceived good of the self as a whole.' On the other hand, it is bound to be realised that ends of this sort, although ingredient in our ideal and thus claiming our allegiance, are distinguished in a rather important way from such ends as paying one's debts, honouring parents, etc. For they are, as it were, not 'ours to command.' It is in most persons' power to strive towards them, but to achieve them is possible only in proportion to certain capacities which are gifts, not matters of volition. While, therefore, there is nothing transparently absurd in regarding such constituents of the ideal as 'paying one's debts' as possessed of moral value in their own right, to ascribe moral value to such constituents as 'culture' is a paradox too great even for common sense. Hence a compromise. Value of some sort can hardly be denied to 'culture' and ascribed to the other constituents of the ideal. But that value seems clearly not to be moral value. So we come to postulate a new kind of 'non-moral' value, standing alongside moral value. And thus arises the fiction that the 'cultured' moral man is somehow 'better,' though not 'morally better,' than the 'uncultured' moral man.

But there is no need whatever to make this discrimination in 'objective values' if one will only avoid the original error of assuming that moral value attaches to concrete ends in their own right. On my view nothing has moral value—neither paying one's debts nor anything else,—save as manifesting the agent's devotion to his ideal, and, ultimately, in proportion to the will-energy involved. Such an end as the acquirement of culture may thus be treated on precisely the same basis as any other possible constituent of one's ideal. In proportion as the acquirement of culture manifests the agent's devotion to his ideal—and of course very different degrees of culture may manifest an equal devotion in differently constituted agents—the acquirement of culture possesses moral value. There is no ground for supposing that it possesses some further kind of objective value, any more than in the case of the other objects of the dominant interests which are the material out of which one's moral ideal is constructed.

I must, however, seek to remove a possible misunderstanding which may be made the ground of an objection to this view. It is of the essence of the theory that has been advocated in these pages that there is no value save that which resides in the will to the ideal. Any value ascribed to content is entirely derivative from this. 'But,' it may be asked, 'does this position not involve you in an obvious ὕστερον πρότερον? Is it not evident that certain concrete ends must be recognised as good, as "values," as a *prior condition of* the construction of the ideal—which, indeed, your own account of that construction in the previous chapter seemed to imply. The "conceived good of the self as a whole," the "end of the self as such," was constructed out of the material supplied by the different particular goods which the self's particular interests led it to recognise. Does this not mean that there is a recognition of "value" prior to, and therefore independent of, the willing of the ideal?'

The objection is to be welcomed, for it furnishes an opportunity of calling attention to a distinction which I ought, perhaps, to have adverted to at an earlier stage; the distinction between 'value-for-self,' or 'subjective value,' and 'intrinsic' or 'objective' value. Undoubtedly the ends out of which we construct the conceived good of the self as a whole—the objects of our desires—are 'values' in the *former* sense. As I tried to show in a previous discussion, they are in the nature of the case conceived as 'personal goods.' To desire an object *is* to think of it as a 'value-for-self.' But merely to say this is enough to indicate that this kind of value is not 'value' in the significant, 'controversial' sense of that term. When one makes the claim that such and such a thing is a 'value,' one commonly means a great deal more than just that it is a thing which some people, or even all people, happen to want. One means that the thing is valuable in itself, irrespective of anyone actually happening to want it—'intrinsically' or 'objectively' valuable.

Now, so far as I can judge, this conception of something as 'intrinsically' valuable originates in moral experience, in which the willing of the ideal (the good will) is recognised as something which 'unconditionally ought' to be. And ultimately it has no other legitimate application. No mere end of desire, however exalted, presents itself as the bearer of an *inherent* worth. In moral experience an entirely new element enters which transforms the value-situation. In recognising an 'unconditional obligation' to will the conceived good of the self as a whole (in whatever concrete embodiment it may find expression), we are *ipso facto* recognising that the willing of it is something that is good whether we happen to want it or not. In short, the consciousness of the unconditionally binding, the 'categorical imperative,' is precisely the consciousness of something as good 'intrinsically' or 'objectively,' good 'in the nature of things.'

Hence the 'utterness' of the contrast, which might otherwise seem anomalous, that is felt between the end representing the good of the self as a whole, and opposing ends representing goods of only partial aspects of the self. The difference is not one of 'degree,' as a superficial glance might suggest. It is fundamentally one of kind. For the former end, inasmuch as it is that towards which we are conscious of unconditional obligation, becomes invested derivatively with intrinsic or objective value. As such, it presents itself with unique authority—or, perhaps more accurately, alone presents itself with any 'authority.'

There is one further matter to which it seems desirable to refer before bringing this chapter to a close. My view denies categorically that Truth and Beauty are intrinsic values. And I hold by this position without reserve. But I am naturally aware that in so doing I am controverting an axiological doctrine that has a wide currency in modern thought. Truth, Beauty, and Goodness, we hear on all sides, represent a 'trinity' of intrinsic values. I want to make a few comments upon this undoubtedly attractive, but I think untenable, doctrine.

I have already explained how, in my view, the fiction of 'non-moral' values arises. The explanation applies directly (as was, indeed, suggested) to the 'values' of Truth and Beauty. To the man (or the community) of more than embryonic culture, the achievement of Truth and the creation or appreciation of Beauty naturally tend to become objects of quite outstanding interests, and to assume accordingly a prominent position in the ideal of the good of the self as a whole. But, unlike the other constituents of the ideal, these ends cannot with any plausibility sustain the appearance of being 'moral' values in their own right. Hence—since they have just as much (or as little) claim to be regarded as values in their own right as have the other constituents—they come to be accepted as values of a 'non-moral' kind. Thus emerges the conception of Truth and Beauty as two independent values, alongside, as it were, the value of Goodness. And once this step is taken, they tend to be regarded as of equal status with Goodness. Truth, Beauty, and Goodness now come to be treated as the three Supreme Values, the triunal goal of all rightly directed human aspiration.

But, quite apart from questions of origin, it seems to me that there are very grave, and most inadequately noticed, difficulties in the 'trinitarian' conception of value. I cannot see how there possibly can be two, let alone three, different ends *each* of which is recognised as an 'intrinsic' value, or an 'intrinsic' good. For what, we must ask, will be the mental situation when any two of these so-called intrinsic goods conflict in our experience, the Truth-value (let us say) dictating one course, and the Goodness-value, or Moral-value, a different course? It cannot be maintained that *each* makes an absolute claim upon the agent. For that would amount to the same thing as saying that *neither* makes an absolute claim. And if, on the other hand, respecting the facts, we admit that it is the Moral-value which by its very nature must make absolute claim, it is not easy to see what remains of the supposed 'intrinsic' character of the Truth-value. The agent's recognition that he ought not to follow here the end dictated by the latter seems to imply the recognition that the achievement of Truth is just not a good-in-itself, a self-justifying, 'intrinsic' value.

In spite of the protestations of theory that Truth, Beauty, and Goodness are co-ordinate values, in actual practice the pre-eminence of Goodness is acknowledged, and no impasse occurs. The self, just because it is one self and not three selves, recognises but one supreme objective claim, the claim of the conceived good of its self as a whole. Truth and Beauty make objective claim only in the measure that they express, in the particular situation, the conceived good of the self as a whole. It may sometimes be that the interests of the agent engaged are so overwhelmingly artistic (or scientific) that Beauty (or Truth) almost completely comprehends the conceived good of the self as a whole, and thus becomes, for all practical purposes, itself an 'absolute value.' But that is the limiting case. And even here Beauty or Truth is an 'absolute value' only, as it were, derivatively; *i.e.* by reason of its *de facto* identity, for the agent in question, with the moral end. In the normal case, however, there are manifold interests besides the interests in Beauty or Truth which must contribute significantly to the conceived good of the self as a whole. And hence a reciprocal limitation which is quite incompatible with the object of any one interest being accepted as an absolute value.

I cannot agree, then, with the doctrine of the Trinity of Values in any form of it (and this seems to be its natural implication) which would assign to Truth and Beauty a value-status co-equal with Moral Goodness. As far as I can see, it would be just as justifiable in principle to exalt such an end as 'Humanity' or 'The Brotherhood of Man' to the rank of intrinsic value. As human nature develops, 'Humanity' too tends to become an object of surpassing interest. In fact, there would be far more propriety in speaking of the Trinity of 'Truth, Beauty, and Humanity,' than of the Trinity of 'Truth, Beauty, and Goodness.' The former are, in a real sense, 'co-ordinate' ends. They represent what are perhaps the three most fundamental interests of developed human nature. But *none* of these ends is co-ordinate with the end of Moral Goodness itself. They are at most typical forms of the expression of Moral Goodness. The latter end is supreme; not as *primus inter pares* (as some compromise theories would have it), but with a supremacy that can brook no competition.

Section 8. Metaphysical Significance of Present Doctrine

A very few words must suffice to remind the reader of the significance of the doctrine of this chapter in our general philosophical scheme. I have been arguing that if we are in real earnest with the implications of moral praise and blame, we are forced to the conclusion that the one thing to which moral value can ultimately be ascribed is will-energy. And I have tried to show that the appearances which suggest that the moral consciousness takes account of the nature of the 'content' of will are only 'appearances.' But this criterion of moral valuation presupposes the validity of the conception of will-energy. And the validity of the conception of will-energy presupposes the validity of the conception of Reality as *not* intelligibly continuous. It follows that the one criterion which, as I hold, can give meaning to moral valuation, is itself meaningless save for a metaphysic which at least goes so far with our Supra-rationalist doctrine as to deny that Reality is 'rational.' It may fairly be claimed, therefore, that the moral doctrine of this chapter, in so far as it is true, affords an appreciable confirmation of the Supra-rationalist metaphysics —save, of course, for those who, for one reason or another, decline to admit that the so-called 'moral' side of our experience has ineluctable claims to be respected in philosophic construction.

CHAPTER VIII

SUPRA-RATIONALISM AND RELIGION

Section 1. Introductory

I HAVE been arguing in these recent chapters (IV. to VII.) that the critical consideration of 'practical experience' leads to the same conclusion as our earlier investigation of 'theoretical experience,' viz. the necessity of recognising the 'supra-rational' (or at the very least the 'non-intelligible') character of ultimate reality. Important evidence of the truth of this metaphysical doctrine is, I believe, derivable from 'religious experience' also. This final chapter will be occupied with the endeavour to show how this is so.

It will prevent misunderstanding, however, if I make it clear at once that I do not claim for the argument from religion the same formal type of cogency as in the previous instances. In the case of freedom, the argument claimed, so far as valid, to establish the Supra-rational Reality with apodeictic certainty. For (so the argument ran) freedom implies such a Reality, and freedom is an indubitable fact. But while I shall try to show that the religious consciousness, like freedom, implies the Supra-rational Reality, I am unable to show that the religious consciousness is a foundational and irremovable aspect of experience, and that what in its essence it affirms must therefore be taken as 'fact.' My conclusion here must accordingly remain at the level of the hypothetical. I say no more than that *if* you admit the validity of the religious consciousness, you must go on to admit that Reality is Supra-rational.

This is one respect, then, in which our claims in the present chapter must be qualified. But there is a further respect also. Even those who are prepared to accord to the religious consciousness the same autonomy that is commonly claimed for the moral may disagree as to the essential marks by which the religious consciousness is to be known. It is fair, I think, to assume general consent to the proposition that the distinguishing mark of the 'moral' consciousness is the 'ought.' But it is difficult to secure universal agreement as to almost any specific characteristic of the 'religious' consciousness. Let it be frankly stated, then, that my argument here makes no pretensions to be a formal proof of the necessity of the Suprarational Absolute save to those who, first of all, believe in the autonomy of religious experience—its irresolubility into anything other than itself—and who, secondly, agree that any genuine religious experience must include *at least* the two features from which my argument will start. Those who (perhaps the larger number) neither accept nor reject, but maintain a suspended judgment upon these matters, may still regard the present chapter as offering, so far as its reasoning is valid, some reinforcement of the results arrived at in the body of the book.

In saying so much, I may have inadvertently prepared the reader to expect a somewhat idiosyncratic reading of the nature of the religious consciousness. Such, however, is very far from being the case. On the contrary, the two features of the religious consciousness from which as data my whole argument proceeds are recognised as integral to religion by, I should say, the vast majority of theologians and philosophers of religion, as well as by ordinary religious thought. Let us note briefly what they are.

Section 2. *Alleged Contradictoriness of Religious Experience.* *'Finite God' Solution*

There is, first, what is commonly called the 'peace of religion'; the tranquil and joyous confidence that flows (as it appears) from an assured faith that the Universe is permeated throughout by the Divine Presence. A religion which could not confer this spiritual serenity, we should most of us say, would be so overwhelmingly impoverished as to cease to command the title of 'religion' at all.

And, in the second place, there is the feature which we may call the 'moral dynamic of religion'; the heightened urge to cleanse the world and our own souls of all impurity and imperfection, and to lessen thereby the vast gulf that, as we feel, divides our erring humanity from the Perfection of God. And here, again, it is natural to say, I think, that a religious experience void of this feature is a religious experience mutilated beyond recognition.

Now that either, or both, of these features *may* be denied to be integral to religion, I have already admitted. But it must be granted, I think, that at least they can claim immensely widespread recognition, to a degree, at all events, which suffices to make our problem a very living one. The great historical religions furnish abundant evidence of this. And it is significant that even where the theology of a great religion is (as is not infrequently the case) somewhat sharply opposed in logic to the propriety of one or other of these features, the sacred utterances of its devotees continue to recognise the reality of *both* moments, joyous confidence *and* moral fervour. Or again, if we care to regard the matter from the level of our own everyday assumptions, we shall find, I think, that a similar recognition is present here too. Most of us are accustomed to look with a good deal of suspicion upon professions of profound religious experience by those whose conduct betrays the lack *either* of 'the tranquil heart' *or* of any inward drive towards purity and goodness.

The religious consciousness, then, as I shall understand it in this chapter, has at least these two features as intrinsic characteristics. What I shall attempt to prove is that a religious consciousness so constituted can only preserve itself from being rent asunder by internal contradiction on the condition that it recognises the Supra-rational character of Reality.

The *prima facie* contradiction that arises is, of course, very well known. Let us see as plainly as may be wherein precisely it consists. It is most succinctly expressed, perhaps, in the saying that for the religious consciousness what 'ought to be' both 'is' and 'is not.' The 'peace of religion' seems to rest upon the postulate that what ought to be really *is*. Its overpowering sense of an inviolable security seems born of, and to imply, the steadfast assurance that the indwelling spirit of the all-perfect God animates the whole scheme of things, that existence in all of its phases would reveal itself for ultimate vision as the manifestation of Divine Perfection.[1] While just as surely, on the other hand, the moral dynamic of religion seems to rest upon the postulate that what ought to be *is not*. For the urge to purify the world, it appears obvious, must imply the conviction that evil and corruption really do exist. Hence, on the surface at least, a religion for which both of these moments are intrinsic would seem to be involved in flat self-contradiction, since it asserts that Reality is at once perfect throughout and shot through with imperfection.

One way of resolving the difficulty—tempting but at bottom illusory—we may briefly notice. It may be urged that the above account weights the balance unduly, and that contradiction only arises when (as in that account) we identify the God of religion with the Absolute of Philosophy. On that assumption it is true that faith in the Divine Perfection conflicts with the belief in actual imperfection. But if, taking a different view, we are content to accept God as less than the Universe, if, in short, we frankly embrace the conception of the 'Finite God,' whom we may identify with the active principle of

---

[1] Cp. Bosanquet, *Value and Destiny of the Individual*, p. 242. 'The characteristic faith of religion is not merely that the good is real, but that nothing else than the good is real.'

SUPRA-RATIONALISM AND RELIGION

Good in the system of things, then no reason remains why our faith in Him should be felt as conflicting with moral endeavour. Indeed, the conception of a God with whom we may ally ourselves in the high enterprise of consummating the triumph of the Good over the powers of Darkness is one that may well fire the imagination and inspire the will to an heroic devotion.

I do not think that either this or any cognate hypothesis provides a real way of escape from our impasse. If we are to be in earnest in claiming for religion the 'peace that passeth understanding,' then we must go on to say, I think, that this serenity of the spirit is not capable of consorting with faith in a merely finite God. For, on the supposition of a Finite God, it is surely clear that the only ground for the consummate confidence of religion must be that somehow we are assured that (to put the matter bluntly) God is going to *win* in the cosmic struggle. Now on what can such assurance be based? Only, surely, upon some insight into the cosmic principle itself—alongside which both God and the opposing forces of Evil now shrink to the status of subordinate and determined elements. And if we do possess this assurance as to the excellence of the Cosmic Principle, must it not be this Supreme Cosmic Principle that we now bow down to and worship, and acclaim as God? The Finite God can be, I think, but a temporary halting-place for religion. Ultimately the abiding peace of religion can find no justification save in faith in the character of the All, faith in a God who is the Absolute of philosophy.

I am not suggesting, of course, that the religious consciousness, even in developed religions, has uniformly expressed itself in terms which imply the identity of God with the Whole. It has very frequently done so, notably through the mouths of the mystics, but elsewhere also whenever the aspect of faith rather than practice has been uppermost in the mind. But the very fact that there is the difficulty which we are at present examining of reconciling moral striving with an Absolute God has naturally led, where it is the practical aspect of religious experience that is being stressed, to utterances which suggest belief in a merely finite God who is at war with an opposing principle of Evil. The oscillations of religion between the Finite and the Infinite God we may take, then, as simply registering and emphasising our problem. They do not in any way cast doubt upon the ultimate inadequacy for religion of the conception of the Finite God.

Section 3. *The 'Supra-rational God'—the Meaning of the Conception, and its Value as a Solution*

Must we then, rejecting the Finite God, acquiesce in the view held by many thinkers, that religion is inherently self-contradictory? Religion maintains now that all things flow from the Divine Perfection, now that the imperfect has incontrovertible existence: just as (to illustrate what is at bottom the same difficulty from a different side) religion also maintains now that man is utterly God-dependent, now that man is free to enter into union with God, or, as in sin, to alienate himself from Him. If we are forced to conclude that the two attitudes cannot co-exist without collision, then there is, I think, no alternative but to relegate religion (as, for example, Bosanquet, with whatever reluctance, finds himself obliged to relegate it) [1] to the realm of the non-ultimate, of 'appearance.' For nothing seems surer than that the soul of man cannot find the haven of real being which it seeks in an experience which involves the disruption of its own unity.

Or is there, perhaps, some way of understanding the matter that will reconcile these apparent opposites, and vindicate the adoption of the religious attitude by rational beings? I think that there is. But it involves recourse to a principle that is, for what are in the main very good reasons, unwelcome in the

---

[1] *Value and Destiny of the Individual,* chap. viii. See especially closing pages.

courts of philosophy and theology. Yet this principle has never been far remote from the simple in heart, from the ordinary devout man who has no cognisance of logical shibboleths [1] which may limit the scope of possible solutions. And it is to be found in diverse guises not here and there, but well-nigh everywhere (as Rudolf Otto has taught us) in the direct expressions of religious experience which precede the conceptual reconstruction of theology. In a word, it is the principle of the 'Unknowable' God.

Unknowable God! Is not this a contradiction in terms? Yes, taken rigidly, I think that it is. By the term 'God' we mean *something*; and the qualification 'unknowable' implies strictly that we can mean *nothing*. But no one, I imagine, who has contended for an 'unknowable' God has ever held to this absolute sense of 'unknowable.' At least such characteristics have been supposed to be known as will make significant the use of the term 'God.' Otherwise our assertion may be 'it is unknowable whether there is a God,' but not 'God is unknowable.'

But if certain known characteristics are thus admitted—as in some sense they must be—what is meant by saying that the Being who possesses these characteristics is nevertheless 'unknowable'? 'For,' it may be objected, 'you cannot mean that God is "unknowable" merely in the sense that a fully articulated knowledge of Him is beyond human capacity. So much almost no one would dispute. You must mean something very much more thoroughgoing than that. Yet if you allow that characteristics such as Infinite Power, Wisdom, and Goodness are known (and something of the sort seems needful to vindicate the propriety of your employment of the term "God") it is hard to see how there is any difference save of detail between your view and ours: and harder to see how you

---

[1] The use of this term implies no disrespect to Logic. The 'culprit' is the philosophy which takes the canons of Logic for more than they really are, failing to apprehend the limitations of the field within which they apply.

can hope by your view to resolve the contradiction which seems intractable upon ours.'

But there *is* a difference, and that of the most radical order. It is vitally important to understand how this is possible. Those of us who assert the essential unknowability of God may quite well agree that God is 'Infinite in Power, Wisdom, and Goodness'—but we should stress the word *Infinite*. And this makes just all the difference. When the attributes in question are raised to Infinitude or Perfection as in the Deity, then, as we believe, these attributes necessarily pass beyond themselves, pass beyond the natures by which we recognise them in our finite experience. Accordingly when we call God 'Perfect in Wisdom,' for example, we are, on the one hand, meaning something quite relevant and definitive, viz. that God enjoys that ideal of wisdom which is the ultimate goal of our human aspirations in the life of knowledge: while on the other hand we are not, we hold, at all compromising God's essential unknowability, since 'perfected wisdom' has by the very nature of the case transcended the character which wisdom reveals in finite life.

And there is nothing really so very strange about this position after all. It is a view whose grounds are quite familiar to us—whether or not they be deemed adequate grounds—that thought in reaching its ideal goal, its perfection, 'commits suicide': as also that morality, were it to succeed finally in its mission of reconciling the 'is' with the 'ought to be,' would pass beyond morality. And it is hardly less evident, although it is a matter of less common comment, that if power should attain its goal of utter mastery over the external, it would thereby, in virtue of its translation of all externality into internality, become something other and higher than that which we think of as 'power' in our finite experience. The doctrine, then, expresses a reasonable philosophic hypothesis. It is no mere *ad hoc* invention. And if we adopt it I submit that there is no self-contradiction whatever in asserting the reality of a God who is 'Infinite in Power, Wisdom, and Goodness' and who is, nevertheless, essentially 'unknowable.' (How we can arrive at such an assertion is, of course, not here in question. All that I am insisting upon is that to make the assertion is not to maintain a sheer self-contradiction.) To put the whole matter in its briefest compass, the Unknowable God is called 'God' because in Him, as it is believed, our human aspirations attain their complete consummation: and He is called 'Unknowable,' because the consummation of these aspirations carries with it the transcendence of the character they assume in their finite functioning, the character by which alone we are enabled to assign to them definitive conceptual meaning.

So much it seemed necessary to say by way of a general vindication of the collocation 'Unknowable God.' We have seen with what qualification the term 'unknowable' is here applied; a qualification, however, which does not disturb the essential purport of the term, which consists in the denial of the possibility of definite conceptual meaning. And it has also become clear that what is being contended for is perhaps more suggestively designated by the expression 'Supra-rational God' rather than 'Unknowable God.' We may now resume the main thread of our discourse and endeavour to see, if possible, how the conception of the Supra-rational God actually functions in resolving the paradox of religion which has been engaging us. I propose to sketch the general answer in preliminary fashion by outlining the sort of defence which, on this basis, the religious man might actually make if confronted with, and challenged to reconcile, the two aspects of his experience which are in *prima facie* contradiction.

'You argue,' so his answer might run, 'that it is contradictory for me to believe that this universe in which we live is throughout the manifestation of a God who is Perfect, while I believe at the same time that there is much imperfection which it is my duty to remove. And so it would be a contradiction if I supposed for a moment that the Perfection which belongs to God is of the same type as the inadequate perfections of which alone we finite beings have cognisance. If I supposed God to be perfect on the basis of human analogies of perfection, then it would be the merest foolishness to unite with that the assertion of the existence of imperfection. But I do not commit this absurdity—for so it will seem to all who possess authentic religious experience—of imagining God's Perfection to be measurable by human standards. To attempt to conceive the Infinite under categories drawn from the finite can result in nothing but a gratuitous distortion of the Divine Nature. When I call God " Perfect " (as I do), what I mean is not that He is to be conceived after the manner of an ideal extension of the kind of " perfect " with which we are acquainted in our spatio-temporal existence: but simply *this*, that in Him, as I believe, all the aspirations of the human heart after perfection meet with their full and final consummation. The final satisfaction of our human aspirations *must*, when we think it out, have a character different in principle from all finite " goods," which, however fully developed in imagination or in fact, are incapable of reaching the all-sufficing harmony which our spirits lust after. The Divine Being, therefore, I conceive to transcend in principle all finite imaginings, to be supra-rational or " beyond knowledge," but to merit the title Perfection in the sense that He is the ultimate goal after which the soul of man everlastingly yearns. And on this view of God, no contradiction remains in my assertion of the existence of what we finite beings call " imperfection." For the imperfection that is asserted is not the contradictory of the Perfection which is God. It is contradictory only of the human analogues of perfection.'

Now this defence, which does not seem to me to do much more than make explicit the logic that is implicit in the minds of many simple religious men, is, I think, intelligible enough so far as it goes. But it is, of course, very far from bringing us a full release from our difficulties. A critic may very well rejoin in this wise: 'Let us agree with you that what we commonly regard as imperfection is contradictory only of human analogues of perfection, not of the Perfection that characterises God. On that hypothesis we may grant your consistency in affirming at once the Perfection of God (or Reality) and the existence of imperfection. But since imperfection, as we now understand it, is not in contradiction with God's Perfection, not in contradiction with what you have yourself described as "the consummation of all the aspirations of the human heart," but is in fact an actual expression of Divine Perfection, have you not now quite as serious a difficulty on your hands? For if this is what you believe, how can you legitimately experience any impulsion to remove this so-called imperfection, which you know to be the expression of Divine Perfection? In a word, if the All is Perfection, then everything already is as it ought to be, and there is no possible way of preserving significance for our infinite strivings.'

The difficulty is serious. And even when we see the fallacy it is not easy to lay it bare in words. But the fallacy is there. And the clue to it is the use of the word '*already.*' It is of crucial importance to see that the assurance of religious experience as to the Perfection of Ultimate Reality is *intrinsically void of temporal reference*, and is utterly distorted if given a meaning in the temporal order. What is felt as Perfect is Reality in its Eternal Being, in its time-transcending (though not time-*less*) character. This is obvious in the case of a religious consciousness that explicitly recognises the Suprarational nature of Divine Perfection. But even where such a recognition is not explicit, the same thing is true. That of which religion *qua* religion is conscious, that which confers upon it its supreme assurance, is always taken to be the deeper reality that lies at the heart of appearances, including within itself (although we know not how or why) the temporal order itself. Religious Faith or Religious Intuition claims, if it claims anything, to be insight into the Eternal. And the Eternal, we must always remember, is not the 'everlasting' or the 'permanent'—which is just an indefinitely prolongated temporal—but essentially that which transcends and is other than Time. Now it follows—and if this is not grasped the paradox of religion must seem forever sheer self-contradiction—that the attempt to give to this assurance of the Eternal Perfection a concrete significance in the temporal order (within which the moral life proceeds) is absolutely meaningless. The two orders are for human consciousness not merely different, but utterly disparate. We have no notion whatever of how the temporal order connects with Eternity. It is not so much false, as just meaningless, to say that the Suprarational Perfection *already* exists, and to repudiate moral endeavour in consequence. It is a proposition of which the affirmation and the denial are equally beside the point. When we carry on our thinking in terms of the temporal order (as the conditions of human life require that we should, even if we be vouchsafed also the insight of faith into the Eternal) nothing but dire confusion can result from the effort to give a meaning within this order to an assurance which is rooted in intuition of the Eternal. The religious man himself makes no mistake. We do not find that intensity of Faith breeds a relaxation of moral effort. And what explanation can there be of this save that in the moment of religious experience we are so profoundly aware of the 'otherness' of nature of the Eternal Reality whose Perfection we apprehend, that we are not even tempted towards the impropriety of a temporal translation of our assurance?

There is then no contradiction whatever between the faith of religion in a God whose Perfection is supra-rational and the moral urge of religion to banish all imperfection. When our thinking is directed to the temporal order, as it necessarily is in all matters affecting the conduct of life, there is nothing, literally nothing, derivable from our intuition of the Eternal

SUPRA-RATIONALISM AND RELIGION

Perfection, which can be legitimately set against any principles which we find that the temporal order of experience imposes upon us. If, then, the obligation to remove whatever is conceived as opposing itself to our human conception of perfected being is ultimate for our temporal experience (and in an earlier chapter [VI.] we have seen reason to believe that it is), this ultimacy is in no way jeopardised by that Faith which appears on the surface—and from the outside—to stand in such radical opposition to it.

In these last few pages I have been trying to show how the charge of embracing self-contradictory moments may be rebutted by the religious man who is prepared to base his defence upon the supra-rational character of the Divine Perfection. And one thing has become abundantly clear. We have got to be in thorough earnest in holding fast to the implications of this supra-rationality, and especially to the implications of Time-transcendence, if we are not to find the old difficulty recoiling upon us in another form and with equal force. If we are in earnest with it, the supposed contradiction does, as I believe, utterly vanish.

And it is undeniable, I think, that the defence I have outlined finds abundant historical precedent, at least as respects its substance, in the actual utterances of religions. No one can read at all deeply in religious (as distinct from theological) literature without being impressed by the mass of testimony to the ultimate mystery that envelops the God-head—which is yet felt as 'God-head,' because felt to be as indubitably Supreme Value as it is indubitably impenetrable to the mind of man. Anyone who doubts this, as an historical judgment, may be referred to the works of Rudolf Otto, as furnishing evidence which, to the present writer at least, seems irrefragable. The famous *Das Heilige* is suffering in this country something of the temporary reaction that follows in the wake of sensational success, and of an often uncritical appreciation. But its ultimate rehabilitation as one of the most profound and original contributions made by our generation to the philosophy of the spirit is, in the opinion of the present writer, about as certain as the destiny of any book can be.

I am less anxious, however, to claim that the defence I have indicated has enjoyed historical favour, than that it is really in principle the only defence of the religious attitude that is logically open: on the postulates, of course—surely not extravagant—as to the nature of that attitude which have been here adopted. This is a bold claim to make, but I see no way to modify it. For consider once again the utter crassness of the contradiction upon any but a 'mystical' theory of the Divine Perfection. On the one hand religion holds that all that is flows from God's Perfection. On the other hand it holds that much that confronts it in experience is imperfect and cries aloud for reform. How can the two positions possibly be consistently united unless we mean something *different* by 'perfect' in the two statements?—unless, in a word, we recognise Divine Perfection to be different in kind from the types of perfection which we can envisage on the analogy of finite experience. If we are to be true to religious experience as we have consented to understand it, then we *must* hold that God transcends human knowledge. Religion stands or falls with the Supra-rational God.

Section 4. Harmony of this Solution with General Principles of Bradley's Philosophy. Bradley's own Solution

This brings us to the next phase of our discussion. If the conclusion which we have reached is sound, if, that is, religious experience implies recognition of the Supra-rational character of the Absolute, the consequences for philosophy must be frankly faced. Only a metaphysic which at least closely resembles the Bradleian, we must agree, is compatible with the validity of religious experience. Every rationalist metaphysic, every metaphysic which, like Idealism, asserts the intelligible continuity of Reality, must be held to be opposed in principle to that which religion affirms. Accordingly, the whole weight of religion's authority attaches itself to the type of philosophy which maintains the Supra-rational Absolute. There will, of course, be diverse opinions as to the value of the authority of religion. But not many will contend, I imagine, that its support is wholly negligible.

Now not every variety of sceptical philosophy, of course, can claim to derive support from religion, as we have come to understand religion. But a glance at Bradley's doctrine does suggest, I think, that here we do have a sceptical philosophy peculiarly well fitted to consort with religion. Indeed, there seems no immediate reason why Bradley's Absolute should not rank as the philosophic counterpart of the God of Religion. Reality or the Absolute, for Bradley, is, as we have previously seen, a single, all-inclusive, and completely harmonious experience, the principles of whose nature are impenetrable by the finite intellect. Moreover, this Whole may fairly lay claim to the title 'Perfection.' For when we ask ourselves what it is that would ultimately satisfy the self, whether in will, thought, or feeling, we find that nothing short of *being this Whole* will meet the case. Being the Whole *is* Perfection, as it seems. So far then, at all events, Bradley's principles appear to be in full harmony with religious experience.

I shall shortly proceed to argue that Bradley's principles are likewise consistent with a further aspect of the religious consciousness to which I have not yet called attention. But at this juncture it seems proper to say something respecting the manner in which Bradley himself deals with the apparent contradiction at the heart of religion and its philosophical implications. The solution which our present chapter offers is suggested by consideration of Bradley's doctrines. But it is far indeed from representing Bradley's own treatment. On the contrary, Bradley flatly maintains that contradiction is of the essence of religion, that to make it consistent is possible only by destruction of its integrity as religion. And yet, on

Bradley's view, this inherent contradictoriness is of no great consequence, even for religion. Such an unusual position calls for some examination.

The contradictoriness of religion manifests itself for Bradley in a variety of guises, and, among others, in the particular guise that we have elected to concentrate upon in this chapter. 'The Whole is at once actually to be good, and, at the same time, is actually to make itself good. Neither its perfect goodness, nor yet its struggle, may be degraded to an appearance.'[1] This is Bradley's statement of the dilemma which has occupied us, the dilemma of being forced to assert the reality of imperfection in a Perfect Reality. But for Bradley the contradiction is not merely apparent, but real. There is no way out of the dilemma. 'The religious consciousness rests on the felt unity of unreduced opposites: and either to combine these consistently, or upon the other hand to transform them is impossible for religion. And hence self-contradiction in theory, and oscillation in sentiment, is inseparable from its essence.'[2]

But what is of special interest for us is not Bradley's insistence upon the finality of contradictoriness for religion. Such a view has no novelty, and, so far as I can detect, Bradley adduces no fresh point of principle which the solution suggested in this chapter would require to take into account. Bradley's omission to avail himself of that solution will seem a merit or a defect according to the reader's judgment upon the thesis of this chapter. What is of interest is, as I have already hinted, Bradley's interpretation of the significance of the contradiction which he finds. The natural view would be that the apprehension of a contradiction in our experience would forthwith lead to the abandonment, or at least the radical modification, of that experience. That is what we should be led to expect from a common-sense survey of ordinary life, and not least in the sphere of religious experience. It is with something of a shock, therefore, that we find Bradley

[1] *Appearance and Reality*, p. 442. [2] *Ibid.*, p. 443.

explicitly holding that contradiction should not be regarded as really a very serious matter for religion at all. On what grounds does he adopt this apparently paradoxical attitude?

We can detect, I think, two distinct, although allied, arguments. The first of these rests upon his belief that 'the essence of religion is not knowledge.'[1] The implication of this is apparently taken to be that the whole question of knowledge, or of theoretical consistency, is really not vital to religion. Religion, *qua* religion, has no direct concern with the objective truth of its ideas. It is enough for religion if the ideas it entertains are suitable to religion's purpose, which is, 'to express the complete reality of goodness through every aspect of our being.'[2] If the ideas fulfil this purpose, then they do all that religion requires of them, and may be said to be 'true for religion.'

I cannot think, however, that this line of argument will bring conviction to many. It is true, no doubt, that 'the essence of religion is not knowledge.' But that does not exclude the possibility that knowledge—at least in the sense of true ideas, however these may be come by—is *of* the essence of religion. And this seems to be the real state of the case. The ideal side of religion is emphatically not regarded by the religious man as something whose significance lies solely in adequately expressing a feeling or a purpose. It is taken as doing this, but as *also* expressing objective truth. And we cannot ignore this aspect without doing violence to the religious consciousness. It may be the case, as has sometimes been suggested,[3] that religious feelings come first and that religious ideas follow as an inference from these feelings. But whatever the genetic relation, it seems certain that religious ideas are actually taken to express not merely feelings, but the truth about reality. If we find that ideas expressing these feelings

---
[1] *Appearance and Reality*, p. 453.   [2] *Ibid.*
[3] See an interesting article by Professor G. C. Field on ' Some Modern Proofs of the Existence of God,' in the *Journal of Philosophic Studies*, Vol. iii., No. 11.

contradict one another, we are not content to say: 'So much the worse for theoretical consistency. Religion needs these ideas, so they're true for religion whether they contradict one another or not.' Rather do we say: 'If these contradictory ideas really express my feelings, so much the worse for these feelings and my religion generally. I must reconstruct.'

The second reason which, if I have understood rightly, underlies Bradley's position on this matter, does not seem to possess greater cogency than the first. Bradley points out, in accordance with the general principles of his philosophy, that complete theoretical consistency is *nowhere* to be found in finite experience. It is absurd for us therefore, he suggests, to withhold our belief on the mere ground that theoretical consistency is absent, if, on the other hand, the beliefs in question correspond with our deepest needs. Such beliefs we must not, of course, fall into the error of regarding as expressive of ultimate truth. Yet, 'in proportion as the need to which they answer is wider and deeper, these ideas already have attained actual truth.'[1]

Now it is true enough, no doubt (granted Bradley's general principles), that to make belief wait upon a proposition that enjoys complete theoretical consistency is just to eliminate the possibility of belief altogether. But does this imply that religion, or any other attitude of mind, can accept with equanimity a stark contradiction? It is one thing, surely, to maintain at once two propositions whose consistency is not clear to us: quite another thing to maintain two propositions whose inconsistency is clear to us. Even as a 'working belief,' I should think, a mutually destructive complex of ideas cannot be understood to *be* such, and at the same time continue to be happily entertained. Bradley might perhaps reply that the religious consciousness, even if it *understands* the complex as mutually destructive, still *feels* it to be a unity, and that this feeling more than counterbalances the intellectual apprehen-

[1] *Essays*, p. 431.

sion of discord. But being unable to accept the possibility of the permanence of a feeling in a mind which recognises that the ideas expressive of it are in blank contradiction with one another, I must still, for myself, hold that religion must either resolve its paradox or perish.

Section 5. Relation of Faith and Moral Fervour. Justification of this Relation on the Metaphysical Theory of the Present Work

We may now return to consider the relation of Bradley's philosophy to that further aspect of the religious consciousness to which I referred some pages back. Hitherto we have been treating the religious consciousness abstractly: and 'abstractly' not only in the sense (which would be legitimate enough for our present purpose) of leaving out the wealth of actual but variable content in the concrete religious consciousness, but also in the sense that nothing has been said of the *relation* which tranquil faith and moral fervour bear to one another within the religious consciousness. I have spoken as though the two aspects merely 'co-existed,' and have been concerned to show only that their co-existence is not self-contradictory. Nothing can be plainer, however, than that the relation in question is not one of mere 'co-existence.' Faith in God is experienced in religion as the most powerful of all driving forces to moral endeavour. It is not merely co-ordinate with the moral moment, but rather its effective stimulus. Upon this there is no need to enlarge, for there is no likelihood of dispute. Nor is it necessary to attempt to appraise the precise influence of 'faith' upon morality. It is enough if we agree that in the religious consciousness faith in God works as a spur to moral endeavour. And this is so obviously true that it is possible that religion would be quite adequately defined simply as 'faith in God,' since, given this, the moral aspect, whose presence we also demand for true religion, is an inevitable emanation.

This, then, is the relationship which we have to explain and, if possible, to justify.

From the point of view of religion itself, however, the relationship is not very difficult to explain. The important point to bear in mind is that for the religious consciousness God is not only Supra-rational but is also Supreme Value—the consummated reality of human aspirations. Now because God is taken as 'Supra-rational,' we saw, moral endeavour is not felt as inconsistent with our faith in the Divine Perfection. And it is because God is also taken as 'Supreme Value' that faith in Him, the assurance of His Reality, is felt as an actual incitement to moral endeavour. For the assurance of God's Reality, the reality of Supreme Value, is *ipso facto* the assurance that our ideals are no mere 'high-blown fancies' but in the deepest sense *are*: not (if I may emphasise this once more) *already* are, but 'are' in that sense in which, as Plato knew, the Form of the Good transcends being and knowing alike. And how can this assurance that the goal of our aspirations is no figment of the imagination, but the very heart of Reality itself, do other than charge our spirits with a new and profounder zeal in its quest?

So far, and in so far as it is accurate, what we have here is no more than the account of the actual forces at work in the religious consciousness. But we have to note now one thing that is implied in this account. It is implied that the religious consciousness, at the same time as it recognises the Supra-rational character of Divine Perfection, and therefore its difference in kind from human ideals of perfection, also asserts a certain *affinity* between the two kinds of perfection. For it is assurance of the reality of the former kind that acts as the impetus to our pursuit of our moral ideal, which must inevitably be, in so far as envisaged, of the latter type. It is clear, therefore, that the religious consciousness does implicitly assert an affinity between two orders whose relations are, *ex hypothesi*, not apprehensible by intelligence. The assured

SUPRA-RATIONALISM AND RELIGION 307

reality of Supra-rational perfection is felt, however illogically, to validate the quest of humanly conceived perfection. Religion is boldly asserting that, despite the admitted disparity of God and 'good,' the path of 'good' is for man the path to God.

Now for religion itself such an assertion is well enough. Religion, although it claims to be true, does not claim that its assertions are built up like scientific theories upon a basis of inferential reasoning. It would even say, through at least many of its spokesmen, that the most important of its assertions could not be so arrived at. Its fundamental apprehensions are not merely admitted, but claimed, to be intuitive. If religion is asked to explain, therefore, how it knows that there is this affinity which it pronounces between God and 'good,' when by its own avowal God's nature is inscrutable, its inability to answer should involve no diminution of its prestige *qua* religion.

When it comes to the question of the philosophical vindication of religious beliefs, however, the case is somewhat different. I have committed myself to the contention that the Supra-rational philosophy which derives from Bradley is in essential harmony with religious experience. I should wish to show, therefore, that this philosophy can justify such an affinity between God and 'good' as the religious consciousness asserts. But here we seem to be confronted by a difficulty. For it is the business of philosophy to give grounds for that which it asserts, and here we appear to have a case in which 'grounds' are strictly impossible. How can our philosophy assert that God's nature is inscrutable, and at the same time assert, as philosophic truth, that we 'know' of this unique affinity between God and 'good'? Does not the latter assertion imply some apprehension of the nature of the inscrutable God, and thereby contradict the former assertion?

In truth, however, the ἀπορία is capable of a fairly easy solution. There are two ways, we have to observe, in which philosophic vindication of a belief is possible. In the one case, the more common, philosophy may endeavour to show that a belief which, as ordinarily held, may be almost wholly unmediated, reveals itself upon a thorough examination of the relevant data as capable of support by the most comprehensive mediation. That is one way—but a way which is plainly closed to us in the present instance. It is impossible, by the very terms of the problem, to see *how* 'good' connects with God. But there is another way, the validity of which is equally unquestionable. Philosophy may try to show that the belief or assertion in question, although incapable of the mediation proper in the former case, is nevertheless an assertion which the very constitution of human experience renders necessary.[1] This type of vindication, of which, of course, we have already had examples in earlier chapters of this book, is, I take it, quite as cogent as the other. And it is the type which, clearly, is proper to our present instance. It is of the very essence of Supra-rationalism, we may remind the reader, to recognise the possibility of such 'datum beliefs.' Supra-rationalism denies the omni-competence of mind, denies that 'mind is in a manner all things' (if we interpret that maxim in its strictness). It contends that mind is a function limited by definitive conditions, and that the apprehension of these conditions must in the nature of the case be a 'knowing that,' never a 'knowing how'—since a 'knowing how' would imply that the conditions in question were *not* limiting conditions. Accordingly Supra-rationalism may properly, while retaining its full philosophic integrity, give its sanction to unmediated assertions, where these assertions concern the actual basic conditions of experience itself.

And I think we may see that the Supra-rational philosophy can offer not merely a general but also a particular vindication of the assertion of affinity between God and 'good'—that is,

---

[1] This, as I understand it, is Kant's manner of establishing the philosophical vindication of the categorical imperative of the ' pure law ' in Section C of the *Groundwork of the Metaphysic of Ethics*.

that it not only gives its assent to the general principle of unmediated judgments, within a prescribed range, but also confirms this unmediated judgment in particular. This will become evident if we recall certain features of the Supra-rationalist interpretation of experience. For this philosophy, the ideal which animates the life-process of mind is the ideal of a self-sufficing or self-explanatory union of differences. Nothing short of this, no unity of differences in which the unity is still partially external to the differences, will afford rest or final satisfaction for the mind. And this means that nothing short of such a unity can accredit itself as 'reality.' But, we saw, the inner nature of the process whereby mind endeavours to attain to a true union of differents—the pursuit of 'grounds' ever more and more comprehensive—is such that mind is in principle incapacitated from attaining the type of unity which it craves. The ideal in so far as concretised in actual experience, the ideal in the form in which it is directly operative in guiding what we call 'advances' in our search for reality, reveals itself to criticism as but the shadow of the ideal in whose attainment mind can alone rest as the real. We found it imperative, therefore, to make a sharp distinction between the 'noumenal' and the 'phenomenal ideal,' or between the ideal in its purity and the ideal in its spatio-temporal expression. But—and this is vital for our present argument—the phenomenal ideal *is* the spatio-temporal expression of the noumenal ideal. It is the yearning after utter harmony which incites us to pursue the inadequate 'copy.' We aim at the ideal unity, and spontaneously, by the very nature of our being, we take the path of the phenomenal ideal. It is no matter of inference, on the basis of a conceived identity (which might be subject to correction), but an intuitive acceptance which we cannot help if we are to think or act at all.

Herein, I think, lies the philosophical vindication of the affinity that is assumed between God and Good, between supra-rational harmony and humanly conceived harmony.

The true answer to the question, 'How can man believe that his phenomenal ideal prescribes his proper path to the noumenal ideal?' is that he *can* believe it because he *cannot help* believing it. He can do no other. If he thinks or acts at all, this is the necessary condition of his thinking or acting. The phenomenal ideal we are forced to construe as the veritable incarnation of the Absolute, the 'Word made flesh,' the true medium of union between finite beings and the Infinite Perfection of Divinity.

But in concluding this section of the argument, I wish to caution the reader against a possible misinterpretation of my view. I do *not* believe that philosophy can, in the full sense, 'prove God.' What philosophy can do is to prove the reality of a Being which, with respect to its *formal* character, answers to the God of religious experience. Philosophy can thereby rebut the charges made by philosophy, which concern (in the main) the possibility of the reality of a Being whose formal character is thus. But this is not *God* that philosophy is proving. God is something more than an 'Inevitable Inference.'[1] The religious man would scoff, and rightly so, at the philosopher who believed that because he could demonstrate that Reality as a whole is a supra-rational harmony, or what not, he thereby 'knew God.' The form has a filling. But the filling is not for philosophy. If at all, it must be for direct experience. And with this we pass beyond the province of philosophy.

Let me pause here in order to recapitulate, in a very few words, the main stages in the advance of the argument to the present point. I began, then, by asking your recognition (provisional, if need be) of two features as fundamental in any genuine religious experience—serenity of soul and moral fervour. These two features, I allowed, contradict one another upon a *prima facie* interpretation of their objective implications. And the most plausible attempt at reconciliation of

---

[1] Cf. James, *Varieties of Religious Experience* (1928 ed.), p. 502, note (2).

SUPRA-RATIONALISM AND RELIGION

them, by way of the conception of the Finite God, I found it necessary to rule out as incapable ultimately of doing justice to the former of these features. The only solution, I then urged, lies in the frank acceptance of the supra-rational character of God's Perfection. And I sought to show how, from this point of view, the religious man may reply to the accusation of internal contradiction. The problem then arose as to whether *philosophy* can justify the world-view which this solution implies. I argued that on Bradley's principles it can, and that the Absolute of Bradley may legitimately claim to be the philosophic counterpart of the God of Religion. After a brief treatment of Bradley's own attitude to the alleged contradiction in religious experience, I went on to draw attention to the relation which exists for religion between the two features in question—a relation from which our previous account had abstracted. And I endeavoured to show that on this head the Supra-rational philosophy which derives from Bradley has not only nothing to condemn, but is in fact able to offer all the support which it is within the power of philosophy to offer to religious experience.

Section 6. *Implications of Above Doctrine with Respect to Theology*

So much then for the central theme of the present chapter. I have tried to show that the metaphysic expounded throughout the book may rightfully claim such authority as attaches to religious experience, since such experience involves postulates which can enjoy philosophic sanction only on the basis of Supra-rationalism. If the particular form of Supra-rationalism need not be identical with that here set forth, the cardinal tenets at least must closely approximate. I want now, in a few concluding pages, to call attention to some of the implications and consequences of the conclusions we have reached. It seems to me of importance to do so. For it must be remembered that the presuppositions with which we set out as to certain essential marks of the religious consciousness, although offered as hypothetical, are nevertheless hypotheses which receive very widespread acknowledgment in contemporary religious thought. Accordingly, if our reasoning from these presuppositions has been valid, the conclusion at which we have arrived must be regarded as something more significant than the mere termination of a dialectical exercise. On the contrary, it can claim to be the intellectual formulation of that which we essentially *mean* in religious experience. It is worth while, therefore, to inquire into the relation of our doctrine to certain much-discussed aspects of religious life and thought.

The first of the implications which I wish to draw out is with respect to credal dogma, and theology in general. In so far as the view to which we have been led can be stated in the form of a creed, the following may be said to express its essence—'I believe in an Infinite God, who is Perfect with a Perfection that transcends human conception, and with whom I enter into such union as befits a finite being by wholehearted devotion to my ideal of good.' These words express what we have found to be implied in the religious consciousness, and they express it in a way which, if our metaphysics is true, is not subversive of sound philosophic doctrine. But what I want to insist upon here is that these words, bare as they are, are not a mere *part* of the true creed, later to be elaborated into a whole series of theological 'articles.' The term 'creed' implies, I think, the claim to literal and absolute acceptance with respect to the articles therein. If this is so, then the words we have set out above express substantially the *whole* of our creed. The theology which evolves a collection of 'articles' is engaged in the attempt to render into conceptual terms, through the application of principles derived from spatio-temporal experience, the nature of the Divine Being and his relationship to man: and this, unless we have been wholly wrong, is the veriest vanity of vanities. Theology's aim—the knowledge of God—is in fatal conflict with its method—the play of the intelligence. That theology may construct doctrines which are of immense 'symbolic' value, and which prove themselves genuinely efficacious in stimulating the attitude of soul characteristic of religion, is not to be doubted. But 'symbolic representation' is one thing; a 'creed' is another. The dogmas of the Church are not taken as symbols by the laity, they are not taught as such by the clergy, and they are emphatically not believed to be such at the time of incorporation into the various creeds.

The practice of 'grading' religions according to the 'enlightenment' of their creeds, where this means according to the degree of 'truth' with which the nature of God is set forth in the several articles, is indeed radically vicious. So far as this aspect is concerned, all creeds are equally false. When we survey the panorama of religions from the point of view which we have here reached, it is much nearer the truth to say —as has often been surmised—that the great historical religions 'differ only in opinion.' In that which is for us the central and irrefragable truth of religion, its mystical doctrine, the great religions are substantially at one. The rationalisations of the too ambitious intellect may often obscure, but never wholly extinguish it, and we can detect its influence even where the letter of the official 'articles' would seem to forbid it utterly. What of that strange 'meeting of extremes' which is exhibited by the fundamental identity in the utterances of mystics nurtured under the most diverse religious auspices? These 'God-intoxicated' beings, who are acclaimed (later, if not sooner) even by their own communities as the bearers of the purest and loftiest religious experience, are nearer to one another, it has often been remarked, than they are to orthodox adherents of their own order. How is this growing approximation in what are admittedly the higher reaches of separate religions to be explained, if not by the recognition that religions, *qua* religion, are fundamentally one? It is not religion that divides 'religions.' It is the diversity of cosmological, ethical, and other ideas, which form the background of any historic interpretation of religious experience into conceptual terms—a body of beliefs, in short, which is intrinsically irrelevant to religion.

It is a familiar maxim among religious writers, and one of which they feel it necessary constantly to remind the academic philosopher of religion, that we must go to the concrete religious consciousness in order to know what religion means. Within limits, of course, the maxim is sound enough. We shall not find what religion is if we omit to do so. But, on the other hand, we may very well not find what religion is if we do go. For the concrete religious consciousness in its historical actuality is constituted not only by that which is constant and essential in religion, but also by a whole host of elements, drawn from credal and other sources, which are in a high degree variable and accidental. And nothing is commoner than the confounding of the accident with the essence. How often do we hear the appeal made to the 'actual facts' of the religious consciousness as substantiating this, that, or the other belief, when it is perfectly clear to the independent investigator that the belief in question is begotten upon religious experience by the intellect and the imagination working within a definitive cultural context—is, in other words, not part of the essence of, but merely accidental to, religion. There is a feeling, which is all but universal, that the deliverances of the religious consciousness are deserving of the highest respect. But if we are to admit this, it is fundamental that we should distinguish what it is that religion says, from what it is that the intellect says by way of conceptual interpretation. It is the latter that is the source of so-called 'religious' strife. It seems odd that those who very properly deprecate the dissipation of the Christian fellowship into a multitude of mutually warring sects, on the ground that in the real 'substance' of Christianity they are all at one, should seldom suspect that perhaps the same is true (*mutatis mutandis*) of the division of 'religion' into 'religions.'

SUPRA-RATIONALISM AND RELIGION

What has been said above may convey the impression that I am unprepared to recognise any 'higher and lower' with respect to credal doctrine or, more generally, with respect to that body of belief which differentiates one historical religion from another. This, however, is not my view. I do accept a criterion for grading the value of creeds, only it is not the criterion of 'enlightenment' referred to on p. 313. The criterion has already been hinted at in an earlier remark. It is plainly the case that some creeds far excel others in their capacity for producing the 'religious' state of soul in those who meditate their meaning. They are, that is, peculiarly efficacious as 'media' for the suggestion of the mystical doctrine which I have tried to show to be the central thing in religion. This may happen through their very incoherences—which are, very probably, symptomatic of a resolute determination to be true to all sides of religious experience, no matter what paradoxes the intellectual interpretation is going to present. Now creeds which are redolent of this mystical significance are naturally to be taken (if the argument of this chapter has been sound) as the intellectual expression of an unusually pure and vivid religious experience. Religious experience, it seems fair to say, has been powerful enough to remain the dominant controlling influence in their formulation. The grading of creeds in terms of their strictly religious value, therefore, is, I think, a quite valid procedure, if we adopt the criterion here suggested—capacity to act as media for the suggestion of the mystical doctrine. And I cannot but think it a signal merit, rather than a demerit, of this criterion that we are no longer compelled to look for the 'higher' religions among those which are in the van of what is called 'civilisation.' A religion may be 'higher' now in spite of much crudity in intellectual formulae, if only the religious experience which is its foundation be pure and vital. This at least seems a more appropriate test of a religion's religious status than the intellectual elaboration of its systematic theology can be.

Section 7. Defence against the Criticism of 'Undue Abstractness'

I pass on to the next point. The 'faith' or creed which I am advocating is certainly one which is deficient in the concreteness commonly attaching to religious creeds. I want to inquire now as to whether this admitted bareness and abstractness may legitimately be made a ground of objection. Does religion, to be active and effectual in the human soul, necessitate a more definitive content? A short, but I think relevant, answer would be to insist that for those who have become alive to the *prima facie* contradictoriness of religious experience, the choice is not between an abstract and a concrete religion, but between an abstract religion and no religion at all. I do not wish, however, to press this argument at the present juncture, and least of all do I wish to give the impression that recourse to abstract religion is a sort of 'Hobson's choice.' It will be profitable, I think, to try to determine what lies at the root of the objection.

There is one possible meaning of the objection, however, which does not seem to require very serious consideration. It may be maintained that the average man will never be satisfied with a creed which does not offer him something definite and concrete, something that is capable of imaginative embodiment. I shall not stop to ask whether it is not a defect in spiritual experience itself, rather than in intellectual culture, that thus exalts the palpable above the impalpable. I wish merely to say that whether or not mankind in general will ever attain to the level of recognising the aids of imagination for what they are is a matter of quite secondary importance for our present discussion. I offer no opinion upon it. What is of the first importance, however, and what does constitute a genuine crux for our theory, is the question of whether our creed lacks something without which the nature of man is intrinsically incapable of enjoying the full satisfyingness that is characteristic of religious experience. Is there something fundamentally wanting in a religion which is summed up in the faith that God is the Supreme Reality, that His Perfection transcends all human conception, and that devotion to the ideal of good is our appropriate mode of union with Him?[1]

What essential feature, then, does our religion lack? Some will say, perhaps, the definite recognition that God is a *Person*. And it is indeed a common enough belief that the very bottom falls out of religion if the Personality of God is denied. But how is it possible really to hold this view in face of the patent facts of experience? Are we to deny religion to those religions, such as Buddhism, which appear very well able to dispense with such a conception? Or again (if I may be permitted one more reference to the mystics), are we to deny religion to those persons who are commonly regarded as the very geniuses of religion? It is difficult to see how anyone who faces the facts squarely can continue to insist that God's Personality is an indispensable article of religion. The main cause of the insistence, I suppose, is the failure to realise that 'not to be Personal' is not necessarily to be 'sub-personal.' It may be (as of course with me it is) to be 'Supra-personal.' If it were understood that the very state after which developing personality aspires, the consummation of personality, is a state in which the attributes of personality as we know them cease to be, there would perhaps be an end of this superstition. And as to attempted philosophical vindications of God's personality, all, as it appears to me, founder upon the same rock. Sooner or later the God of Personal Attributes reveals himself as a God who is in essential relationship to an 'other,' not Himself. And with this we are back to the doctrine of the Finite God. It is true, indeed, that many of the philosophers who have been forward to assail the conception of Divine Personality have laid themselves open to an effective *argumentum ad hominem*. As

[1] The criticism that in speaking of 'Him' I am implying the 'Personality' of God would of course be frivolous. I say 'Him' rather than 'It' as being the less misleading course, for God is Supra-personal, not sub-personal. See more below.

von Hügel very justly points out, those writers who most trenchantly denounce as 'anthropomorphic' the ascription of Personality to God appear to feel no scruple in availing themselves of metaphysical concepts which are liable to precisely the same objections, often in an intensified form. 'Thus Thought or Love or Law, or even Substance, nothing of this is, for such thinkers, anthropomorphic or sub-human: but everything personal is rank anthropomorphism.'[1] The argument is fair, I think, against those upon whom it is directed. But it is not, of course, in itself a philosophical vindication of Divine Personality. And it is not effective even as an *argumentum ad hominem* in regard to the metaphysics of Supra-rationalism.

I cannot admit, then, that the replacement of the Personal God by the Supra-personal God in any way jeopardises the tenability of our creed. Let us turn now to another 'defect' which may be laid to our charge. We have, by implication at least, ruled out the doctrine of the 'personal mediator.' The path to God, we have urged, lies in devotion to the moral ideal, not in devotion to, or spiritual identification with, an historic person. Is this a blemish upon the power or purity of our faith?

I want to reply to this quite frankly and plainly. It is a matter upon which one is too often tempted to 'hedge,' and if in what follows I incline to the other extreme I may perhaps be pardoned. I do not regard our substitution of the moral ideal for the historic person as a blemish, or a loss, but as an incomparable gain. So long as devotion to an historic person is believed to be the true medium of union with God, the one way of salvation, so long will the ideal of perfection be stabilised in a manner fundamentally contradictory of man's nature, with its limitless potentialities of fresh and fruitful advances. It is no use saying that this is not so, on the ground that the person who is our exemplar is to be conceived 'spiritually' rather than 'bodily,' as an attitude of will rather than as a

---

[1] *Essays and Addresses*, 1st series, p. 50.

concrete system of willing. If we abstract from the historical content we do, or at least may, get rid of the disadvantages of an 'embodied' ideal. But it is only because we have really replaced the historic person by the moral ideal itself. For there is a sense in which the moral ideal is itself devotion to the moral ideal. The 'highest we know' is, formally, devotion to the 'highest we know.' And if the historic person is *not* thus stripped of all temporalities, and taken to be an eternal exemplar solely in virtue of the spiritual attitude of will, the difficulties in the way of accepting such an ideal as 'absolute' seem to me insuperable. If he *is* so taken, let us be open about it, and admit that, apart from the mere fact of concrete embodiment (the value of which is now not obvious, whereas its danger is very obvious indeed) we have nothing here that is not in principle apprehensible by the 'pagan' moral consciousness.

But in actual fact we all know well enough that it is not merely with respect to the formal attitude of the will that personal mediators are, where recognised at all, accepted as external exemplars. The concrete content does have attributed to it a like finality of perfection. The result can only be that the living spirit of man is torn, and progressively torn as culture widens, by conflicting loyalties. On the one hand is his loyalty to the personal mediator. On the other hand is his loyalty to his ideal of perfection. The latter, defined for him through his rationally developing appreciation of what form of life is really to be desired, can no more be repudiated than the obligation to follow the historic person. The conflict may be more or less sharp, according to circumstances, but it is fundamentally irreconcilable. The attempts to reconcile it may follow two distinct courses. Either there may be organised discouragement of what would otherwise appear as 'emancipation' in ethical ideas: or else, by dint of disingenuous reinterpretations of the character and ideals of the historic person, it may be sought to show that modern advances are not really 'advances' at all, but have all been foreseen and provided for. Whether or not either or both of these efforts at solution possess historic actuality, it may be left to the reader to decide. But that they express the direction in which the solution will naturally be sought is, I think, undeniable. It is surely no slight advantage in the creed which I am defending that it offers no temptation to a shuffling obscurantism, which shows ten times the uglier through its association with the name of true religion.

No one, of course, would desire to deprecate without qualification the value of taking a concrete person as the exemplar of the good life. The contemplation of a beautiful and noble character has well-proven effects upon the springs of conduct. But it is not a *sine qua non* of goodness, and unless we are careful to concentrate upon the formal aspect—which is the beginning of the abandonment of the 'concrete person'— it is an actual danger. Conduct at its best is not imitation but creation. It requires us, as Aristotle taught, to make just the precise adjustment which the individual situation, always more or less novel, calls for. If we have little confidence in the creative insight of our practical reason then we shall do well, as Aristotle again taught, to model ourselves upon the man of 'proved practical wisdom.' But this is a compromise to save us from a worse fall, not one of the loftier flights of human achievement. Surely the right attitude to the historical exemplars of goodness is not to sit at their feet but to stand on their shoulders.

There is one further 'omission' upon which I wish to touch now, but very briefly indeed. Our creed says nothing concerning the 'hope of immortality' in any of its very many meanings. And it is not uncommon to hear it said that no religion can be potent over the heart of man which fails to convey specific assurance of survival of bodily death. Should this be regarded as a serious defect in our doctrine?

It would be ridiculous (even had I the competence under any conditions, which I have not) to attempt to make a contribution to the tremendous problem of Immortality in the concluding pages of a concluding chapter. My purpose here is of a much more humble character. I shall merely set out in principle the reply which seems relevant and sufficient upon our doctrine to this, and any similar, charge of omission.

I might, indeed, appeal to the facts. I might ask whether in the Old Testament, for example, we do not learn of a life in which religion is potent, and immortality is disbelieved. But I lay no stress on this. 'Facts are chiels that winna ding' no doubt, but then it is often astonishingly hard to know just what the 'facts' are. What I wish to point out is this. For anyone who embraces in a living form the creed which I am defending, the question of personal survival of bodily death, in whatever form, cannot be an independent issue of vital import. For if we have faith in the Perfection of the Whole (as on this creed), we have, *ipso facto*, faith that Reality is such as to satisfy in full our aspirations after perfection. This in turn means, not indeed that all our desires but (to use an expression of Bosanquet's) our 'criticised desires' meet with their fulfilment. But this again implies that our faith must include a faith in immortality *just in so far as we believe immortality to be genuinely worthy of desire*, i.e. an element in true perfection. We cannot believe both that Reality is the consummation of our aspirations after perfection, and that Reality is opposed to the satisfaction of *one* such aspiration. And if, on the other hand, immortality presents itself to us as something which, although we desire it, ought not to be desired, then of course we have no right to insist upon it in religion, or be filled with despondency at the prospect of not achieving it.[1]

In this last Section I have sought to answer some of the objections which might be felt against our creed on the score of its abstractness. I have tried to show that its abstract-

[1] The reader may be referred to an illuminating, if brief, discussion of the so-called 'religious' demand for finite immortality, in Professor J. S. Haldane's recent Gifford Lectures published under the title *The Sciences and Philosophy*.

ness involves no diminution of 'satisfyingness.' It is easy to imagine other objections of the same general character, but it is questionable if their discussion would elicit any new principle of interest. At any rate, I do not propose to dwell further upon this relatively unimportant aspect of our theme. So much defence did seem called for, however, in view of the very great prominence in religious life and thought of the conceptions whose claims we have just considered.

For Product Safety Concerns and Information please contact our EU representative GPSR@taylorandfrancis.com
Taylor & Francis Verlag GmbH, Kaufingerstraße 24, 80331 München, Germany

www.ingramcontent.com/pod-product-compliance
Lightning Source LLC
Chambersburg PA
CBHW061425300426
44114CB00014B/1545